POCKET
ENCYCLOPEDIA

HOME REPAIR

POCKET
ENCYCLOPEDIA
HOME
REPAIR

Contributing authors
John McGowan · Roger DuBern

DORLING KINDERSLEY
London · New York · Stuttgart

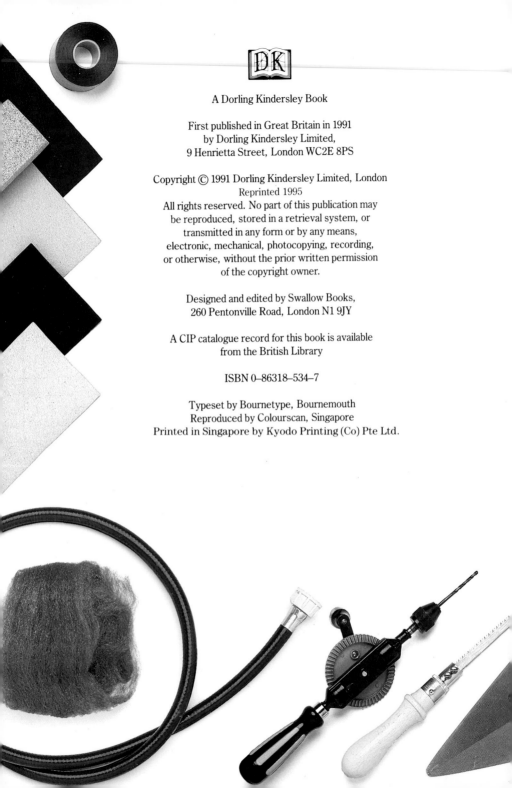

A Dorling Kindersley Book

First published in Great Britain in 1991
by Dorling Kindersley Limited,
9 Henrietta Street, London WC2E 8PS

Designed and edited by Swallow Books,
260 Pentonville Road, London N1 9JY

A CIP catalogue record for this book is available
from the British Library

ISBN 0–86318–534–7

Typeset by Bournetype, Bournemouth
Reproduced by Colourscan, Singapore
Printed in Singapore by Kyodo Printing (Co) Pte Ltd.

CONTENTS

Introduction 6

INTRODUCTION

Carrying out home repairs yourself gives threefold savings. You will save money, of course, because it will not be necessary to call in a professional. You will save time, since you can make repairs at your own convenience rather than having to wait in for a carpenter or plumber to arrive. Lastly, you will save trouble because dealing with a minor problem early will prevent it from escalating into a major task: leaking pipes are a classic example of this.

This book gives you the technical back-up that you need to tackle a whole range of potential problems that arise at some time in any home, both indoors and outside. You do not have to be an expert; you do not even need to have tried any do-it-yourself repairs before. The book is compact enough to be carried from one job to another, and is designed to be easy to follow, with clear, step-by-step instructions. All that you need to know in order to achieve a high standard of workmanship and a professional finish is detailed.

The *DK Pocket Encyclopedia of Home Repair* is a comprehensive manual. Divided into ten chapters, each covering a different area of work, it deals with repairs to both the contents and furnishings of your home, and the fabric of the building itself. Each chapter begins by detailing and illustrating the tools and materials necessary for the repairs that follow so that you are well prepared in advance and do not have to break off in the middle of a job for lack of a vital tool.

Chapter One examines furniture repairs, covering everything from everyday knocks and scratches to major renovations, such as mending legs, renewing upholstery and making loose covers. In Chapter Two you will find information on the care and repair of home contents and ornaments, whether made from china or glass, metal, plastic or leather. Here you can

REPAIRING YOUR HOME

Regular checking and maintenance will enable you to catch any problems early, when they are easier to deal with. Neglect routine maintenance and you could be faced with a major repair. Here is a concise guide to the main areas where problems arise, and the chapters within this book where you will find the advice and information that you need in order to maintain and repair each of them.

Lofts
Bare joists in the loft should be insulated to conserve heat and cut bills (Chapter Eight).

Roof
Check your roof regularly for any damage and repair it at the first opportunity (Chapter Nine).

Flashing
Loose flashing around dormer windows and chimney pots should be replaced to prevent damp (Chapter Nine).

Ceilings and solid walls
Check for damp and condensation (Chapter Nine) and repair any cracks in walls and ceilings (Chapter Three).

Windows
Windows and frames should be checked regularly inside and out for signs of damp and damaged paintwork (Chapter Five).

External walls
Loose and cracked rendering, damaged pointing, or a defective damp-proof course will lead to damp penetrating the walls (Chapter Nine).

Floors
Damaged floor coverings will need to be patched or repaired (Chapter Four).

Tiles
Wall and floor tiles may become damaged and need repairing or replacing (Chapters Three and Four).

Hollow walls
Light partition walls can be repaired very easily with plasterboard (Chapter Three).

Windowsills
Window- and doorsills need regular maintenance to protect them from damp and rot (Chapter Nine).

Doors
Internal and external doors and frames will need to be repaired or replaced if they stick, are damaged or are rotten (Chapter Nine).

find out how to remove stains, repair broken china- and glassware, and restore damaged metalwork.

Walls and ceilings form the subject matter of Chapter Three, which tells you how to fill and smooth any cracks, bulges and areas of rough plasterwork prior to decoration. Chapter Four deals with floors, discussing the care and repair of different floors and floor coverings. Chapter Five examines doors and windows, showing how to repair jamming, sticking, warped or rotten windows, doors, and frames.

You must be particularly careful when undertaking electrical repairs, so the information contained in Chapter Six is indispensable. As well as dealing with everyday faults, the chapter has a special section on faulty appliances. Chapter Seven contains information on plumbing, and will be vital in an emergency. Following the advice given in this chapter, you will be able to avoid a flood and the extensive redecorating that this would involve.

Heating and insulation is discussed in Chapter Eight, which gives details of the different central heating systems available. Methods of insulation are examined, helping you to cut heating bills and save energy. Chapter Nine deals with the external repairs necessary to help your home to withstand water, wind, and temperature changes. It also gives advice on how to detect and deal with damp, rot, and infestation, enabling you to keep the fabric of your house in good condition. To finish, home safety is covered in Chapter Ten, ensuring the security and protection of your family and possessions.

Throughout the book, great care has been taken to give preference wherever possible to those materials that are environmentally friendly, in order to help to protect our planet. Make it a rule, for instance, to use only ozone-friendly aerosols, and wood preservatives should be water-based where possible to avoid harm to children, pets, and garden plants. Conserve water, and help to protect the quality of your water supply by observing the latest water regulations.

· CHAPTER ONE ·

FURNITURE

However well you care for your home, sooner or later most pieces of furniture will need renovating, repairing or replacing. Replacing some items, particularly large pieces of furniture, can be very expensive, so it is always worth considering renovating articles you are fond of. A fresh coat of varnish on a fading table, or a freshly caned seat on an old chair, can make it feel like new. A number of basic furniture repairs can be effected without specialist skills or equipment and prove cheaper and more satisfying than buying a replacement. Any valuable antiques, however, should be taken to a professional restorer.

Tools and materials

The nature of furniture repair is so varied that there are many tools which you will find useful. Although you may have some woodworking tools already, you will probably want to supplement them with a few more specialized items. Power tools, such as power drills, circular saws and power sanders, can be expensive, but are well worth the investment in terms of time saving and accuracy.

Accurate measuring and marking up is essential, particularly in woodwork. The most useful measuring and marking tools are a good retractable measuring tape, a steel rule, a try square and a good-quality spirit level. Treat these tools very carefully; if they are damaged, they will become inaccurate. Buy the best quality measuring and marking tools you can afford, and make sure that wooden and metal parts are firmly attached.

Saws are the most versatile cutting tools, particularly for wood. They come in a variety of types and sizes, but the most useful are a panel saw and a tenon saw. You will need at least one large cabinet screwdriver and one small cross-head screwdriver, and a range of chisels in different sizes and blade shapes. Use a wooden carpenters' mallet for driving chisels and for tapping components together.

Carpenters' pincers

Snipe-nosed pliers

Pincers and pliers
Use carpenters' pincers for extracting nails and tacks. Use pliers with pointed and rounded jaws for small items and to crop wire and manipulate small sections of metal.

Tenon saw and mitre box
This saw has a straight, rectangular blade with a stiffened back. It is used for cutting wood accurately, especially when making joints. The angled slots in the sides of a mitre box guide a saw blade when cutting mitres or right-angle joints with a tenon saw.

Sash clamp
A couple of medium-sized sash clamps are needed for regluing frames and clamping boards together.

Bradawl

Bradawl
The chisel-like tip of a bradawl cuts across wood fibres to make a starter hole for screws.

Sash clamp

Tenon saw

Mitre box

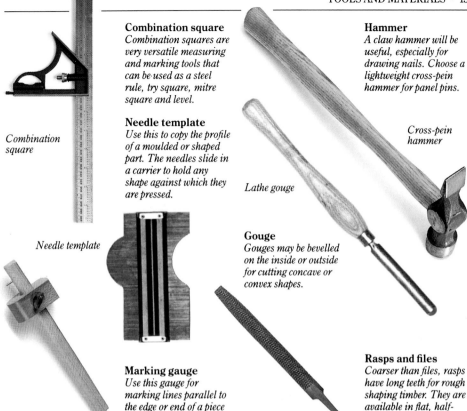

Combination square
Combination squares are very versatile measuring and marking tools that can be used as a steel rule, try square, mitre square and level.

Combination square

Needle template
Use this to copy the profile of a moulded or shaped part. The needles slide in a carrier to hold any shape against which they are pressed.

Needle template

Lathe gouge

Gouge
Gouges may be bevelled on the inside or outside for cutting concave or convex shapes.

Hammer
A claw hammer will be useful, especially for drawing nails. Choose a lightweight cross-pein hammer for panel pins.

Cross-pein hammer

Marking gauge
Use this gauge for marking lines parallel to the edge or end of a piece of timber or board.

Marking gauge

Wood rasp

Rasps and files
Coarser than files, rasps have long teeth for rough shaping timber. They are available in flat, half-round and round shapes.

MATERIALS

● White spirit: Use this turpentine substitute to thin finishes and to clean furniture.
● Linseed oil: Mix this oil with white spirit to make a furniture cleaner. Linseed is traditionally used for oiling wood, but takes a long time to dry. Better finishing oils are available today.
● Wire wool: Use very fine-grade wire wool to matt down gloss finishes and clean off old wax polish.
● Liquid abrasives: Burnishing cream, car paint cleaner and metal polish are all abrasive enough to remove stains from a polished surface and to revive a dull one.
● Oxalic acid: Available from chemists as white crystals, this

makes a bleach when dissolved in water. It is highly poisonous.
● Two-part bleach: A strong commercial bleach which may even take the colour out of wood, so apply with care.
● Methylated spirits: This will remove some ink stains and will strip shellac from furniture. It is also used to lift out linseed oil during French polishing.
● Wax crayons: Melt these down and use them to fill tiny holes and chips.
● Stopper: A commercial product for filling medium and large holes in timber.
● Plastic wood: This filler sets hard enough to rebuild chipped or broken edges.
● Woodworm fluid: A chemical

insecticide which kills the larva of the furniture beetle and prevents reinfestation.
● Candle wax: This can be used to lubricate sticking drawers and doors.
● Chemical stripper: There are several products which will safely dissolve old paint and varnish from woof surfaces.
● Grain filler: This is made from china clay or whiting plus colouring pigments bound together by a mixture of white spirit and linseed oil. It can be used to fill up the pores in open-grained timber.
● Abrasives: Abrasive papers are available in coarse, medium and fine grades (these refer to the relative size of the grit).

Identifying wood

A vast range of timbers has been used for making furniture, and you would have to be an expert to identify most of them. Here we describe some of the popular woods which have been in continuous use for centuries and which are frequently found today.

Oak

Oak
This has a beige to pale grey background with a darker brown flecked grain pattern. It is very hard, with open pores.

Pine
Pine

Yellowy cream in colour, pine has a pale beige, sometimes very wild, grain. Veneers adhere well to it. Nowadays, pine is often finished in a clear polish, but in the past it was usually either painted or veneered.

Elm

Elm
Because elm has a high resistance to splitting, it was often used for carved solid chair seats. It is very pale beige in colour.

Maple
This light-coloured wood has a close, heavily figured grain. Some types are used for decorative veneering.

Maple

Satinwood

Satinwood
This is a light, yellowish wood which can be very figured. It was used a great deal for veneered cabinet work from the end of the eighteenth century until the early twentieth century.

Mahogany

English walnut

GLUES

- Animal glue: This is the kind of glue that you will most often find in old joints. It is still available today in the form of cakes or beads which you have to melt in a heated glue pot. There are better glues today for jointing timber, but animal glue (also called scotch glue) is still the glue that is most often used for sticking decorative veneers to the backing wood.
- Polyvinyl acetate: This modern water-thinned adhesive is ideal for gluing timber. It is white in colour and sold in all DIY stockists.
- Glue film: Specially developed for gluing veneers, this is a sheet of glue that you lay between the veneer and the groundwork and activate by heat.
- Epoxy resin: This is not used a great deal in furniture restoration, but you may need it for gluing back small pieces of inlay.

Mahogany
Mahogany is a popular wood for all kinds of furniture. The earliest and best types of mahogany came from Cuba, then Honduras. The colour ranges from a reddish to a dark brown. It is a dense wood with an even grain, which makes it ideal for furniture, particularly when carved.

American walnut

Walnut
This has a creamy brown background with a highly figured dark brown to black grain. Its main use is as a decorative veneer, but it is also used in solid form to make chairs and table frames.

Drawer and cabinet furniture

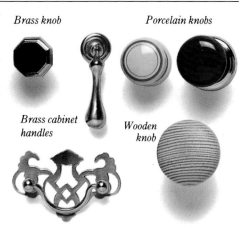

Brass knob   *Porcelain knobs*

Brass cabinet handles   *Wooden knob*

If you have an old piece that has lost a handle or has been fitted with out-of-style handles that you wish to replace, make sure that you choose handles of the right period. It is almost impossible to find original sets of brass handles, but reproduction brass handles are usually available, as are metal key escutcheons and wooden knobs.

Most handles are attached with threaded rods which pass through the wood and are secured by a nut on the inside. Metal or china knobs usually have a single screw projecting from their back face, while wooden knobs have their own coarse screw thread. These screw into matching holes on the drawer front.

If the thread on the back of a wooden knob is allowed to work loose, it is likely to wear. To prevent this, reglue it immediately. If serious wear has occurred, make a saw cut down the centre of the knob's worn thread and glue and wedge it from inside the drawer front.

Clean metal fittings with the appropriate metal cleaner. It is best to remove metal

Cabinet furniture
Smaller knobs and handles, used for cupboard and cabinet doors and drawers, are made in a variety of decorative shapes, in wood, metal, glass and plastic.

knobs, handles and key escutcheons before cleaning them. If they are difficult to remove, protect the surrounding wood with masking tape to prevent dirty metal cleaner from being rubbed into it. You will also need to mask plated metal when you clean the wood.

Treating woodworm

All beetles attack timber in the same way. A beetle lays its eggs in cracks or crevices in the wood. Larvae hatch out and spend several years tunnelling through the wood, eating, on average, about 2in (50mm) of wood each year. Hundreds of tiny tunnels can be created, making badly infested timber liable to collapse.

Woodworm
The most obvious sign of woodworm is a spattering of pin-sized holes in the surface. It is often difficult to tell whether the attack has died out; if in doubt, treat the timber by cleaning it thoroughly and brushing or spraying it with woodworm fluid.

Many old pieces of furniture have been victims of woodworm in the past, but often they will have been treated successfully. The way to tell whether or not the woodworm is still active is to look carefully at the holes. Fresh flight holes will be clean and lighter in colour than the surrounding wood, whereas old ones will have darkened. Signs of fine powder in or around flight holes are another clue.

If you think that a newly acquired piece has woodworm, treat it as soon as you can, preferably before bringing it into the house. Cut out and replace any serious damage and treat sound timber with a commercial fluid.

Squirt the fluid into the flight holes using a can with a pointed nozzle or an aerosol spray with a special applicator. As the internal tunnels are interconnected, there is no need to treat every flight hole – one every 2in (50mm) will be sufficient. Brush or spray the fluid over all unfinished timber and treat finished surfaces with an insecticidal polish.

Repairing veneers

Veneers are thin sheets of real wood glued to a thicker backing, usually either a solid softwood or cheap hardwood. Coloured woods (marquetry) and other thin sheet materials like brass, tortoiseshell and ivory (inlays) are often let into a veneered surface to make decorative patterns. Veneers can be bought from most specialist suppliers. You can buy ready-made stringing, banding, patterns and even complete pictorial motifs in a range of woods to replace missing components.

You can cut out damaged sections of veneer and replace them with a new patch. This must be thicker than the original, so that you can sand it flush. If necessary, glue two thinner pieces of veneer together.

Treating loose veneers

If a veneer is lifting up at one edge or corner, glue it back as soon as possible before it breaks off and is lost. Dust and grease will have contaminated the old glue, so scrape it from the veneer and ground. Brush fresh glue under the veneer and clamp it flat, or weight it down, for 24 hours.

If a whole piece of veneer has become detached, clean off the old glue, apply fresh glue and replace it. Clamp it in place until the glue has set. If the original veneer is missing or badly damaged, you will have to patch or replace it with a new veneer.

Treating dented veneers

You can raise dents by using the steaming method described on page 23. But because the steam will soften the glue holding the veneer to its ground, you must clamp or weight the veneer as soon as you have eliminated the dent. Put a block of softwood over the area and fix it in place with a G-clamp. To apply pressure in the middle of a table top, place two strips of stout timber across the table, one on top and one beneath, with a clamp at each end. Leave in place until the glue has set.

When raising dents, work carefully and keep the iron moving to avoid scorching the wood. Be prepared for the wood fibres to take several hours to swell and fill the dent.

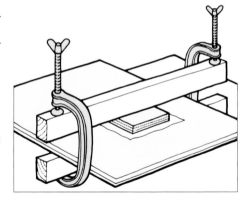

Clamping dented veneer
Once you have steamed out the dent, place a block of softwood on the area and clamp it up. This will prevent the veneer from lifting.

Treating veneer blisters

Patches of veneer can become detached from the solid wood ground, and if these swell they will form a raised blister. It is sometimes possible to soften the original glue and press back the blister. Steam the area with a wet cloth and heated iron until the blister is flat. Then clamp it as described for raising a dent.

If this is unsuccessful, cut a slit along the blister and work glue under it with a knife blade. Press the blister down with a wallpaper seam roller and wipe off excess glue with a damp cloth. Close the slit with gummed paper and clamp or weight it for 24 hours.

Patching damaged veneers

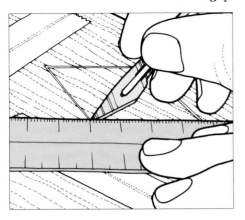

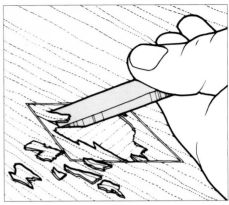

1 *Tape an oversized piece of veneer over the damage, aligning the grain closely. Using a scalpel and a straight edge, cut a diamond shape through the two layers across the grain.*

2 *Lay the patch aside and carefully chisel out the veneer within the cut area. Then scrape out all the old glue. Trim the patch to fit tightly, using a file or garnet paper and working with the grain.*

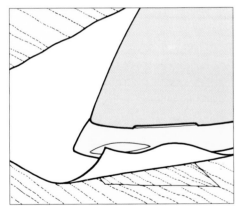

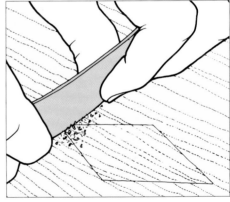

3 *Iron glue film on to the back of the patch and lay it in place. Protecting it with brown paper, press flat with a cool iron. The patch should stand very slightly proud of the surface.*

4 *Rub a block of softwood gently over the patch until the glue has cooled, so that the edges do not lift. When the glue is completely dry, you can sand or scrape the new veneer flush.*

REPAIRING INLAYS AND MARQUETRY

Once inlay or marquetry begins to lift, it is easily broken off and lost. This will make your repair job more difficult, so replace the loose piece as soon as possible.

Clean brass, ivory or tortoiseshell inlay and glue it back with epoxy resin glue. Tape or clamp the inlay until the glue sets. Glue veneer pieces with PVA, scotch glue or, if the piece is large enough, glue film.

If a whole central or corner marquetry motif is missing, you may be able to buy a close match. If only a small piece is missing, take a rubbing of the area by laying a piece of paper over it and shade in the shape with a soft pencil. Tape the rubbing on to the replacement veneer, prick it through with a needle to reproduce the shape, and trim it out with a knife.

Stripping and staining wood

Before you attempt to refinish a piece of furniture, it must be perfectly sound and clean. Never fall into the trap of believing that polish will hide minor blemishes; on the contrary, it will emphasize them. Begin by stripping off the old finish, either locally or over the entire piece, depending on its condition. Next, if the wood is stained or discoloured, it might be necessary to bleach it. Finally, sand the surface perfectly flat.

When a piece of furniture has been stripped and sanded, it may look too new, and you may want to put the colour back into the wood by staining it. If you have to cope with a light patch left by bleaching or colouring a new piece of wood, staining it to match the surrounding timber is a difficult task which needs practice.

You may need to smooth and seal the surface with a grain filler – a runny cream which comes in different colours – before applying the finish. You will need a natural wood colour for light and bleached woods and the appropriate wood shade for darker woods. The grain filler is applied across the grain, using a piece of hessian or coarse rag, and left to harden overnight. The grain filler and stain can be mixed and applied in one operation. When using chemicals of any kind to treat furniture, make sure that you are well protected against fumes and splashes.

Stripping the finish

In some cases you will have to strip all the old finish from a piece of furniture in order to restore it. If possible, however, it is preferable to keep the area of wood stripped as small as you can.

Stripping local areas
There are several ways of stripping a small area: by using a scraper, methylated spirits or a commercial chemical stripper. Scraping has advantages if surrounding areas are badly affected by a liquid stripper. On veneered furniture, make sure that you do not scrape through to the groundwork. Scrape more or less in the direction of the grain, changing the angle slightly from time to time so that you do not scrape a hollow in the wood. Sand the area lightly to feather the polished edges of the patch before refinishing.

Methylated spirits are good for stripping small areas of polish. Apply with a coarse cloth or very fine wire wool.

Chemical stripper will also strip a patch of finish. Dip a small ball of 000 gauge wire wool in it and rub the polish off in the direction of the grain. Neutralize the area with either white spirit or water.

INDUSTRIAL STRIPPING

There are several commercial processes for stripping finishes from timber and metal. Most of them involve dipping the item into a tank of hot caustic soda, then hosing it off with water. This can be very damaging to furniture, leading to weakened joints, peeled veneers, splits in solid panels and raised grain.

However, there are other methods which do not immerse pieces in caustic for long periods. These cold chemical strippers do not harm joints or split the wood, but the grain is raised slightly and will require light sanding. Always ask the company's advice before going ahead and make sure that you never submit a valuable item to any industrial process.

Stripping a whole piece
Use a chemical stripper to strip a whole piece of furniture. The most versatile strippers are in a liquid or light, jelly-like form and are painted on and then scraped off along with the softened paint. Use fine wire wool to remove the residue and clean out moulded areas. Wash the wood with white spirit and wire wool, rubbing in the direction of the grain. When the spirit has evaporated, sand the wood lightly with a fine abrasive to prepare it for polishing.

If the piece is covered with layers of paint, it is best to use a hot-air stripper. This tool blows air heated to 570°F (300°C), lifting paint in a matter of seconds.

Bleaching

Once wood has been stripped, it may be necessary to bleach it, either to remove stains or to lighten discoloured timber. You can bleach out mild staining with a saturated hot-water solution of oxalic acid crystals (available from pharmacists). Wash this off with clean water. Wear protective gloves and avoid splashing other parts of the furniture or your clothes.

To remove serious stains or discolouration, use a commercial two-part bleach. Apply with an old bristle or nylon brush. After about 4 hours wipe the surface with a damp cloth, then neutralize with a solution of 1 teaspoon of white vinegar in a pint (½ litre) of water.

Sanding

Before you apply a stain or a finish you will need to sand the wood to provide a smooth surface. This stage is essential before the application of a water-based stain. After this, sanding will reduce the depth of colour. If you have bleached the wood, the final washing stage will have raised the grain; otherwise wipe a damp rag over the wood before sanding.

Use a medium-grade abrasive paper wrapped around a cork or softwood block. Sand the wood in the direction of the grain only. Switch to a fine-grade paper for the final sanding. For shaped surfaces, use a small piece of abrasive paper and your fingertips.

Blending wood stains

To match a patch to the surrounding wood, build up the background colour gradually by applying several coats of light stain. As you approach the right colour you should begin to copy the grain pattern with streaks of darker colour while the background is still wet. Blend the stain into the surrounding area by blotting it with a damp cloth or brush: avoid a hard edge at all costs. Before attempting to colour a patch, try blending stains and paints on scrap wood. If the stain seems uneven, remember that absorbency differs with the angle at which the grain meets the surface.

Simulating grain
With a fine sable brush and artists' oil paints, break up the edge of a patch by continuing the existing grain with lines of paint, blending the colours with turpentine.

Disguising filler
Paint in the background colour, extending it on to the wood. While the paint is wet, fake the grain. Brush the paint out well so that it does not show as a raised texture.

TYPES OF STAIN

Stains are available as powdered pigments for mixing yourself, but you will find it easier to use one of the ready-made stains from any DIY shop. You can blend compatible stains to alter their colour.

Water-based stains
These are easy for an amateur to use. They flow nicely, and if you apply too dark a colour, you can lighten the tone by wiping the stain off the surface with a damp cloth while it is still wet. This

quality allows you to shade when you are matching a patched area to surrounding grain patterns.

Any finish can be applied over a water-based stain. However, it will raise the grain unless you wet and sand the wood first. Also, these stains will encourage certain veneers to blister, so it is better to use the oil-based types to stain any veneered pieces.

Oil-based stains
Not truly oil-based at all, these stains are a solution of naphtha

and white spirit. (They are not spirit-based stains either; those are made with methylated spirits and can only be obtained from a specialist supplier.) With oil-based stains you will have to mix your own colours. Some polyurethanes react badly with oil-based stains, so test the combination on scrap timber first. You can also use them to colour French polish. Always add the stain to the polish, as they separate if you mix the other way around.

Wood finishes

Wood can be given a variety of protective finishes – including stain, varnish, wax, polish and oil – to prevent moisture, heat, scratches and insects from penetrating the surface. In each case the wood should be prepared carefully: stripped of old paint or varnish, filled with wood filler or stopper, sealed with knotting and smoothed ready for finishing (pages 18–19). Applying the surface finish to a piece of furniture is a particularly rewarding part of repair and restoration. It may well bring out the beauty of the wood for the first time. The type of finish you should use will depend on the style of the piece, the wood from which it is made and the use to which it will be put.

Varnishes and lacquers

Today it is possible to buy extremely durable finishes which will resist alcohol, water and even direct heat, ideal for chairs and tables which receive hard use. If, however, you can replace a finish with the appropriate traditional type, you should do so.

Polyurethanes
You can buy ready-coloured polyurethane finishes, but the clear sort is the most widely used for furniture. Matt, semi-matt or gloss finishes are available.

Apply polyurethane varnish as you would a coat of paint. Use a good-quality brush and avoid going over an area twice once the varnish has begun to set. You will need to paint at least two coats on to bare wood.

If you decide to treat an old piece with polyurethane, either use a matt varnish and liven it with a coat of wax polish, or apply a gloss varnish, then dip fine wire wool in wax polish and apply it to the surface in the direction of the grain.

Applying a varnish
Use a good-quality, clean paint brush and leave to dry for at least 6–12 hours in a dust-free atmosphere. When dry, lightly abrade the surface. For the best results, thin the first coat with 10 per cent white spirit and apply at least four coats.

Two-part cold cure lacquer
This two-part lacquer produces a tough, glossy finish, but is not easy to apply and can make timber look artificial. Unlike a polyurethane, it does not darken with age. When applying, use a face mask to protect against fumes.

Mix the two parts together, then paint the lacquer on to the wood. Leave it to harden for two hours, rub out any imperfections with silicon carbide paper, then apply a second coat. Leave to dry overnight. Once it has set, either polish it to a high gloss with a burnishing agent, or give it a satin finish by rubbing it down with wire wool and then applying wax.

Traditional finishes

Many dealers and collectors prefer these authentic finishes. Although they are not as durable as modern varnishes, it is important to use them for old or valuable pieces.

An oil finish can be used on any timber, but will look particularly good on teak or open-grained woods like oak. Stripped pine looks very mellow when it is oiled. It is best to use a commercial teak oil. Linseed oil looks just as good, but it takes so long to dry that it becomes sticky and collects dust. Wipe a generous coating of oil on to the wood with a soft cloth, rubbing it into the grain, then wiping any excess off. You may need to apply two or three coats. Allow each coat to dry for 24 hours, then rub down the surface with a clean cloth and apply the next coat.

Applying oils and waxes

Using a clean, lint-free rag, spread a first coat sparingly over the surface, working with the grain. With wax, apply two coats for a good finish. With teak oil, apply a second, thinner coat, leave it to dry for 24 hours, then rub with wire wool and polish.

Wax polishes for furniture are widely available, but should not be applied directly to timber. Although it is a beautiful finish, wax may collect dust which can be carried into the wood. The safest approach is to seal the wood with shellac or varnish, then apply the polish.

French polish was a very popular finish in the nineteenth century. Its appeal is for its appearance, not for its function. It is very soft and easily damaged by water, alcohol and heat, and best reserved for furniture which will not receive hard use.

Applying French polish

Small specks of dust will ruin this finish, so work in a clean, draught-free, daylit area. Avoid damp, as the polish goes cloudy. Pour polish into the cotton wool before you wrap the rubber (below). Gently press the pad on to a spare piece of wood to remove excess polish, and so prevent runs from forming. Dab a few drops of linseed oil on the pad with your fingertip to keep it lubricated.

It is most important to distribute the polish evenly, making sure that there are no bare patches, and never to allow the rubber to stop on the surface. Sweep the rubber on to the surface, using overlapping, circular strokes. When you have covered an area once, go over it again with figure-of-eight movements. Finish with straight strokes across the grain, sweeping on and off the surface at each end. As

the rubber begins to dry, increase the pressure slightly. If it starts to stick, apply a little more oil to the sole.

Leave the first coat to harden for about 20 minutes, then apply a second coat. After applying four or five coats, leave it to harden overnight. Rub it down lightly with self-lubricating silicon carbide paper and wipe dust from the surface with a cloth dampened in methylated spirits. Continue building up coats.

When you have built up a good body of polish you must lift out the linseed oil. To do this, add methylated spirits to the rubber and apply straight strokes to the polished wood. Leave it to evaporate for a few minutes, then "spirit off" again. If the surface clears and then clouds over again, it means that the rag is too dirty to lift the oil out, so change to a cleaner one. Use a clean, soft cloth for the final polish, then leave the piece in a dust-free atmosphere for a few days to harden off.

Making a rubber

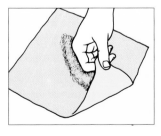

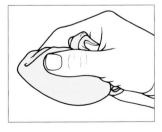

1 *Place a handful of cotton wool or wadding in the centre of a lint-free, colourless linen square and fold one corner over it.*

2 *Fold in the loose fabric at the sides and twist it into a tail behind the pad. There should be a point at one end for getting into corners.*

3 *Fold the tail up into the palm of your hand, squeezing the pad until it is egg-shaped. Store the rubber in an airtight jar when not in use.*

Cleaning and repairing furniture

Over the years a layer of dust and old wax builds up on wood, until a dull film gradually obscures its colour and grain. Eventually, you will need to use a reviver to clean off this film and bring out the full beauty of the wood again.

If your piece of furniture is stained, the type of treatment it requires will depend on whether the damage is just in the depth of the polish or has reached the wood itself.

Cleaning wood
Wash grime from furniture with a reviver – a mixture of 4 parts white spirit to 1 part linseed oil – on a cloth. This will not affect any finish other than wax polish, which it lifts off along with accumulated dirt. It will not lift veneer nor raise the grain of the wood. From time to time refold the cloth so that its surface is clean. If your furniture is really dirty, use the reviver on a ball of 000 grade wire wool. Do not apply too much pressure, and work in the direction of the grain so that you do not scratch the finish beneath. Then wipe the wood with a clean cloth dampened in white spirit. After cleaning apply a fresh coat of wax or French polish.

Cleaning painted furniture
To remove greasy deposits from painted or lacquered pieces, wash them with a rag dipped in warm, soapy water. Do not flood the surface, as water can penetrate the joints and make them swell. Shellac and lacquer will cloud if water is left lying on them, and veneer will lift if water gets underneath. You should wash larger items a little at a time, working upwards from the bottom to avoid streaking. Finally, rinse the piece carefully with a rag dipped in clean water and then rub the surface dry with a clean, soft cloth.

Removing stains

White blemishes are a result of the surface of soft finishes breaking up. To eradicate them, apply a liquid metal polish on a soft, damp cloth, rubbing to below the level of the stain. Repolish when no traces of the blemish remain. If water finds its way below the finish, it often leaves a dark stain. Cutting back the finish with metal polish may be successful, but you may have to strip or even bleach the area (page 19).

Ink stains can also respond to metal polish if the ink has not penetrated the finish and methylated spirits will remove some artists' inks. If neither of these methods works, you will have to strip the polish locally with methylated spirits or chemical stripper, then apply bleach to the stain with a small paint brush. Touch in the resulting patch with wood stain and repolish it.

If candle wax falls on a piece of furniture, wait until it solidifies, then pick it off with your fingernail or a plastic spatula. Use reviver to wash any remaining wax from the surface, then apply some fresh wax polish.

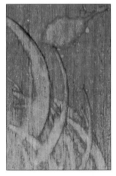

White ring stains
A wet glass left on a table overnight will etch a ring into the polish. Alcohol or nail varnish remover will also dissolve the finish, and heat will melt it. These marks are often no deeper than the top layer of polish and can be removed with a liquid metal polish or car paint cleaner.

Ink stains
Where the ink has penetrated the finish, moisten a cloth with methylated spirits, wrap it around your finger and rub the area of the stain. Use as little methylated spirits as possible – it dissolves polish.

Repairing surface damage

You can expect to find dents, scratches and other minor damage on regularly used furniture. These are important clues to the authenticity of antiques, and makers of reproduction furniture often age pieces artificially. You may wish to ignore minor scratches and dents, but if not, the remedies are relatively simple. Either way, polish wood regularly to protect it, use mats and cloths on dining tables and try to remove spills before a stain develops.

If the finish is scorched, you can improve it by rubbing it with metal polish. But if the wood is charred, you must scrape it off with a sharp, rounded blade. Fill the resulting hole with a stopper or, if it is shallow, level it with polish.

The materials you use for filling will depend on the extent of the damage. To disguise the repair, match the colour carefully.

Wax is an ideal medium for filling small, woodworm-type holes. Using a small soldering iron, mix wax crayons in a tin lid to get the right colour. When cool, press scrapings into the holes with a knife or chisel blade, then burnish the area with the back of a piece of abrasive paper. Finally, seal with polish.

Use a commercial stopper to fill large holes. They are sold in a range of wood-simulating colours. Press the stopper in, using a flexible blade, and leave it standing slightly proud, then finish it off with very fine abrasive paper when it has set. Plastic wood is a commercial filler which sets hard. It is useful for repairing damage on an unsupported edge. Press it into place with a knife blade, shaping it roughly to match the contour. When set, sand it flush with the original surface.

A dent can be disguised by treating it with a clear or stained finish, although if it is deep, you will have to use wood filler or stopping of the appropriate colour first, to build up the surface. Bruises and small dents can be removed by using water to swell the wood. The finish is removed with white spirit, then water and heat is applied. After the wood has swelled, it must be allowed to dry before sanding, recolouring, if necessary, with a matching stain, and repolishing.

You can polish out fine scratches with a metal polish, or disguise them by rubbing them with shoe polish or a commercial scratch remover. Fill deep scratches with wax polish, lacquer, or a thinned varnish stain. Modern lacquers are thick enough to use directly from the tin. But with French polish, you must pour a little into a shallow dish and leave it to evaporate until it stiffens slightly. A severe scratch which has penetrated below the surface finish and into the wood can only be repaired by stripping and refinishing the area (pages 18–21).

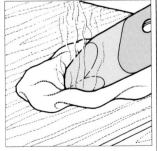

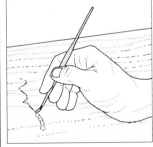

Using a hot iron and steam to raise a dent
Place a damp cloth on the area and run a hot domestic (above left) or soldering (above right) iron over it, keeping the iron on the move to avoid scorching. Eventually, the wood will swell to fill the dent. Alternatively, wrap a wad of cotton wool in clean linen and soak it in boiling water before applying it. Repeat several times. In either case, allow a few hours for the wood fibres to rise, sand and finish.

Filling deep scratches
Take a brushload of your chosen polish and "paint" several coats along the scratch, making sure that the repair stands proud. Sand the surface flush and finish with metal polish.

Repairing joints

Some pieces of furniture may need more drastic treatment than simply repairing surface damage. Chairs in particular are subject to a lot of wear and tear, especially on rails and joints, so it is quite likely that you will have to tackle a few of the repairs outlined here. When a piece you already have is damaged, it is best to mend it as soon as possible – you are more likely to get an invisible repair, as the two edges will not be dirty or worn. If you buy a broken chair, make sure that you are capable of restoring it.

Repairing broken tenons
A tenon fits into the slot of the mortise in a mortise and tenon joint. Unfortunately, when you dismantle a chair for regluing, you will often find that a tenon has broken inside the joint. If this is the case, you will have to cut out any remaining tenon in the joint in order to free the mortise and then repair the broken tenon.

Repairing a dowel joint
Dowel joints are made with hardwood pegs that are glued into both the pieces of wood being joined together. They are often used to join the cresting rail to the back legs, or to hold arms on carver chairs in place, and to reinforce other joints.

Repairing a split mortise
Mortise and tenon joints are widely used for tables and chairs, where they are usually found between the seat rails and the back legs and between stretcher rails and legs. Sideways pressure on this type of joint can split the leg.

Replacing a broken tenon

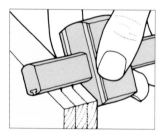
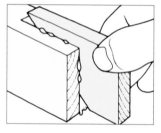
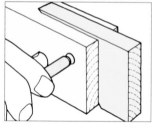

1 *First, square off the rail. Then use a mortise gauge to mark out an angled housing for the new tenon on the end and underside of the rail, making sure that the housing is three times as long as the original tenon.*

2 *Saw and pare out the waste from the new housing with a chisel. Cut a tenon to fit the angled housing from similar timber to that of the rail, matching the direction of the grain. Leave it slightly larger to make it easier to plane flush.*

3 *Glue the tenon that holds the housing closed, keeping it in place with a small G-clamp. Before planing the tenon to size, drill a hole through the wood and glue in a dowel: this will lock the tenon and rail together.*

SOFTENING GLUE

There are times when you will have to soften the glue of a sound joint – to remove a broken component, for instance. You should soften water-soluble glues with water or steam rather than brute force. You could wrap wet rags around a joint until water seeps into it, but this is a slow process. It is best to make a steam generator to inject steam straight into the joint. Both methods will damage surrounding polish, so be prepared for some refinishing.

To make a steam generator, plug a tight-fitting cork into a kettle. Drill a hole through the cork for a piece of brass tubing. Fit a length of rubber or heat-resistant plastic tubing on the brass tube and plug a second piece of brass tubing into the other end to make a nozzle. Half fill the kettle with water and heat it until the water is boiling. Drill a small hole in the joint and, wearing thick gloves to protect your hands, plug the steaming nozzle into the hole until the glue softens and the joint slackens. You should then be able to pull it apart easily.

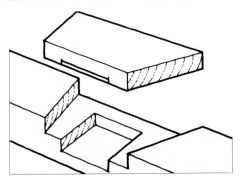

Repairing a split mortise

Introduce glue into the split with a brush or knife blade, then clamp it up. If the side of the mortise is broken away completely, you must first insert a strengthening patch of matching wood. Begin by making an angled saw cut at each side of the mortise down to the level of the damage. Pare out the waste so that the bottom surface of the housing is flush. Cut a patch to fit the housing, glue it and clamp it up. Once the glue has set, plane the patch flush and recut the side of the mortise.

Repairing a dowel joint

First remove any remaining dowel. Grip any protruding pieces with pincers, twisting and pulling them out. If the dowel has broken off below the surface, choose a drill bit that matches the hole and drill it out. Use the sides of the holes to centre the drill. If the dowel has broken off flush, a large drill could wander sideways and enlarge the hole, so drill out the centre with a small drill bit, then pick out the rest with a small gouge.

Ready-made hardwood dowels are available in a limited range of sizes. Buy them to suit the diameter of the holes. Cut lengths of dowel slightly shorter than the combined depths of the holes in the two halves of the joint. Chamfer the ends with a pencil sharpener and, using a saw, cut a groove through which trapped glue can escape. Glue the joint and clamp it in place until it sets hard.

Repairing loose chair joints

Chair joints are often heavily stressed, causing them to work loose. If the joint is covered in upholstery, you will have to remove it and take note of how it should be replaced. In this case, because the repair is to be concealed, joints can be repaired by screwing an L-shaped metal bracket to the inside of the frame. However, remaking the joint will produce a stronger repair – even though doing so will involve taking several joints apart and, if the joint links the seat to a leg, removing a triangular reinforcing block. If the joint is visible, you will also need to take it apart to make a neat repair.

Remaking the joint

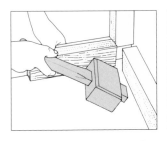

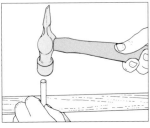

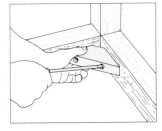

1 *Unscrew the reinforcing block, then tap it sharply with a hammer or mallet to break the glue bond. Separate the two pieces of wood and, if the dowels have sheared off, use a drill to remove them.*

2 *Measure the hole depth and cut a dowel ¼in (6mm) shorter than the combined depth of the matching holes. Cut a groove down each dowel, fill it with adhesive, then tap each into position with a hammer.*

3 *Tap the joint together with a mallet and either refit the original corner blocks or, if they are worn, screw new ones in place. Leave the chair on one side until the adhesive is completely dry.*

Levelling uneven chair and table legs

Every now and again you will come across a chair or table that rocks from leg to leg, even when you place it on a flat surface. To cure this, first make sure that there are no obvious faults, such as a tack driven into one foot, and check that a chair frame is true by looking across the seat rails to see if they are parallel. The simplest solution is either to trim the three longer legs, or to add a sliver of wood to the shorter leg.

To trim the legs, stand the chair on a flat board and let it come to rest in its optimum position. Measure from the short leg to the floor and, using a fine saw or sharp chisel, trim this amount off the other three legs. To ensure a perfect balance, sand rather than saw off the last millimetre or so.

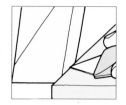

An over-length leg
Stand the chair on a board with the longest leg hanging over one edge. Mark where the leg meets the top of the board, then cut it to size.

Building up a short leg
Stand the chair on a flat board, making sure that the three longer legs are in contact with the surface. By trial and error, plane down a scrap of wood until it fits snugly under the short leg. Glue and screw the packing block in place and allow it to dry.

Rebuilding a damaged leg

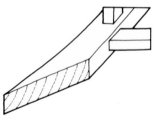

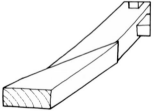

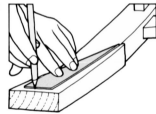

1 *If one end of a leg is badly broken or worm-eaten, you should glue on a new section. Cut and plane a 1 in 4 angle on the end of the leg.*

2 *Cut a similar angle on an oversize block of wood which has a similar grain direction to the original leg. Glue and clamp the block to the leg.*

3 *Mark the shape of the original leg on the block using a cardboard template. Shape the block with a saw and spokeshave. Reinforce the joint with dowels or screws.*

Mending broken chair rails

When a rail splits, it always follows the line of the grain. If a serious split occurs, but the rail is still in one piece, glue it immediately and bind it tightly with waxed string. If the rail has broken in two, you should reinforce the repair after gluing and binding with hardwood dowels or wood screws. Insert a screw or dowel from each side. The screws should be countersunk

and plugged. When this is done, bind up the joint again with the waxed string. Leave the string in place until the glue has completely set; then unwind it carefully and remove any excess glue. Refinish if necessary.

If a rail used to reinforce chair legs dislodges where the rail enters the hole, you can usually fix a dowel through the leg and the rail end to secure it back in place. If this is unsuccessful, however, you will either have to search for a matching rail or ask a carpenter to make up a new one.

Replacing a rail

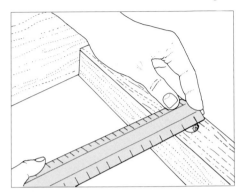

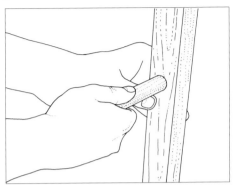

1 *Remove the old rail with a tenon saw, drill out the remaining stubs and clean the holes with a small file. Cut the new rail to length, allowing for the ends which enter the legs. Measure the diameter of the holes in the legs and draw a circle of the same diameter on the new rail using a compass, then file the ends of the rail until they fit snugly in the holes. Use an old brush to apply PVA woodworking adhesive inside the holes and on the rail ends.*

2 *Pull the chair legs slightly apart to allow the rail to fit into position, but try not to dislodge the other joints. Wipe off any excess glue and wind a string or fabric tourniquet around the chair legs to hold the rail in place until the adhesive has set firmly. To prevent marks from forming on the legs, insert cotton-wool pads under the tourniquet at the points of highest pressure. If necessary, stain the rail to match the colour of the rest of the chair.*

Mending castors

A castor will run badly or even jam if the small axle of the wheel is badly worn. If the castors have become stiff, you may be able to repair them by oiling them lightly. If the screws holding the castors to the legs have worked loose, fill the worn screw holes with slivers of wood and replace the screws. If the wheel starts to buckle under the chair, tighten the shaft by tapping it lightly with a hammer and punch. In cases where the castor has simply snapped off, it must be replaced. You should be able to buy a replacement castor from a DIY shop. Castors for chairs and sofas are readily available, but you may have to go to a specialist ironmonger or hardware shop to find more unusual types, such as toe castors, used on the tripod legs of pedestal tables, and cup castors, used on gateleg tables. If you cannot get a good match, replace all the castors. Castors are usually fixed to the legs by a central screw or via a cup socket. Keep castors in good condition by oiling them regularly.

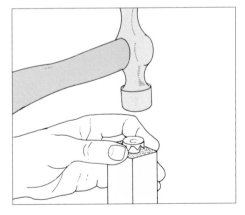

Replacing a castor
If the castor has a cup fitting, first remove the brass screws at the side of the cup and lightly tap around the base of the leg to release the castor. If it has a screw fitting, remove the wood screws and unscrew the castor by hand. Then check the new castor for fit. If the leg is too wide, trim it with a chisel or file; if it is too thin, pack it out with slivers of wood (above). If the fixing holes do not line up, plug the old ones and drill new holes, then screw the new castor in place.

Repairing tables

When a table top is fixed rigidly to the frame, shrinkage of the wood can lead to splits along the grain, or the glued joints that hold the separate planks together can open up. When this happens, you must take the top off the frame to make repairs. Take out retaining screws or knock out the glued blocks with a blunt chisel, then dismantle the frame.

Taking joints apart

Once the glue has failed, you may find that simple butt joints, or ones held by a tongue of ply or dowels, fall apart as soon as the top is freed from the underframe. However, if a joint is difficult to dismantle, try playing steam along it to soften the glue (page 24).

To loosen a joint, place a softening block at the end of one of the planks and tap it sharply with a mallet. If no movement occurs, try tapping in the other direction.

Regluing the top

You will need at least three sash clamps and softening blocks to glue up a table top. Place one clamp at each end on the underside and the other centrally on top, to prevent the top from

Regluing
Clamping a square or rectangular top.

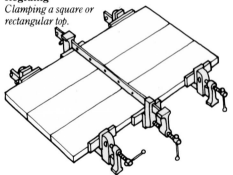

bowing as you apply pressure to the clamps. The softening blocks between the clamp heads and the edges of the top avoid bruising the wood. If the edges are moulded, shape the blocks to suit. Glue the edges, rub the joints together to squeeze out excess glue, then apply light pressure to the clamps. Wipe off any glue and inspect the joints. If they are not lying flush, lay a block of wood across each joint and strike it with a hammer until the edges line up perfectly. Put extra pressure on the clamp and clean off the glue again. Check that the top is flat by laying a straight-edge across it and raise or lower the clamps to take out any slight bowing.

To clamp up round or oval tops, you will have to make up a cradle for each side which will allow the clamps to apply force directly across the joints. This should be made of softwood blocks, shaped to fit the table and held in place with plywood.

Repairing a split panel

Any furniture which has solid panels is designed to cope with the fact that the wood will shrink across the grain. However, if the panel is held too rigidly, shrinkage will occur and the panel will eventually split.

You can fill a narrow split by opening it up slightly with the point of a tenon saw, then tapping in a piece of glued veneer and planing it smooth with the surface. In some pieces of furniture, the base frame or drawer runners prevent movement. Instead of the wood itself splitting, the glued joints may open up.

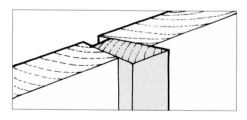

Filling a split
If the gap is wide enough, choose a strip of matching timber that is slightly wider than the open joint and plane a shallow taper along it. Scrape out the old glue from the joint with a knife blade, put glue on the strip and tap it into the gap until it jams in tightly. When set, scrape and sand the strip flush with the panel.

Rebuilding broken mouldings

Many table tops have shaped, moulded, decorative edges. If part of a moulding is split away, glue it back as soon as possible and either clamp or tape it tightly in place until the glue sets hard. If the piece of moulding is missing, you will have to rebuild the edge with a patch of matching wood. After you have glued the patch firmly in place, shape it and sand it to match the rest of the moulding.

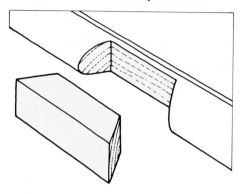

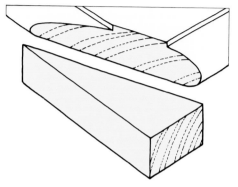

Mending damage in the centre
If the damage occurs in the centre of the moulding, let in a piece which is angled at each end. This not only makes the joint less visible, but also allows you to make trial fittings without forcing the piece into a tight gap in the moulding. You can then make sure that the new piece fits exactly.

Repairing a broken corner
Plane the damaged area flat and square, and cut and plane a block with the same grain direction. Glue both faces of the joint and rub them together until suction holds the block in place. Tape it tightly until the glue sets. Finally, shape the patch with a plane, files and a shaped sanding block to match the moulding.

Repairing drawers

Drawers are often mishandled. If they are used frequently and roughly, worn runners may cause them to stick; if they have been stored in damp or hot conditions, the sides may swell or warp, also causing them to stick. If they are overloaded, the bottom panel may bow, making the drawer impossible to open, or the panel may break away completely. Some older drawers have grooves and rails. Worn grooves should be recut with a circular saw and worn rails replaced.

If the runners are worn, simply remove the old ones and replace them. If the sides are swollen, allow to dry out in warm conditions for a couple of weeks or sandpaper the sides and runners and lubricate them with candle wax. To cure a bowed drawer, lever out the bottom panel with a knife or steel rule and apply fresh adhesive to the grooves before reassembling.

Replacing a drawer base
Cut a sheet of plywood to fit into the grooves on three sides of the drawer. If you cannot find plywood of the required thickness, buy it in the closest thickness and plane off a shallow angle on the underside at three edges. Slide in the new bottom and fix it with small, countersunk screws.

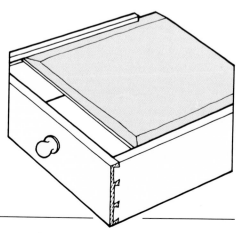

Cane and rush seating

Canework first became popular in Europe and America in the seventeenth century. Originally, it had a simple, open mesh, but gradually a closer, more decorative pattern was used. Rush-seated chairs are known to have been made in Europe since the Middle Ages. They have been in use in America since the arrival of the Pilgrim Fathers. Pre-woven panels of split cane for seats are available, but are difficult to fix to an adequate tension, so it is best to use the traditional method. It will take about 6–8 hours to weave a new seat for an average-sized chair.

Caring for cane and rush

Canework will dry out and become brittle in a dry, centrally heated atmosphere: a humidifier will prevent this. To wash dirty cane or rush, dip a cloth in warm, soapy water, wring it out and wipe over the surface. Rinse several times with clean water, as residues of soap may encourage mould. Rush is particularly vulnerable to mould, so leave the piece out in the sun to dry.

Preparing a chair for caning

The first thing to do is to remove the worn seat. Cut out the main panel inside the frame with a sharp trimming or craft knife, keeping a small sample of the caning as a pattern guide. If necessary, drill out the old wooden pegs and bits of cane from the holes in the seat frame. Carefully pull out any remaining pieces of cane with pliers. At this stage you should also check that the frame of the chair is sound and carry out any necessary repairs (pages 22–9).

Tools and materials for cane seats

Very few tools and materials are needed to work with either cane or rush seating, and most of these will probably be in your basic tool kit already. You will not need a workshop: just set the chair up so that you can work at a comfortable height in good daylight.

A craft knife is useful for cutting out the old seats, taper-nosed pliers will help to manipulate the cane, and end- or side-cutting nippers or scissors are useful for cutting lengths of cane or trimming the ends that hang below the seat. A spring needle can be used to lever up tight canes. Plastic golf tees are ideal for pegging the canes in place while you work. Use a stiff metal rod of suitable diameter – such as a large nail with the point filed flat, or the tip ground from an old cross-head screwdriver – for clearing old pegs from frame holes.

Types of seating cane

Cane used for seating is split into standard widths, numbered from 1 to 6. As a guide, use No. 2 cane for all the front-to-back and side-to-side work and for looping over the beading cane, No. 3 or 4 cane, which is slightly wider, for the diagonals, and No. 6 cane for beading edges. Before you use cane, soak it in warm water for a couple of minutes to make it supple, then put it in a plastic bag to keep it moist. If the cane starts to dry out, wipe it over with a wet cloth. Cane is smoother in one direction than the other; weave it in the smoother direction, with the shiny side uppermost, so that it will not catch.

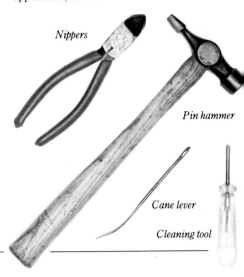

Nippers

Pin hammer

Cane lever

Cleaning tool

Fixing the first layer of cane

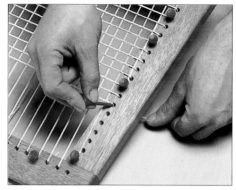

1 *Push one end of the cane through the central hole in the back rail until about 6in (15cm) protrudes underneath. Peg the cane in place, glossy side up, then draw it forwards to the central hole in the front rail. Check that the cane is neither twisted nor too tight and peg it in place. Then bring the strand up through the next hole to the right and pull it back to the corresponding hole in the back rail, so that the strands are parallel. Continue in this way until the right-hand side of the seat is filled with parallel canes, holding new canes in place with the tees. Fill the left-hand side in the same way.*

2 *Next, take canes across the seat at right angles to the first line of canes. Leave the front and back corner holes free: these will be needed for the diagonal layer. Peg a cane into the hole next to the back corner on the side rail and take it across to the back right-hand corner, then back across to the left-hand side, and so on until the seat is filled with a layer of parallel canes running from side to side on top of the vertical canes to form the first layer. Each time you use a new length of cane, leave at least 3in (75mm) hanging below the rail. Move the pegs along as you work, only leaving those holding new canes in place.*

Adding the second layer of cane

1 *The second layer is built up in the same way as the first. Take a second set of canes from front to back on top of the previous layer, using the existing strands as a guide, and easing the second layer of canes to the right of the first layer when threading through the holes. When the second row of front-to-back canes is complete, the weaving can begin with the second row of cross canes.*

2 *First moisten the canes by spraying with a mist of water, to prevent them from cracking while you weave. Secure the first cane in the back left-hand corner and weave it under and over both sets of canes running from front to back until you reach the back right-hand corner. Insert it into a hole, back through the next, and weave back from right to left. Continue weaving until the layer is complete.*

Weaving the diagonal layer

1 *Any weaving errors will be noticeable in this top layer, so work carefully. Start at the back left-hand corner, this time using the extreme corner hole, and take the cane to the opposite corner, weaving it under each pair of cross canes and over each pair of front-to-back canes. At the front corner take the cane down into the extreme corner hole and up through the next hole to the left. Weave this strand diagonally back across the seat, keeping it parallel with the first. When the left-hand side of the seat is filled, return to the back left-hand corner and continue working to the right to complete the seat.*

2 *Working from the back right-hand corner to the front left-hand corner, weave a second set of diagonals at right angles to the first. This time take the canes over the cross canes and under the front-to-back canes and fill the right-hand side of the seat first. Return to the back right-hand corner and fill the left-hand side. As the holes become more crowded, you may need to use a bodkin to help fit the canes through the holes.*

To keep the diagonals parallel on a tapered seat you will sometimes have to use a hole in the side rails twice. If you do, make sure that the pattern on the two diagonal layers matches.

Finishing off

The neatest way to finish off a cane chair seat is to plug alternate holes to lodge the canes in position, and fix a strand of beading over the peg holes. You will need No. 6 beading cane and No. 2 cane to secure it in position. Alternatively, the canes can be fixed in place by plugging each hole with a permanent peg. Finally, the beading needs to be plugged into the corner holes and any loose ends trimmed.

Plugging
To prevent the cane from slipping out of place, plug the holes. Cut the 3/16in (4.5mm) wide basket cane into 3/4in (20mm) lengths and smear each with a little PVA woodworking glue. Using a hammer, drive the plugs into alternate holes all around the edge of the seat until they lie just below the surface, but keep the corner holes clear. If the plugs will not fit easily into the holes, taper the ends with a sharp knife. If you find that a hole you do not plan to peg has a loose end of cane, push the end into an adjacent hole and plug that.

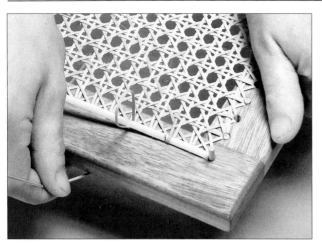

Beading

Cut four pieces of beading cane 2in (50mm) longer than each seat rail and cut one end of each strand into a taper. Take one strand and peg it into a corner of the frame. Then take a strand of ordinary (No. 2) cane, pass it up through the next unplugged hole, loop it over the beading cane and take it down the same hole to hold the beading flat against the seat. Take the securing cane along to the next unplugged hole and again up and over the beading cane, and so on until each side of the seat has been beaded. Before tightening the last loop, tuck the end into a corner hole.

Finishing off

Finally, hammer cane plugs into each corner of the seat to secure the ends of the beading. Turn the chair upside-down, apply glue to the remaining pieces of plugging cane and hammer them into the unplugged holes. Once the adhesive has set, trim off the untidy ends on the underside. If the chair has a rounded seat, apply the beading in a single strip and, when you reach the hole where you started, remove the peg and drive in the end of the beading strip. If the chair was dismantled to extract the seat frame before starting work, reassemble it, using PVA woodworking adhesive for a firm bond (pages 24–5).

Tools and materials for rush seats

Like caning, renewing a rush seat is a reasonably simple procedure, and few tools are needed. Use a large bundle of rush or seagrass for an average-sized seat. You will need a craft knife for removing the old seat and for trimming off rough ends. An old, worn screwdriver or chisel is useful for levering the last few cords into place and for manipulating knots, and an old lawnmower roller for flattening the seat.

Rush lever

Roller

Craft knife

Working out the sequence for rushing

Before you begin working, sprinkle your bundle of rushes with water and leave it to soften for a few minutes to make it pliable. For a strong seat, it is best to have the minimum of joins, so wind as much as you can handle on to a cardboard winder (shaped like a broad I). To join strands, tie them together on the underside of the seat. As a rough guide, allow 2–3 hours for re-rushing an average-sized chair. Removing the old seat produces a lot of dust and rush splinters, so work outside if you can, or lay down an old dust sheet.

The job involves winding the rushes around the frame from corner to corner. If, however, the seat is wider at the front than at the back, you will need to fill in the ends of the front rail to make it the same length as the back rail. Likewise, with a rectangular seat, when the left and right segments are full, you will have to take extra turns over the front and back rails to fill the gaps.

To fill in the front rail, tie the rushes to the left-hand seat rail with soft string. Twist the rushes into a cord, then wrap this cord over

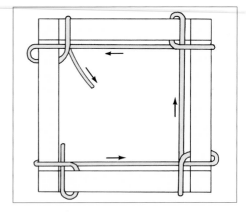

Filling a square frame
A pattern automatically forms as a strand of rush is woven around the frame and looped over each corner. This gives the impression that diagonal seams divide the chair into four segments.

the front rail close to the leg, up through frame, over the side rail and back up through the frame. Take the cord over the right-hand rail, through the frame and over the front, fastening it to the inside of the right-hand side rail. Continue in this way until the front corners are filled.

Weaving in the rushes

1 *Start in the front left-hand corner and tie the rush on to the frame, so that it exits from under a rail. Work around the seat in an anti-clockwise direction, taking the rush over the rail in the front right-hand corner of the seat. The strand is taken around this corner so that it exits from under the front rail and on to the back right-hand corner, and so on.*

2 *Continue winding anti-clockwise in the same sequence, building up the seat from the corners and working towards the centre of the seat. As you pass strands over a rail, twist them to ensure a neat finish. Leave lower strands untwisted. Tie each new strand on to the end of the previous one on the underside of the seat.*

Tightening and packing the rushes

1 *To ensure that the frame is well covered and that the diagonals lie straight, the strands need to be pushed tightly and evenly together after about eight rows have been woven in each corner. Use your fingers to pull the strands firmly towards the frame. Take a few strands at a time, lodge your knee against the frame and ease the strands together so that the rail is not visible underneath. Repeat after every eight strands.*

As an alternative, you can use a scrap of wood and a mallet to drive the strands together, again so that the chair frame is not visible. Insert the piece of wood vertically between the strands and tap it firmly with the mallet.

2 *Each time you tighten the rushes, pack the gap between the top and bottom layers with broken pieces of rush to give the seat greater comfort and strength and to prevent it from sagging. Use a knife to trim off the loose ends of any rushes protruding from the bottom of the seat. Fold the offcuts in half and push them into the pocket formed between the two layers at the corners, using a rush lever, blunt knife or scissors to ensure a tight fit. Continue pushing in the offcuts until you can push no more in. Once you have packed the corners, continue to weave in the same way, squeezing up the corners and packing every eight or nine rows until you reach the centre.*

Securing and finishing

1 *Wrap the last strand over the rail to the underside of the seat. Pull it to the centre and gently ease down a woven strand far enough to allow the final strand to be slipped underneath. Tie a stopper knot in it to prevent it from slipping out of place, and trim off any free ends. Alternatively, push the last two strands through the hole in the centre of the seat to the underside as shown.*

2 *Tie the strands together with a firm knot and tidy up the loose ends. If the chair was dismantled before work started, reassemble it, using PVA adhesive to ensure strong joints (pages 24–5). To finish, you can add a coat of wax or polish to give the rush a rich and protective finish and a lustrous sheen.*

Renewing upholstery

If a chair seat is sagging or lumpy, it needs to be stripped, and the old webbing, padding and springs replaced. In many cases the outer fabric wears before the inner padding, but it is still wise to renew the padding when re-covering the seat. Always use a strong fabric that is recommended for upholstery when choosing your cover material.

There are two basic types of upholstered seat: a fixed seat, which forms an integral part of the chair, and a loose, padded seat, which contains no springs and simply drops into the

chair frame. Although the same basic upholstery technique is used for all types of chair, a drop-in seat pad (below left) is easier to work on than a fixed seat, because it can be detached and turned to any angle, and because it contains no springs. To re-upholster a chair which does not have springs, fix the webbing, hessian and stuffing in the same way as you do for the drop-in seat pad (page 44), make rows of blind and top stitching (page 41) around the perimeter to build a firm edge to the cushion, and then complete as for the sprung seat.

Sprung chair seat
Once you can successfully repair a sprung stuffed-over chair (right), you are well on the way to becoming an upholsterer. This job contains all the elements of traditional upholstery – sewing and lacing a coil spring platform, judging the amount and shape of stuffing, and sculpting it with stitches. The top cover is either tacked and trimmed to the side of the seat frame, or wrapped and tacked underneath.

Drop-in seat pad
Although no upholstery task can be described as easy, a drop-in seat pad (below) is the simplest project for a complete beginner. Because the pad itself is removable, you can work on it unhindered by the frame.

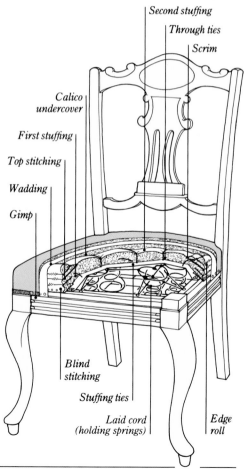

Second stuffing

Through ties

Scrim

Calico undercover

First stuffing

Top stitching

Wadding

Gimp

Blind stitching

Stuffing ties

Laid cord (holding springs)

Edge roll

Calico undercover

Wadding

Top cover

Stuffing

Stuffing ties

Hessian platform

Removable frame

Webbing

Tools and materials

Specialist upholstery tools and materials, available from needlework and DIY shops and upholsterers, are essential. Woven webbing, which comes in jute, linen or cotton mixtures, is used for traditional upholstery. Rubber webbing, used with foam rubber padding, is for modern furniture. Use 2in (50mm) webbing for chair seats. The hessian should be the 16oz (450g) "tarpaulin" type.

For traditional upholstery, horsehair and sheep's wool are the best stuffing materials, but those mixed with other animal hairs are less expensive and more readily available. You will need a tack lifter to remove old tacks and a sharp knife to cut the springs free from the webbing. Webbing, hessian and calico are secured with ⅝in (16mm) tin tacks and the covering material with ⅜in (10mm) or ½in (12mm) fine-headed tacks.

Tacks are driven in with a small tacking hammer. The springs are attached with No. 1 upholsterers' twine and a 5–6in (12.5–15cm) spring needle, and the padding with light-weight upholsterers' twine and a 10in (25cm) stitching needle. Scissors are useful for cutting all materials and latex adhesive is needed for gluing the gimp over the tacks.

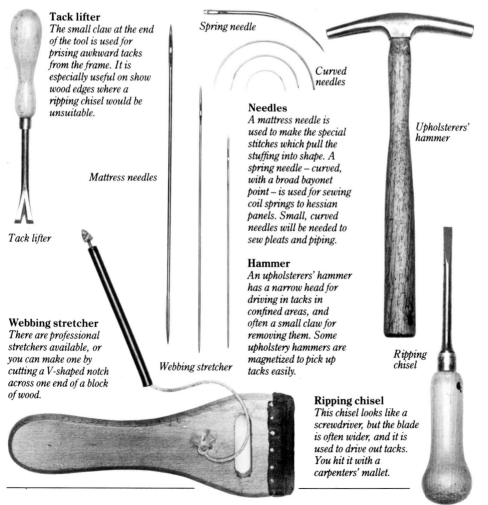

Tack lifter
The small claw at the end of the tool is used for prising awkward tacks from the frame. It is especially useful on show wood edges where a ripping chisel would be unsuitable.

Tack lifter

Spring needle

Curved needles

Needles
A mattress needle is used to make the special stitches which pull the stuffing into shape. A spring needle – curved, with a broad bayonet point – is used for sewing coil springs to hessian panels. Small, curved needles will be needed to sew pleats and piping.

Mattress needles

Hammer
An upholsterers' hammer has a narrow head for driving in tacks in confined areas, and often a small claw for removing them. Some upholstery hammers are magnetized to pick up tacks easily.

Upholsterers' hammer

Webbing stretcher
There are professional stretchers available, or you can make one by cutting a V-shaped notch across one end of a block of wood.

Webbing stretcher

Ripping chisel

Ripping chisel
This chisel looks like a screwdriver, but the blade is often wider, and it is used to drive out tacks. You hit it with a carpenters' mallet.

Ripping off

Ripping off is an upholsterers' term for removing old upholstery. This is a filthy job, so put on old clothes and wear a face mask. Begin by removing the dust panel, covering fabrics and webbing, using a ripping chisel or tack lifter (for show wood) to get the tacks out. Work all around the frame, always driving in the direction of the grain to avoid splitting the rail. You will have to hold a drop-in seat pad in a bench vice.

Cut the twine holding the springs to the coverings and compress them with your hands. As long as they are not broken and will return well, you can reuse them.

Discard all the old covering material, unless you find horsehair. This top-quality stuffing material can be revived and used again. Tease the horsehair apart to shake out all the dust, then wash it in warm, soapy water. Tease it out once more and leave it to dry.

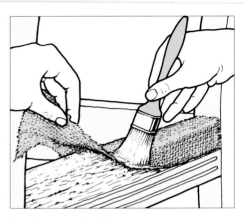

Reinforcing a chair frame
Before you begin to upholster, carry out any repairs (pages 24–7). The rails on an old chair that has been upholstered many times may be splintered and need reinforcing. Stipple woodworking glue on to the rails and then lay a piece of hessian over it. Paint more glue on top to saturate the hessian, then rub it down on to the rail with a block of wood.

Renewing webbing

On a traditional chair you will need woven webbing, which is fixed in a series of strips, first from front to back, then from left to right, until it forms a criss-cross network over the bottom of the seat. It is best to keep the webbing in one long strip and to cut as you go, to be sure of the correct measurements.

On a modern chair you may need rubber webbing, which stretches when pulled or sat upon, so it is important that each strip is fixed under the same tension. For dining and other small chairs you only need to fix rubber webbing in one direction, but for larger chairs you should interweave a second row for extra strength. With both types of webbing you will finally have to attach the springs to the new webbing (opposite).

Replacing woven webbing
Fold under 1in (25mm) of webbing, position the folded edge halfway across the back rail of the seat and hammer in three tacks ½in (12mm) from the fold. Add two more tacks, evenly

Tacking webbing
When replacing webbing, make sure that you hammer in the tacks to one side of the old tack holes. Keep the webbing taut and interweave the strips as shown here. A web should "ring" when it is tapped.

spaced below the first row. Pull the webbing taut and fasten it to the front rail, using three tacks as before. Cut off the excess, fold over 1in (25mm) and hammer in two more tacks to secure it. Fix the rest of the strips, weaving the cross strips to form a network.

Using rubber webbing
Measure the distance from the centre of the back rail to the centre of the front rail. To transfer this on to the webbing, first draw a line ½in (12mm) from one end of the webbing, then measure off the chair span from this line and draw a second line. Next, mark a third line 1in (25mm) inside the second. Position the webbing on the chair with the first line lying

halfway across the back rail and hammer in four tacks across it at equal distances. Lay the webbing straight across the frame so that the third line lies halfway across the front rail, then fix it in position and cut off the surplus.

To ensure that each strip has the same tension, measure and fix each in the same way until equally spaced strips span the frame. On a large chair add a second row in the same way, stretched evenly, but running from left to right and interweaving the first layer.

USING A WEBBING STRETCHER

When the webbing is tacked at one end, wrap the other end over the stretcher and tuck it into the notch, trapping it against the frame with the tool. Lever down on the stretcher to pull the length of webbing taut across the frame, then tack the webbing in place.

You may find it easier to use the webbing stretcher against the top side of the rail, so that the webbing is held firmly against the bottom side of the chair for you to drive in the tacks.

Replacing springs

If you have just renewed the webbing, you will need to reattach the springs. If you are not reupholstering, but need to secure a loose spring or insert a new one, you will first need to remove the "bottoming" and release the webbing by prising off the securing tacks. To fix the springs to the webbing, cut a length of No. 1 upholsterers' twine and thread it to a spring needle. When you have secured the springs in position on the webbing, you will need to lace them together and to the seat frame with cord, to make sure that they will work in unison.

Sewing the springs to the webbing

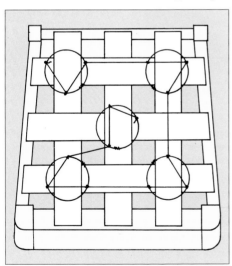

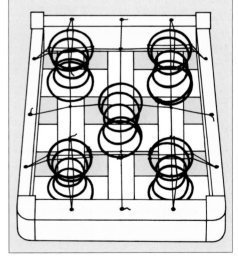

1 *Arrange the springs so that they are evenly supported by the webbing and their ends face the centre of the chair. Then push the threaded needle through the webbing and make a stitch over the base of the spring, using a half-hitch knot to fasten it underneath. Make two more stitches at equal intervals around the spring base. Repeat the process for the other springs, using the same piece of twine.*

2 *Using a ⅝in (15mm) improved tack, secure a length of cord to the back rail, aligning it with the springs. Compress the first spring and tie a half-hitch around the second coil from the top. Tie another knot around the opposite side of the top coil. Compress and tie the next spring and tie the cord around the tack on the front rail. Repeat the process with separate lengths of cord until all the springs are secured.*

Fitting new hessian

The springs must be covered with a layer of strong hessian to support the padding and prevent it from falling through the seat. Cut a piece of strong hessian about 1in (25mm) larger all around than the frame of your chair, centre it over the frame and partially drive in tacks at the centre of each rail to tension it.

When tensioning the hessian, make sure that you do not compress the springs any further. Extra compression may make the lacing slacken so that the springing will not function. Attaching the hessian to the springs prevents movement between them which would wear through the hessian.

Replacing hessian

 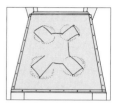

1 *Fold the edge of the hessian over and tack at the centre, then the corners, of the back rail. Tack the centre of the other three sides, then the front corners and finally all around.*

2 *To attach the hessian to the springs, use the same method as when sewing the springs to the webbing (page 39). This will prevent movement which would wear through the hessian.*

Replacing the padding

On traditional chairs, horsehair, wool or vegetable fibre padding is positioned on top of the hessian and is anchored with stuffing ties sewn across the hessian, then covered with a layer of calico. Modern chairs, however, may be padded with foam rubber, which is fitted directly over rubber webbing. The foam rubber is cut to size, with ½in (12mm) extra added all around, and is secured to the frame with a calico surround.

Some modern chairs may have foam rubber padding which is fixed to the frame with four lengths of calico folded in half lengthways and glued to the sides of the foam pad. When the glue has set, the free edge of calico is pulled down tightly and tacked to the chair frame, with tacks about 1in (25mm) apart.

Renewing the stuffing

 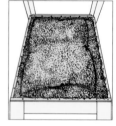

1 *Using a spring needle and a length of stitching twine, sew two large stuffing ties along each side, about 3in (75mm) from the edge of the seat, and loose enough to fit two fingers under each tie.*

2 *Tease out the fibre and tuck bundles of it under each tie, starting at the back and working forwards. When the loops are filled, pile more teased stuffing into a dome about 4in (100mm) high in the middle.*

Renewing the scrim

In some sprung chairs the fibre stuffing is covered with scrim to shape the seat and a second layer of padding put over the first, in turn secured by stuffing ties stitched to the scrim, and covered with a layer of calico. The scrim stage is used to shape and firm up the seat pad. Through ties are made between the

scrim and the hessian to pull down the centre of the seat. Other upholstery stitches, such as blind stitching and top stitching, can be used to firm the edge of the seat even more.

To renew the scrim, begin by cutting a panel large enough to cover the fibre, with at least 2in (50mm) to spare on all sides. Fix it temporarily with one tack in the centre of each rail and make diagonal cuts into the two back corners to fit around the legs.

Fitting the scrim

 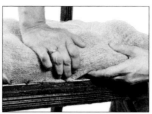 

1 *Make through ties between the scrim and the hessian to pull down the centre of the seat, criss-crossing the seat at 4in (100mm) intervals. At the last corner, tie the thread. The through ties will be pulled tight when the scrim is tacked.*

2 *Remove a tack and firm up the edge by stuffing fibre under the hessian. Tuck the edge of the scrim under the stuffing, pinch it and pull it down, tacking it along the edge of the seat rail. Stuff more fibre in to build up the edge at the corners.*

3 *Fold the edge in at the corner under the stuffing, tacking it to the rail as before. Work around each side in this manner. Pleat the front corners to get rid of any excess fabric. Pull the through ties tight and finish them with a firm knot.*

Making through ties

Thread a mattress needle with twine and start with a slip knot in one corner on top, then pass the needle through the seat. As soon as the unthreaded end of the needle emerges underneath, move it ¾in (19mm) to one side, then push the threaded end back up through the seat so that it emerges near its original entry point. Remove the needle completely, make another stitch about 4in (100mm) to one side, and so on to criss-cross the seat at 4in (100mm) intervals.

Other upholstery stitches

Blind and top stitches are special upholstery stitches used to shape and firm the scrim-covered seat. One row of blind stitches pulls the stuffing against the side wall of the seat cushion, and two rows of top stitches sculpt a square corner to the seat pad.

To make blind stitches, push the mattress needle into the side of the chair near the back at an angle of 45°. Pull the needle through to the top, but just before the eye emerges, angle it back so that it appears in front of the leg above the tack line. Pull the needle out, tie a slip knot and pull the stitch tight. Insert the needle 2in (50mm) along to emerge on the top, 1in (25mm) behind its point of entry. Just before the eye appears, return it again to exit

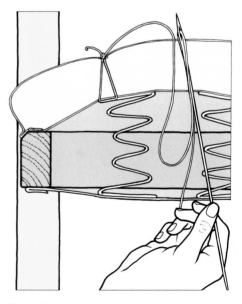

Through ties
These are made between the scrim and the hessian to shape the seat.

next to the first stitch. Before you extract the needle, wind the thread around it three times to bind the stitch. Make a row of stitches around the pad and finish with a double hitch. Top stitches are made in the same way, but the needle is pulled free of the top.

Replacing the calico

Traditional padding, held in place with stuffing ties, needs to be completely covered with a layer of calico to preserve its shape before the final layers of wadding and fabric are added. Smooth the stuffing into an even dome at the same time as you pull down on the calico cover, and try to keep this shape to the seat as you work around the chair frame, tacking the calico securely in place.

Fitting calico

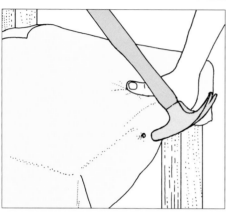

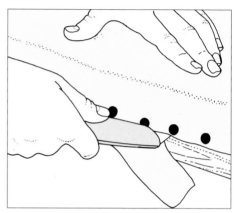

1 *Cut a calico undercover 2–3in (50–75mm) larger than the frame. Spread the calico across the stuffing, partially tacking it in the centre of each rail, just above the show wood. Stretching the fabric diagonally, tension it by pulling each corner over the frame and tacking it in place. Remove one tack in a side rail and smooth the fabric from the centre to the side with your hand before you insert the row of tacks.*

2 *Hold the calico in place while you drive in a row of tacks, about 1in (25mm) apart, from the centre of each rail towards the corners. Make diagonal release cuts at the back corners and trim away the excess to reduce the bulk. Tuck in the fabric to make a neat, folded edge against the leg, and tack. Tack neat pleats in the front corners and trim the fabric close to the tacks, using a sharp knife.*

Re-covering and finishing off

When replacing the cover of a fixed seat or a drop-in pad, the covering fabric will need to be a resilient material intended for upholstery. It is cut to the size of the chair, allowing 3in (75mm) extra material all around for turning and trimming. Before fitting the top cover, cut a piece of cotton wadding slightly larger than the pad and lay it squarely on top, so that it reaches almost to the bottom tack line. Holding the wadding down with one hand, pluck at its edges to feather it off so that it does not show as a ridge under the cover.

On a fixed seat the cover is tacked on to the side of the chair frame, and on a drop-in pad it is tucked around the pad frame and tacked to the underside. To finish both a fixed chair seat and a drop-in pad, a piece of black linen "bottoming" is stretched and fitted to the underside of the seat in a similar way to the first hessian panel (page 40), but with the edges turned under all the way around to give a neat edge. The bottoming should cover all the tacks fixing the top cover of a drop-in pad and follow the edges of the seat or pad.

Finally, a length of braid or gimp is pinned and glued around the edge of a fixed seat to cover the tacks and give a neat finish. Use tacks or gimp pins to attach each end of the braid and latex adhesive to glue along its lengths. You may need to attach a separate length of braid across the back of the chair.

Replacing the top cover

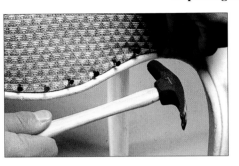

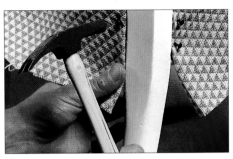

1 *Using fine-headed tacks, temporarily tack the cover to the frame, first at the centre of each side edge to tension it, then drive in the tacks at 1in (25mm) intervals to within 2in (50mm) of the corners, keeping the fabric smooth and taut as you work.*

2 *Turn the corners back and make a diagonal cut to the line of the fold. Fold the resulting triangles to fit neatly against the upright. Trim the excess fabric to within ½in (12mm) of the fold and tack it temporarily to the frame.*

3 *If the front corners are square, fold the surplus fabric into a single pleat and tack it in place. With rounded corners, fold the fabric into a double or inverted pleat (one each side) before tacking.*

4 *Make sure that the cover is not wrinkled and hammer home the temporary tacks. Add extra tacks between them so that they are spaced about ½in (12mm) apart. Trim the excess fabric with a knife.*

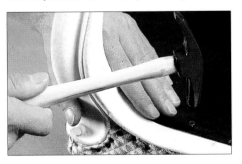

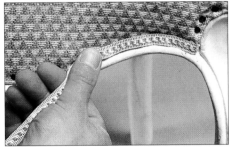

5 *Cut a piece of bottoming slightly larger than the bottom of the chair, centre on the underside of the frame and turn under about ½in (12mm) all around. Secure it with tacks spaced about 2in (50mm) apart, close to the folded edge.*

6 *Fold over ½in (12mm) at one end of a length of braid and tack it to the edge of the chair. Spread adhesive on the inside of the braid and press it into position over the tacks. Fold over ½in (12mm) at the other end and secure it in place.*

Re-covering a loose seat

Many dining chairs have a loose upholstered pad which drops inside the seat rails to rest on rebates. There are no springs in loose drop-in seat pads, but otherwise all the stages are the same as for repairing a sprung seat (that is, webbing, hessian, stuffing, calico, wadding and top cover). Since they can be removed from the chair frame, loose pads are much easier to work with.

Re-covering a loose seat

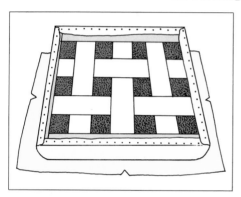

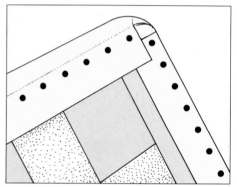

1 *Lay the fabric upside-down on a flat surface. Centre the wadding on top of the seat and lay both seat and wadding upside-down on the fabric. Fold the fabric around the frame along the back edge and temporarily tack at the centre on the underside. Smooth the fabric over the seat and tack in the centre of the other three sides. Working outwards from the centre back, continue tacking at 1in (25mm) intervals to within 2in (50mm) of each corner. Repeat on the other sides, checking that the fabric lies smooth.*

2 *To neaten the corners, pull the fabric down hard diagonally and tack the corner to the underside of the frame. Fold the extra fabric on either side of the tack into a pleat and tack into place. If there are any wrinkles, remove tacks which are pulling too tight and retack. Trim the fabric to within ½in (12mm) of the tacks. Finally, tack a piece of bottoming to the underside of the frame, as for a fixed seat (pages 42–3). Stretch it over the frame in the same way as for hessian (page 40).*

Repairing torn upholstery

Small tears and holes in upholstery should be repaired as soon as possible to prevent them from fraying. Burnt, worn and torn areas can be darned or patched with a small piece of matching fabric from inside a seam or hem or other unobtrusive area, making sure that the design matches closely.

First, snip off any loose threads. If the damage is bad, however, you will have to disguise it. Worn arms on chairs can be covered with a pair of simple arm caps made from remnants. Bad stains can sometimes be disguised by appliqué motifs, provided that the fabrics are of the same weight.

Darning tears
Press the damaged fabric flat and fix a piece of iron-on interfacing, ½in (12mm) larger than the tear, on the wrong side of the fabric over the tear. Darn across the tear.

Patching large holes or tears
Cut a small piece of matching fabric from an unobtrusive area. Slide the patch under the tear and either stick it with a latex adhesive or sew it in place.

Replacing worn piping

The cylindrical raised edge found along some seams on upholstery is known as piping. It is made by covering thick cotton cord with fabric. Piping is often the first part of the upholstery to wear, and it can be replaced as long as the rest of the fabric is in good condition.

Use fine skewers to hold the fabric to the stuffing. Carefully cut the threads holding the original piping in place, making sure that you do not cut the rest of the fabric. Then remove the old piping. Buy piping cord of the same thickness as the original and lay it down in the centre of a fabric strip 1½in (40mm) wide, cut on the bias. (Join two strips of fabric end-to-end by placing them pattern side together and at 90°, and sewing across.) Fold the fabric over the cord and sew the two sides together along the edge of the cord. Place the flange of the piping inside the seam of the upholstery. Close the seam with slip-stitching, passing the thread through the flange close to the piping.

Removing stains from soft furnishings

It is best to deal with spillages and stains as quickly as possible. Blot or scrape a spillage immediately, working from the edge to avoid spreading it. If the stain is greasy, sprinkle on an absorbent, such as talcum powder, leave for 30 minutes, then brush or shake and vacuum, and dry clean (page 46). If it is water-based, rinse immediately in cold water, then wash or shampoo (page 47).

To make up an ammonia or borax solution for use on water-soluble stains, mix one table-spoon of ammonia or borax in 1pint (600ml) of warm water. For a peroxide solution, used to remove such stains as coffee and chocolate, add one part of 20 vol peroxide to four parts cold water and add a drop of ammonia.

CLEANING FURNISHING FABRICS

Regular care and cleaning of soft furnishings will help to prolong their life and keep them looking fresh. Dirt and dust can permanently damage the fabric, so it is worth vacuuming, brushing and shaking out the dust every week. Spills and stains should be treated immediately and fabrics should be washed before the dirt becomes ingrained.

Protective treatments
Use a dirt-repellent spray on new fabric and reapply regularly after cleaning. Slip covers will help to protect the arms and backs of upholstered chairs and sofas, which receive a lot of wear. Similarly, linings help to prolong the life of curtains.

Upholstery
Upholstery should be cleaned two or three times a year with upholstery shampoo. Always test for colour fastness first by wetting a small area and pressing with a warm iron between two pieces of plain white cotton. If no colour comes off on the cotton, the fabric is colourfast and can be washed, but if the colour smudges, the fabric will have to be dry cleaned.

Washable loose covers
Any tears should be mended before the fabric is shampooed. If it is not recommended for machine washing, you will need to launder the fabric gently by hand in warm water and mild detergent. Iron the loose covers while they are still damp, on the wrong side for matt finishes and on the right side for shiny ones. Fabrics with special finishes are best drip-dried; stretch covers can usually be machine washed and do not need ironing. Check any drying recommendations before using a tumble drier.

Curtains
All curtains should be washed or cleaned regularly to prevent the fabric from wearing out quickly. Lined, interlined and heavy fabrics will probably have to be dry cleaned. Before washing or cleaning, remove all the hooks, ease out the gathers and shake out any loose dirt. If you are washing the curtains, soak them in cold water with liquid detergent for 10 minutes, then rinse, wash, drip-dry and iron them while they are still damp.

Fabric lampshades
Turn off the electricity, remove the shade and take off the trimmings if they are not colourfast. Clean washable fabrics in warm, soapy water, rinse in clear, lukewarm water and allow them to dry naturally. Non-washable fabrics, and those that are not colourfast, should be dry cleaned.

REMOVING WATER-SOLUBLE STAINS

Washable fabrics, except for wool, silk and non-colourfast materials, should be soaked immediately in a solution of the suggested cleaner (see below). To remove fresh stains on colourfast linens, stretch the fabric over the sink, sprinkle on some powdered detergent or stain remover, pour boiling water through, then rinse. If the stain remains, rub cleaner gently into it, rinse and wash. With non-washable fabrics, stretch the fabric over a jug and pour cold water through the stain. If the stain remains, put an absorbent pad under it and work in the cleaning solution with a second pad, then sponge the area with clear water and blot it dry. Repeat the process if necessary.

Stain	Method of removal
Beer	Use detergent or shampoo. For dried stains, add one egg cup of white vinegar to 1 pint (600ml) of water.
Blood	Soak fresh stains in cold water – never boil, as this sets the stain. For dried stains, sponge with salt water (½ tsp salt to 1 pint – 600ml – water) or use biological detergent or carpet shampoo.
Coffee, tea and chocolate	Use borax or peroxide solution or carpet shampoo. With dried stains, loosen with glycerine first.
Fruit juice and jam	On white table linen, pour salt on the fresh stain to stop it from spreading, then rinse with boiling water. Otherwise use peroxide or borax solution, or carpet shampoo.
Ink	Rinse in cold water and wash.
Lemon juice	Use borax solution, then wash.
Mildew	Brush off excess, then use upholstery shampoo.
Milk	Rinse fresh stains in lukewarm water. For dried stains, use borax solution or carpet shampoo.
Nicotine	As an alternative to the dry-cleaning method, try detergent or peroxide solution.
Soft drinks	Rinse with boiling water, then wash.
Soot	On washables and carpets, vacuum the excess, then try using detergent or shampoo before dry cleaner.
Urine	Use biological detergent or carpet shampoo, adding one egg cup of white vinegar to 1 pint (600ml) of water to the shampoo solution.
Vomit and faeces	If necessary, use an absorbent first, then biological detergent, borax solution or carpet shampoo.
Water	Rainspots on felt, velvet and taffeta can be removed by holding the material in the steam from a boiling kettle, not too near the spout. Remove alkaline drinking water marks by sponging with a solution of one teaspoon of white vinegar to 1 pint (600ml) warm water.
Wine	Use an absorbent pad to prevent the stain from spreading, sponge with clean, warm water, then use upholstery shampoo on non-washables. For washables, soak in a borax solution for half an hour before washing.

REMOVING SOLVENT-SOLUBLE STAINS

Stains that cannot be removed by water, or that are on fabrics which are not washable, will need to be dry cleaned. Use a dry-cleaning agent, but test it first on an inconspicuous part of the fabric. Follow the instructions carefully and leave for 15 minutes to check that it does not discolour the fabric. To treat a stain, place a wad of white tissues or cotton wool under the fabric, then apply the cleaner to the right side of the fabric with another pad. Take care not to soak the fabric too much, and work from the outer edge of the stain inwards to prevent it from spreading. Change the pads frequently, and blot dry after each application. When the stain has disappeared, wash or dry clean the fabric.

Stain	Method of removal
Adhesives	**Clear and contact adhesive** Use acetone, amyl acetate or non-oily nail varnish remover until the stain has disappeared, then dry clean. **Latex and model-maker's cement** Remove the worst with a spatula, then use dry cleaner. **Epoxy resin** Cannot remove once hardened. Try acetone, amyl acetate or lighter fuel before the stain dries.
Ballpoint and felt pen marks	Use methylated spirits and dry cleaner.
Candle wax	Scrape off as much as you can with a blunt blade. Place slightly damp blotting paper or tissues over (and if possible under) the fabric and press quickly with a warm iron. Repeat until the wax is absorbed. On furniture, chill with an ice cube, then scrape off. Alternatively, use dry cleaner.
Chewing gum	Chill with an ice cube to harden, then scrape off before using dry cleaner.
Cream, ice cream	Use dry cleaner. For washable fabrics, try biological detergent or borax solution first.
Gravy	If it contains grease, use dry cleaner.
Grease	Remove as much as possible with an absorbent pad, then use dry cleaner. On wallpaper, dab lightly with baby powder on cotton wool, or try holding blotting paper over the stain and pressing quickly with a warm iron, but take care not to scorch the paper.
Mustard	For non-washable fabrics, use methylated spirits or dry cleaner. Soften old stains with glycerine, then rinse with lukewarm water and dry before using dry cleaner.
Nail varnish	Use acetone, amyl acetate or non-oily nail varnish remover.
Nicotine	Use eucalyptus oil or methylated spirits.
Oil and paraffin	Soak up as much as possible with absorbent, then use dry cleaner. For bicycle or motor oil, try eucalyptus oil.
Paint and varnish	For enamel and oil paints, use paint remover or turpentine. For cellulose paint, use acetone or amyl acetate. Fresh emulsion can be rinsed off with cold water. Dried stains cannot usually be removed, but try methylated spirits.

Replacing loose covers

L oose covers can be used to give new life to an old chair or sofa or to co-ordinate new furniture with the rest of the decoration in the room. Making the loose covers takes time and effort, but a favourite, well-worn piece of furniture that has seen better days can be made to look as good as new.

The exact fitting and styling of the loose covers will vary depending on the shape of the chair or sofa. Square shapes are the easiest; curves and scrolls require more attention and care when cutting and fitting the fabric.

The best method is to fit the different pieces on the chair with the right side of the fabric showing. You can then get the pieces into exactly the right position, taking into account any irregularities in the chair's shape. Each section is smoothed and pinned until it fits perfectly. Remove the cover and repin the seams on the wrong side of the fabric ready for stitching.

Another method is to fit the fabric wrong side out. This saves time in repinning the seams ready for sewing, but is not as accurate: it does not allow for any unevenness in the chair's shape and makes matching patterns more difficult. If you are replacing an existing cover, unpick the seams and use it as a pattern. If you are working with an expensive material or complicated print, it may be worthwhile to make a trial cover from cheap material or calico to use as a pattern.

Choosing fabric

The initial choice of the correct kind of fabric is crucial to achieving a professional finish with minimum effort. A department store with a good selection of furnishing fabrics will usually be able to advise you about suitable materials. For heavy daily wear, choose from the more robust and durable fabrics, such as cotton/linen union, damask or heavy cottons.

The best fabrics are firm and closely woven, as these will retain their shape. Ideally, the material chosen should also be shrink- and fade-resistant. Very thick and heavily textured fabrics should be avoided as they are difficult to fit and, where several layers are seamed or overlapped, they create too much bulk.

With plain colours, the weight and texture of the fabric are all-important, especially if you are fitting new covers to an old chair with well-worn lumps and bumps. A light colour or shiny finish will tend to show up any undulations, whereas matt or slightly textured fabrics and deep colours will make them less noticeable. A large print can look very impressive if the motifs are centred on the different sections of the chair or sofa, but this can be wasteful of fabric and requires careful attention when matching the pattern.

Measuring up and estimating fabric

Handling large areas of bulky fabric is often difficult and cumbersome, but the best way of fitting the material accurately is by cutting it directly on the chair or sofa. Tailor the style of the cover to the shape of your chair, cutting as many sections as you need to ensure that the fabric is not stretched or pulled around corners or on the arms. If you are making loose covers for a new chair, the seams of the inner calico cover will provide guide lines for placing the seams on the external cover. Otherwise, look at the existing worn covers which you are replacing to see how they are cut and seamed.

Calculating the amount of fabric
You will need to take three main measurements, as shown opposite, to estimate the amount of fabric needed. Check that the pieces can be cut from a single width of fabric and add together the measurements to find the total amount of material needed, allowing for matching patterns. When you are measuring

the width, remember to allow an extra 3in (75mm) on the back for a centre opening, or 1½in (40mm) on both the side and the back for a side back opening. Make sure that you allow a sufficient amount of material for reasonable seam allowances, otherwise you will find it difficult to cut and fit the fabric on the chair or sofa. The most economical way to do this is to join the widths along a single central seam, but a conspicuous central pattern or motif should be centred on the back with two narrower panels sewn on either side to make up the width. Allow enough fabric for bias strips to cover the piping cord if you are trimming the cover with self-fabric piping, and for a gathered or pleated skirt (pages 52–3).

Taking the measurements

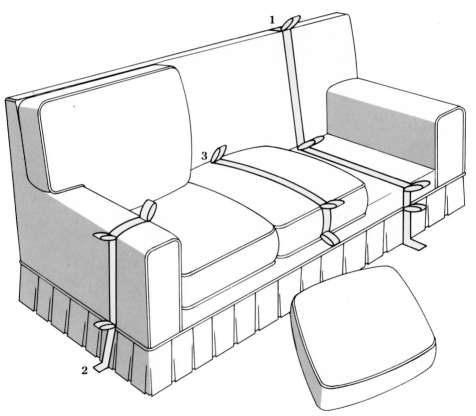

1 *Front and back: measure up the back from the floor, across the top, down the front of the back, across the seat and down to the floor. Add 2in (50mm) for each seam, 12in (30cm) for a tuck-in and 3in (75mm) for the skirt hem. If there is no skirt, measure to the bottom of the chair and add on 10in (25cm) for the facings.*

2 *Side and arm: measure from the floor up the skirt and outer side arm, over the top arm and down the inner arm. Add on 2in (50mm) for each seam crossed, 6in (15cm) for the tuck-in and an allowance for the skirt hem. For a style without a skirt, measure to the bottom of the chair and add on for facings. Double the total amount.*

3 *Cushions: measure the cushion from back to front, adding on the depth. Allow 2in (50mm) for each seam. Multiply the measurement by two (for top and bottom), and then by the number of cushions needed. Remember to allow enough fabric to accommodate patterns: large motifs should be centred on both sides of the cushion.*

Fitting loose covers

A loose cover for a chair is made up of at least ten separate pieces: two outside arms, two inside arms, outside back, inside back, seat, two front arm panels and a front apron panel. For many chairs you can use one arm section as a template for the other. However, with old chairs, the two sides are often not symmetrical, so it is best to measure and cut each section individually. Add an extra 1in (25mm) for the seam allowance.

Begin by pinning the separate sections of fabric to the chair with right sides facing out. This stage allows you to adjust the pieces to accommodate any unevenness in the shape of the chair. Ensure that the grain or nap on plain fabrics and the design on patterned fabrics run in the same direction on each section. Pin each piece along its centre, smooth the fabric out and pin around the edges. As you add each section, pin it to the edges of the sections already in position.

When all the sections are in place, mark the seamlines with tailors' chalk, then trim the seam allowances to ½in (12mm). You will need to allow for the movement that occurs when the chair is sat on, so leave 6in (15cm) around the edge of the seat section. Also, you will need to make an opening to allow the cover to be fitted and removed; it is simplest to place this in the centre of the back section or, if the back of the chair will be visible, the opening can be made at the back corner. When the cover is complete, sew a fastening device such as a zip, velcro strip or hooks and eyes along the edges of the opening.

Measuring and cutting sections is relatively straightforward when the chair is of a uniform shape, but if it has a deep back or is unusually shaped, you may have to cut extra panels for the top sides, and in some cases for the tops of the arms.

Fitting the fabric sections

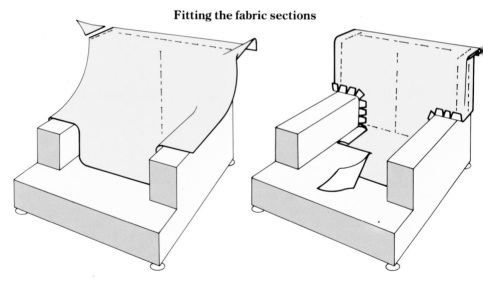

1 *Fit the inside back section, right side out, on the chair. Place large motifs slightly above the centre back. Overlap the top and sides of the back edge by 1in (25mm). Attach the fabric to the chair back with a line of pins down the centre, then smooth it out to the sides and pin along the top and edges. Match the edges of each side panel to the top, then pin together and trim off the excess.*

2 *Fit the fabric, working from the top of the inside back down to the arms, pinning as you go, and trimming away the excess. Make cuts in the seam allowance where the arm meets the back, to ensure a close fit. Allow 6in (15cm) for a tuck-in at the base of the inside back, then trim off the excess. It may also be necessary to leave a 3in (75mm) tuck-in allowance for the back arms.*

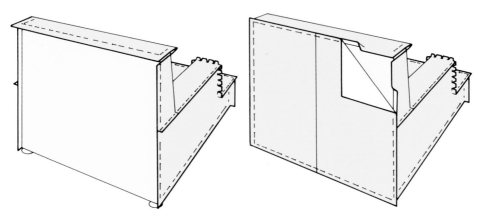

3 *Place the seat section on the chair, allowing for 6in (15cm) tuck-ins at the back and sides and a 1in (25mm) seam at the front edge. Pin along the centre, smooth out to the sides and pin at the edges. Make cuts in the seam allowance to fit the fabric around corners. Pin the front apron panel in the same way, allowing 2in (50mm) at the lower edge and 1in (25mm) seams. Pin the top edge to the seat panel.*

4 *Place the inner arm sections over the arms of the chair; allow 6in (15cm) at the seat edge for a tuck-in and 1in (25mm) for the seams. Pin along the centre of each arm and down the front of each panel. Make cuts in the seam allowance at the back edge and pin to the back section. Position the front arm panels and pin them in place, leaving a 1in (25mm) seam allowance all around.*

5 *Place the outside arm sections on the sides of the chair, leaving a 1in (25mm) seam allowance around the top and sides, and a 2in (50mm) allowance at the lower edge. The generous lower edge allowance ensures that the cover will not be too short. Secure the panel to the chair with a few pins, then pin all the edges to the edges of the other sections. Clip the seam allowance where the side and arm front panels meet.*

6 *Fold the outside back sections in half lengthways. Pin a line from top to bottom 1½in (40mm) from the fold, then cut along the fold to form the opening. Leaving the pins in place, open out the back section and pin it to the rest of the cover, allowing 1in (25mm) at the side and top edges and 2in (50mm) at the lower edge. Unpin the bottom of the centre seam just enough to remove the cover and mark the top of the opening.*

Covering the cushions

When cutting fabric with a pronounced pattern, think how it will look on the finished cushion and centre any large motifs on both of the main sections so that the cushion will be reversible.

The side panel containing the zip should be positioned at the back of the cushion so that it will not be visible. A seam allowance of ½in (12mm) should be sufficient for simple shapes, but with more complex shapes you will need to fit the cushion allowing an extra 1in (25mm) for the seams.

Shaping corners

Chairs and sofas with rounded corners or irregularly shaped backs will need the fullness on the front section taken in so that it will fit

the seam on the back section. This can be done with gathering, tucks or darts. Square corners will need the side back section cut separately as a boxed section. Excess material on the arms may also need to be taken in, using the same techniques.

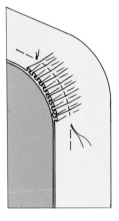 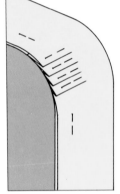 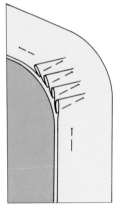 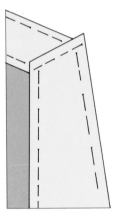

Gathering
Pin the sections together along the sides until you reach the corner. Stitch hand gathering along the seamline and pull it until the sections fit together. Fasten the gathering, pin the sections in place and stitch along the seam.

Tucks
Tucks can also be used to take in the bulk at a corner. Pin the straight sections up to the curve. Starting at the centre of the fullness, pin equal-sized tucks to take in the excess material. Stitch the tucks in place.

Darts
These are formed in the same way as tucks. Pin the section up to the corner and, working from the centre of the excess material, pin small darts to remove the fullness. Sew the darts in place along the seamline.

Boxed sections
If the sides of the back and arms have angular corners or are not rectangular, you will need to cut a separate section so that the fabric grain can run vertically. Allow 1in (25mm) for seams all around.

Lower edge finishes

The lower edge of the chair or sofa can be either left plain, trimmed with piping or finished with a skirt. There are three different types of skirt: plain with an inverted pleat at each corner, continuously pleated, or gathered for a

softer effect. For a continuously pleated frill, measure the front and sides of the chair and find a pleat width which will fit evenly into the measurements, leaving a pleat at each corner. Skirts usually have a finished depth of about 7in (18cm). A plain or piped finish can be fastened to the underside of the chair with either a facing tacked underneath or ties at the legs.

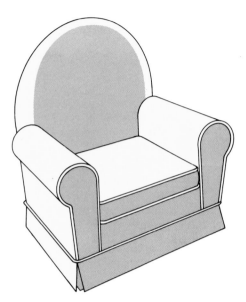
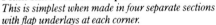

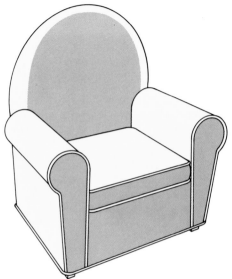

Plain skirt with corner pleats
This is simplest when made in four separate sections with flap underlays at each corner.

Plain skirt with edge piping
This is finished with a facing about 5in (13cm) deep to fit along the four sides.

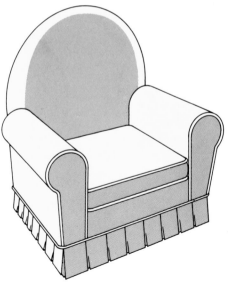

Gathered skirt
Allow about twice the required finished length for the fullness, distributed evenly.

Pleated skirt
Allow three times the required finished length when measuring the material.

CHAPTER TWO

HOME
CONTENTS

Regular care, cleaning and repair extends the life and efficiency of the contents of any home. Having invested in your ornaments and furnishings, it makes good sense to spend a little time ensuring that they continue to look and feel good. When buying anything for the home, you should find out how it should be cleaned. Modern products, including cleaning agents, polishes and glues, are designed for ease of use and for specific materials, so it is important to choose the right one. Valuable antiques and precious glass should be given to an expert for repair, but you can complete most repairs of less valuable objects simply and quickly yourself with the correct tools.

Tools and materials

When repairing household objects, you can work satisfactorily in a spare room or even the kitchen. Good lighting is essential, especially for colour matching, which must be carried out in daylight. The room must be well ventilated (because some chemicals give off unhealthy fumes) and have access to hot and cold water. A large work table is useful for spreading out tools, materials and partly assembled items; a cramped, cluttered area will lead to costly, even dangerous spillages or breakages. Protect the table-top with wipe-clean plastic or old newspaper and keep dangerous materials in a lockable cupboard.

Most forms of ceramic restoration can be carried out with a very basic set of tools, but a few specialized items will make your work easier. Use modelling clay for replacing missing parts. Cocktail sticks or matchsticks are ideal for applying glue and filler. Keep worn-out toothbrushes and shaving brushes for cleaning ceramics. Wear rubber gloves for protection when handling dangerous chemicals.

It is important to choose the right adhesive for repairs (page 61). Epoxy resins, used for china, metal and glass repairs, are strong and heat- and water-resistant. They usually come in two separate tubes to be mixed together. Clear contact adhesive sets almost immediately, so that there is no need to hold the pieces in place. Latex adhesive is used for patching fabrics and carpets. Glues required for mending plastics depend on the type of plastic (page 85). Masking tape and gummed paper strips are useful for holding repairs in place while the glue sets.

Needle files

Junior hacksaw

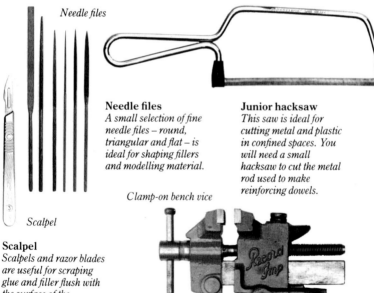

Needle files
A small selection of fine needle files – round, triangular and flat – is ideal for shaping fillers and modelling material.

Junior hacksaw
This saw is ideal for cutting metal and plastic in confined spaces. You will need a small hacksaw to cut the metal rod used to make reinforcing dowels.

Clamp-on bench vice

Scalpel

Scalpel
Scalpels and razor blades are useful for scraping glue and filler flush with the surface of the ceramic, particularly razor blades, as they can be bent to fit curved surfaces. Scalpels are available from artists' suppliers, and a range of interchangeable blades is available.

Vice
A small, clamp-on vice will hold metal rods and other materials while they are cut and shaped.

Boxwood modelling tools

Boxwood tools for modelling
Wooden modelling tools from an artists' suppliers are ideal for shaping and smoothing epoxy paste.

Power drill and flexible drive attachment

A flexible drive attachment for a power drill will enable you to drill ceramics safely. The working end, containing the chuck, is connected by a flexible cable to the power drill (which must be clamped into a bench mounting). If you can afford them, miniature electric drills from model shops are the most accurate type of drill.

Taper-nosed pliers

These are useful for manipulating wire to make supports for modelling material. They also enable you to reach less accessible areas.

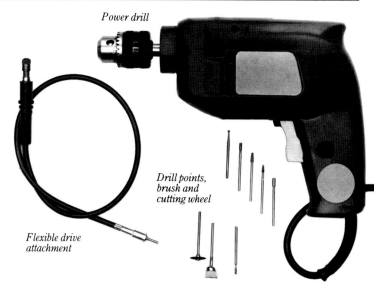

Power drill

Drill points, brush and cutting wheel

Flexible drive attachment

Taper-nosed pliers

Dental tools

Shaped probes and spatulas will reach into awkward spaces when filling or modelling china. If your dentist cannot supply you with second-hand tools, you can obtain them from dental suppliers.

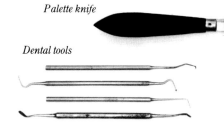

Palette knife

Dental tools

Drill points, brush and cutting wheel

Ceramics are so hard that only diamond-tipped drill points (from dental suppliers) will penetrate them successfully. These are expensive, but you only need one or two points for inserting small, metal reinforcing pins into joints.

Palette knife

An artists' palette knife with a flexible steel blade will be useful for mixing resins and fillers.

MATERIALS

- Abrasive paper: Use to rub down glue, filler and paintwork.
- Acetone: Use this to clean and degrease broken edges. Buy a lanolin-free type.
- Chrome polish: For buffing filler and glaze, buy polish from an auto accessory store.
- Cotton wool: Swabs keep bleach and other chemicals in contact with the piece.
- Hydrogen peroxide: Bleaches stains from ceramics.

- Kaolin: Mix with epoxy glue to make a filler putty.
- Masking tape: Use this to strap glued pieces together.
- Metal rods: Stainless steel and brass rod can be used to make reinforcing pins or dowels.
- Methylated spirits: You will need a doctor's prescription to get clear industrial meths from a pharmacist. Normal methylated spirits may stain ceramics.
- Modelling clay: Use this to

support pieces, for taking impressions and to model a master of a missing component.
- Paint stripper: Breaks down glues in unsatisfactory repairs.
- Plaster of Paris: Fills pottery and forms moulds.
- Rust remover: Commercial removers eliminate rust stains.
- Sand: Support objects in sand while the glue sets.
- Spirits of salts: Hydrochloric acid removes lime scale.

Types of ceramic

Ceramics are made of clay fired in kilns and given a variety of treatments. Identifying these treatments is important because they affect both the value and the method of repair. Start by examining the body of the piece, then look at the glaze and decoration.

Biscuit
This unglazed white porcelain is also known as bisque. Matching colours for retouching unglazed wares is difficult.

Black basaltware
A black stoneware containing ironstone, basalt was first produced at the Wedgwood factory in the eighteenth century.

Bone china
Bone china is a hard paste porcelain with animal bone ash added to make the china very white. It was developed in the later part of the eighteenth century.

Creamware
Stoneware that is fired at a lower temperature than normal is known as creamware. The cream-coloured lead glaze is not resistant to hot water.

Hard paste porcelain
First developed in China in the ninth century, the secret of making hard paste porcelain remained undiscovered in Europe until 1705. Hard paste is a mixture of kaolin (white china clay) and petuntse (china stone), fired at 1600°F (900°C), then glazed and fired again at 2400°F (1300°C). This fuses the glaze into the body of the china, making it extremely hard.

Pottery
This opaque earthenware is made from baked clay. It is porous and requires a glaze to protect it and make it waterproof.

Slipware
This term refers to pottery dipped in a creamy water-and-clay mixture. Slip itself is a decorative feature, and on some pieces this is taken still further by removing part of the slip to form patterns.

Soft paste porcelain
This type of porcelain was made before the technique for producing hard paste became widespread. Soft paste was composed of white clay and a vitreous mixture of sand and flint. The glaze was fired at a lower temperature, so that it lies on the surface and looks thicker than that on hard paste. Obviously, this type of porcelain is much softer than hard paste and can be scratched easily.

Stoneware
A coarse, hard, non-porous pottery made by adding flint or stone dust to clay. Salt-glazed stoneware, which has a slightly pitted appearance, is produced by adding salt to the kiln.

POTTERY AND PORCELAIN

It is useful to be able to distinguish pottery from porcelain because the method of restoration will differ. A broken edge or a chip in pottery will reveal a coarse, granular body. Look at it in good daylight and you will see a distinct edge to the glaze against the earthenware.

The body of porcelain is much lighter and finer, with an almost glassy appearance where the glaze is fused into it. You will find that porcelain is very light and looks translucent when you hold it up to the light. Another characteristic quality of porcelain is the ringing sound it makes when it is struck lightly.

SPECIAL GLAZES

Lustre
Metallic finishes are produced by adding metallic salts to the glaze. It may be an all-over finish imitating metal work, or applied in panels along with printed or painted patterns.

Crackle
Any glaze can begin to craze, forming a network of extremely fine cracks across the surface. Some china, notably certain oriental ware, is deliberately crazed during manufacture. This type of decorative finish is known as crackle glaze or alligator glaze.

Types of glass

Glass is made from silica derived from sand, with the addition of lime and an alkali. In early glass this alkali was either wood ash (making potash glass) or burnt seaweed (making soda glass). However, in the seventeenth century the English glassmaker George Ravenscroft introduced lead oxide as the alkali, resulting in the superior flint glass used today. Far from being merely a plain and practical material, glass has numerous decorative functions and finishes.

Acid-etched glass
Etched glass was originally made by coating a glass with wax, then scratching through with a pointed tool. Acid was applied, which ate into the areas unprotected by wax, leaving the motif permanently on the surface.

Cased or cameo glass
This effect is made by imposing coloured glass on a base layer of clear glass. In the best pieces, the layer of coloured glass is quite thick. Each layer may then be cut through or etched to reveal the colour below.

Cut glass
Glassware can be faceted by cutting it with an abrasive wheel. This technique enhances the reflective and refractive qualities of the material. On early cut drinking glasses the work was restricted to stems – the only part that was thick enough to cut without risk of shattering the piece. Today, all manner of glassware is cut.

Engraved glass
Engraving – a matt white motif on polished glass – is produced by scratching with a diamond point or by grinding a line with a revolving abrasive wheel. Diamond engraving was used as early as the sixteenth century, but wheel engraving became increasingly popular from the eighteenth century onwards.
  A rarer form of engraving known as "stipple" produces a delicate light-and-shade effect by varying the density of minute chips made with the diamond or steel tool.

Millefiori
The patterns in this millefiori paperweight are made with groups of tiny glass rods grouped together and cut across to reveal the pattern, and then set in clear glass.

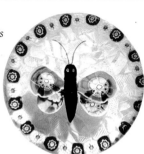

Millefiori
Millefiori was developed in Venice, but it was made famous by French glassmakers. Genuine millefiori is now very expensive.

Moulded glass
To make blown moulded glassware, a bubble of molten glass on the end of a tube is placed inside a metal mould. The glassmaker blows down the tube to force the soft glass out against the shaped inner surface of the mould. Press moulding, a method developed in the 1920s, uses a plunger to squeeze the molten glass into the mould.
  The pattern on blown moulded glass is evident on the inside as well as on the outside, whereas the inside of a press moulded piece is smooth. You can tell a moulded piece from cut glass by examining the edge of the pattern. Cut patterns have crisp, sharp edges, whereas moulded patterns are rounder.

Painted and enamelled glass
Designs painted directly on to glass are often worn, but retouching is usually a fairly simple job (pages 74–5). With back-painted glass, however, the paint is protected and therefore does not wear so easily. This type of painting appears perfectly flat from the front. Glassware was often decorated with gilding, especially on rims (page 68). If blemished, this too, can be retouched.
  Enamelled glass is the most durable finish because, after painting, the enamel is fired in a kiln until it fuses, becoming an integral part of the glass.

Cleaning china

Everyday crockery and glass, such as cups, mugs, plates and bowls, should be washed up soon after use and dried before storing. If you are leaving crockery to soak, use cold, soapy water. Hot water tends to "bake" some food, such as egg yolks, on to the china. If you have a dishwasher, load the crockery as you use it and pre-rinse if the machine has that facility. To remove tea or coffee stains, leave to soak overnight in a washing powder solution. Modern china, even delicate porcelain, may be dishwasher-proof, but always check before loading, and wash by hand if in any doubt. Heat may weaken a repair, so wash any glued items carefully by hand, not in a dishwasher.

Handling ornaments

China and pottery ornaments should be dusted regularly with a light feather duster. If a layer of dirt has built up, place the object on a foam mat or folded cloth in a bowl of warm, soapy water, then rinse and dry thoroughly. It is always worth dusting ornaments prior to washing them to prevent excess dirt from entering any tiny cracks or crazing. Use a soft paintbrush or a shaving brush. Bad stains can be removed with a damp cloth dipped in bicarbonate of soda or borax. Hard-water marks usually respond to vinegar and water, and hard rubbing. Stubborn dirty patches can be removed with chrome polish. Gently burnish the clean piece with a soft cloth.

Removing stains

Ceramics often have ugly stains which washing will not remove. In such a case you should use a bleach solution. You must be particularly careful to treat stained edges of broken pieces before gluing, or an invisible join will be impossible to achieve.

Neat household bleach will remove light staining. Otherwise use hydrogen peroxide (100 vol) available from your pharmacist. Make a solution with one part bleach to three parts water, plus a few drops of ammonia. Wear protective gloves and an apron. If you spill bleach on your skin, wash it off immediately with cold water. You will find that it is best to soak the piece in water before applying bleach.

This will prevent stains from being drawn into the body of the ceramic. Pottery is particularly absorbent, so resoak such pieces every time you apply bleach. Use tweezers to dip cotton wool swabs in the bleach solution and apply them to the stain. Leave them in position for several hours.

Cover the piece with a plastic sheet or seal it in a plastic container to keep the swabs moist. Inspect the staining after a couple of hours and repeat the bleaching process until the stain is completely removed. It may take several weeks to treat badly stained items – try increasing the concentration of bleach.

Caution: Gilding may be affected by strong bleach, so inspect a gilded piece frequently. When the stain has gone, rinse the item in water and leave it to dry.

Removing lime scale

If a ceramic bowl has been used to house a potted plant, for example, hard water may have left a deposit of calcium carbonate (lime scale), through evaporation. This can be removed using spirits of salts (hydrochloric acid), available from any pharmacist.

Warning: Always handle acid with care. Wear old clothing, protective gloves and safety glasses. *Never* add water to acid – it will boil over, causing a serious accident. Only add acid to water. Pour enough water into the bowl to cover the stain. Slowly add acid until the lime scale starts to bubble, then leave this solution in the pot until it has dissolved the scale. If necessary, add more acid. When you have finished, pour the solution into a drain, then wash the article.

Washing off salts

Salts present in the body of an object can accumulate on the surface, causing it to break up. To cure this, the salts must be washed out of the object. If the surface is flaking, consolidate it first by brushing on a solution of polyvinyl alcohol powder and warm distilled water. This will fix the surface, yet still allow the salts to be washed away. Then place the article in a plastic container and add distilled water. Do not immerse the object entirely – some of its surface must be exposed.

Change the water daily until all the salts have gone. To test this, hold a spoonful of the water over a flame so that the water evaporates. There should be no salts left.

Removing metallic stains

The copper and iron rivets once used to reinforce repairs will often stain the surrounding ceramic. Ammonia applied with cotton wool swabs will remove copper stains, and you can use a commercial rust remover (phosphoric acid) on rust marks. When the stains have disappeared, wash the area thoroughly with distilled water.

Metallic stains
Rivets used to reinforce old repairs often stain the surrounding china. Whether or not you intend to remove the rivet and reglue the joint, you will need to clean off any unsightly stains.

ADHESIVES

There are a great many adhesives on the market that claim to bond almost anything permanently. Most of these will be suitable for mending ceramics. The glues described here are reliable and are recommended for the repair of china ornaments.

Epoxy resin glues
Epoxy adhesives are sold in two tubes, the glue itself and a hardener. When the two constituents are mixed, the glue begins to set. Ensure that the two parts are thoroughly mixed before use, and use within an hour. For most work, use standard epoxy adhesive which sets in about 6 hours, although full strength is achieved only after several days. Slow-setting epoxy resin can also be used as the basis for filler. For small, hand-held sub-assemblies, buy a quick-setting variety which hardens after only 5–10 minutes. A special, much thinner epoxy adhesive, available from specialist suppliers, makes it much easier to achieve a hairline joint. Always use this type of glue when casting components.

All epoxy glues have a tendency to yellow. To compensate, mix in a tiny amount of titanium dioxide, available from art shops, to colour the glue without reducing its adhesive quality. For coloured ceramics, add a little pigment in place of the titanium dioxide.

Some epoxy resin glues are heat-resistant and all are resistant to water, oil and acids. Some people are allergic to epoxy resins, so avoid getting any on your skin.

Polyvinyl acetate glue
PVA is a white, water-based, single-tube adhesive that turns transparent when dry and is ideal for gluing earthenware, terracotta and pottery. Dampen the edge of the joint with water before gluing, to prevent adhesive from being absorbed and weakening the bond.

Cyanoacrylate glues
These "superglues" are suitable for hard paste china only. They are water-thinned, and so add nothing to the bulk of the work. However, they are water-soluble and should not be used for vases and other ornaments that are frequently in contact with water. They are useful for multiple breaks, since a build-up of gap-filling glue may force the last pieces out of alignment. The fast setting time – 10–15 seconds under finger pressure – is ideal for bonding tiny pieces which are impossible to tape together successfully.

Warning: These glues bond skin. If you get some on your skin, soak immediately in warm, soapy water to dissolve the glue. Alternatively, acetone or a proprietary solvent may dissolve them. If both of these methods fail, seek medical help.

Repairing breaks in china

Gluing china is not a particularly difficult task, requiring more patience than skill. To get a good repair, you should be prepared to persevere with each and every joint until it is perfect. If you do not, you will have more problems, either because a subsequent piece will not fit, or because a slight misalignment will show.

Small, hollow objects such as cups or bowls are the easiest to mend. Although a plate might appear simpler, broken pieces with exaggerated curves will give you a more positive "feel" as you bring them together; this will indicate to you that they mate exactly.

Modern adhesives have greatly improved the results achieved by gluing broken china and glass. Epoxy resins, which are strong and heat-resistant, do not set immediately and therefore allow time for accurate positioning. Setting times vary, but will be quicker in a warm room and can be accelerated by placing the article near a radiator. Contact adhesives, which are less expensive, set almost immediately, so are more difficult to use, although the thixotropic type allows more time for repositioning. Special adhesives are available for clear glass (pages 72–3).

It is worth repairing cracks and chips in valuable items, or as a means of prolonging the life of a favourite item. Pieces of ordinary domestic china are best thrown away in a newspaper wrapping and replaced.

Repairing simple breaks

Clean, simple breaks in china can be repaired more successfully than fractures and multiple breaks. Repairs in stems and bases will also be less noticeable than, for example, in the rim of a cup or mug. Before mending china, ensure that all pieces are clean. Wipe the pieces with a solvent, such as methylated spirits, white spirit or surgical spirit, ensuring that any old adhesive and grease is removed. Then rinse and allow to dry. Work out how the pieces fit together and use masking tape or gummed paper strips to hold them in position. Never use clear adhesive tape, since it will be difficult to remove without dislodging the pieces. Then remove the pieces and roughen the broken edges with sandpaper before applying adhesive. Mix the adhesive according to the pack instructions and carefully glue the pieces together, removing any excess with methylated spirits.

While the glue is drying, support the pieces in position. With larger breaks, support the item with crumpled kitchen foil, a box of sand, or a plastic bag full of sand. If the item is broken into more than two pieces, glue them one at a time, allowing the adhesive to set between the individual repairs.

Supporting repairs
A repair should be supported so that gravity helps to hold pieces together while the glue is setting. Modelling clay is the most useful material for this purpose – you can embed smaller items in it and use it to prop up larger pieces. Place plates and saucers in a plastic or wooden plate rack, using clay to hold them at the right angle. Do not use a metal rack – it might damage delicate decorations. Support very large items in a box or plastic bag filled with sand, or on crumpled kitchen foil. You can also use modelling clay to hold a cup in position and prevent it from rolling on the workbench when you are gluing on a handle.

Repairing multiple breaks

It is usually only worth mending multiple breaks on large or decorative pieces, such as vases and ornaments. Following the same technique as for simple breaks, use a solvent to clean each individual piece. Work out how the pieces fit together, using masking tape or gummed paper strips – never clear sticky-tape – across the breaks. Then number the pieces with a chinagraph pencil or felt pen. Remove the tape, disassemble the pieces and smear a little epoxy resin along the side of the main item and along the side of the first piece to be attached, then press together.

Working from the inside piece out, secure each piece in place with masking tape and wipe away excess glue with methylated spirits. Squeeze out excess glue, as any increase in size will prevent the final bit from fitting. Use Plasticine, crumpled kitchen foil or a bowl of sand to support the item. When the first piece is dry, glue on the next, apply masking tape, allow to dry and so on until the broken object is complete. If you wish to speed up the drying process, use a hairdryer to blow warm air on to

Gluing breaks
Smear epoxy resin along the broken edge of each piece as you reassemble the broken article, and glue each in place, wiping away any excess adhesive with methylated spirits before it sets.

Taping multiple breaks
Hold the pieces together with masking tape while the glue sets, and support the object in a bowl or bucket of sand. Do not use clear tape, or you may damage the fragile broken edges.

it, or leave the item near a heater. When the adhesive has set, scrape off any ridges with a scalpel or razor blade as you go until the repair lies flush with the rest of the surface, and wipe away the dust. If a handle or stem also has multiple breaks, repair it as a whole before sticking it on to the main item.

Repairing a warped article

Often it will be impossible to coax two pieces of a broken item together, even when the edge is sound and perfectly clean. The reason for this is that when the ceramic broke, tensions were released within the item and one or more of the pieces became distorted. However, slightly warped pieces can be "sprung" into place.

Glue one half of the joint, then strap it together firmly with tape. Tape the unglued section of the joint, but not too tightly. Leave the glue to set thoroughly – say for two to three days – then remove the tape and apply glue to the unbonded half with a knife blade. Warm the joint with a hairdryer. Taking care not to dislodge the glued joint, pull the joint closed with tape, then apply tape all along the joint and leave the glue to set.

REPAIRING A CRACK

Clean and bleach the crack, then warm the item on a radiator, or with a hairdryer. Place a knife or razor blade in the crack to open it up a little. Take great care, because it is easy to turn the crack into a break. Scrape epoxy glue against the edge of the crack from both sides. The heat will encourage the glue to seep into the crack. Remove the blade and strap up the crack tightly with adhesive tape. Leave the piece to dry for at least 12 hours.

REPAIRING A CUP HANDLE

A broken cup handle must be taped back on carefully to ensure a first-rate joint. Apply glue to both surfaces and glue the handle in position. Run one piece of tape straight across the handle. Then stick pieces of tape diagonally across the handle, stretching them first at one end then the other for equal tension. Allow plenty of time for the glue to dry, or you may dislodge the handle while trying to remove the tape. Alternatively, use a quick-setting glue.

Reinforcing a joint

This type of repair will only be necessary where the joint is likely to take more than the average strain (for example, a handle), or when the object is heavy, as in the case of a large bowl. To reinforce a joint, brass or stainless steel pins are glued into holes drilled in both halves of the break. Porcelain is so hard that it can only be drilled with diamond drill points. (These are expensive and are available from dental suppliers.) It is rarely necessary to fit pins larger than ⅛in (3mm) in diameter. Holes for pins this size should not be deeper than ³⁄₁₆in (5mm) and about one-third the thickness of the china. Drill a small hole first, then work up to the correct diameter.

Pinning a joint

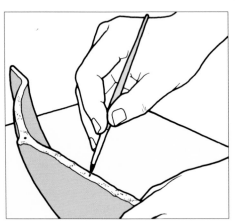

1 *On one edge, mark the position of the pins with small spots of paint. Bring the two halves together carefully to transfer the exact position of the spots.*

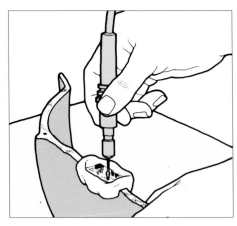

2 *Build a wall of Plasticine and fill with cold water to keep the point cool. Drill a hole slightly larger than the pin, and make any adjustments before gluing.*

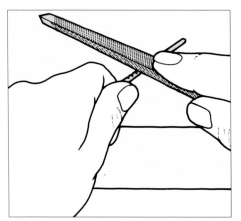

3 *Roughen the metal rod with a file, then remove any traces of grease with acetone before using a hacksaw to cut the pins to the exact length needed.*

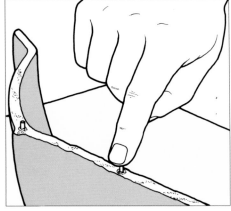

4 *Scrape adhesive into the holes on both sides, bedding the pins into one half. Glue, assemble and strap up the joint in the normal way (pages 62–3).*

Dissolving old glue

Old glues often discolour with age. The only remedy for discoloured joints, or badly repaired pieces where the joins are not aligned properly and hardened glue is left on the surface, is to dismantle the item, clean off the remaining glue, and mend the pieces of china again, with a modern adhesive (page 61).

Using water
Brown animal-based glues can usually be broken down by simply immersing the piece in hot water. PVA glues may also respond to this treatment. To avoid cracking the ceramic, place it on a cloth or foam mat in a plastic bowl of warm water, then gradually add hot water to increase the temperature.

As the glue softens, use a small, stiff paintbrush or toothbrush to remove it. Then try each joint to make sure that it closes perfectly. If it does not, inspect the edges closely for traces of glue. Either brush this away with water, or carefully pick off any specks with a pointed knife blade.

Using methylated spirits
Shellac, which is also brown in colour, may break down in hot water. If this does not work, lay cotton wool swabs soaked in industrial methylated spirits along each side of the joint. Apply fresh swabs until the spirits penetrate the joint and it falls apart. If this, too, is unsuccessful, try paint stripper.

Using acetone
Acetone-soaked cotton wool swabs, laid along either side of the joint, will soften cellulose-based and PVA glues. As acetone evaporates very fast, wrap the item in plastic as soon as you have applied the swabs.

Using paint stripper
Commercial strippers will soften modern epoxy and rubber-based glues, but they may also remove surface paintwork. This can be an advantage if it was from a previous, badly applied restoration, but you must avoid stripping original paint. Where possible, use stripper on the inside of the piece only. Wash it off as soon as the glue has softened and take care not to smear any on the outside. Soak pottery in water before applying stripper.

Warning: When using paint stripper, wear protective gloves, follow the manufacturer's instructions on the packet and avoid contact with the skin. Brush away from yourself at all times to avoid flicking stripper into your eyes. Never pour hot water on to ceramics that have recently been treated with paint stripper, as noxious fumes will be given off.

Dissolving glue with paint stripper

 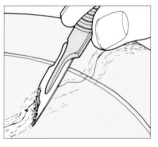 

1 *Paint stripper along the joint with a small brush on the inside of the item only, if possible. A type with a jelly-like consistency is best. Avoid very fluid strippers, as these can run and may cause damage to other areas.*

2 *Do not leave the stripper on for too long, or you may damage the paintwork. As soon as the glue has softened, lift off any excess left on the surface with a scalpel blade so that a second application of stripper can penetrate the joint.*

3 *If the broken pieces will not separate of their own accord, try pulling them apart gently, or insert a scalpel into the crack and gently lever it open. Wash the pieces in water, using an old toothbrush to remove the glue.*

Repairing chips and holes

Cups and mugs are especially prone to chipping around the rim. These chips are unsightly and can attract dirt. Edges also often chip when a china object breaks, and it is quite unusual to be able to just glue two pieces of china together and form a perfect edge. Sometimes small pieces may even be lost. For an invisible repair, you will need to fill these holes and then retouch the surface decoration.

If the hole is deep, you will need to apply the filler in several layers, allowing each to dry before applying the next. To match a colour when painting over the repair, mix in artists' powder colour until you reach the right shade and test it on spare filler. Finish the repair by painting a coat of thinned varnish over it to match the glaze of the china.

Fine edges may be completely broken away, leaving a gap which needs to be backed up to support the filler. Tape alone might bridge the gap, but it is usually safer to use thin plastic or cardboard, bent to follow the curve and taped tightly in place. Dust the support with talcum powder to prevent the glue from sticking to it, and leave it in place until the repair has set.

Keep some acetone and a cotton rag handy for wiping epoxy resin from tools and ceramics. Filler will usually take six to ten hours to dry, depending on room temperature.

Mending small holes and chips

1 *Chips in china can be concealed by filling out the surface and painting over the repair to match the rest of the piece. First clean the chip or hole with methylated, white or surgical spirit. Then make up a mixture of epoxy resin adhesive and titanium dioxide, a white powder available from artists' suppliers. Add powder colour as necessary.*

2 *Press the filler firmly into the crevice with a smooth, rounded stick, eliminating air pockets as you work. When the cavity is well packed and the filler lies proud of the surface, remove any smears with methylated spirits. Wait for the filler to set and rub it down, first with a needle file and then with glasspaper, until it lies flush with the surface.*

Filling a joint

Once the adhesive in a joint has set hard, remove the tape and scrape off any remaining glue with a sharp knife. Remove any smears of glue with a very fine abrasive paper. Look for small chips along the line of repair. Press filler into these with a palette knife or knife blade, working across the line from both directions. Then dampen the knife with methylated spirits or water and draw it along the joint, pressing and smoothing the filler into low points. When set, scrape the filler flush. Use a razor blade for flat surfaces and a round-tipped knife for internal curves. Smooth the surface with the smallest piece of very fine abrasive paper that will cover your fingertip.

You may need to make further applications of filler. Continue until you can rub a finger across the repair without feeling a change in the texture of the surface. Finally, you should buff the whole piece with a light coating of chrome polish to conceal and protect the repair.

Filling holes

Back up holes which pass right through an object with adhesive tape to stop the filler from falling out while it is still soft. Curved surfaces can be backed with modelling clay dusted with talcum powder to prevent the filler from

sticking to it. Stretch two or three lengths of tape across the hole and press filler into the recess. Begin at the edges, scraping the filler against them. Gradually build up the filler to slightly above the ceramic. Dip your finger in methylated spirits or water and smooth the surface of the filler. When it has set, rub it down and buff the surface with chrome polish.

Repairing a teapot spout

It is possible to model the missing piece of a teapot spout directly on to the existing china. To do this, you will need to make a support for the putty. Plug the end of the spout with modelling clay, bending it until it follows the curve of the spout. Cut off any excess clay and dust the rest with talcum powder. Spread a little neat epoxy adhesive on the broken edge, then build up the missing section with epoxy putty, smoothing it to flow into the existing shape. You may need to support the soft putty

Rebuilding a teapot spout
The tip of a teapot spout is vulnerable, and many pots are spoiled because part of the spout has broken off. Modelling the missing piece is a simple job that will make the teapot look and work like new.

by wrapping adhesive tape around the spout. Once the putty has set, remove the clay, shape and abrade the repaired section, then paint it.

TYPES OF FILLER

Epoxy putty
To fill porcelain, use epoxy putty (from a general hardware store). You buy this in two tubes, and mix the two components in equal proportions, setting the hardening process in motion. It sets very hard, but it can be filed and sanded to a smooth finish. The putty will not become too stiff to handle for 45–60 minutes.
  You can make your own putty by mixing epoxy resin glue with titanium dioxide to make it white and a powder such as kaolin or talcum powder to give it body. First make up the glue (page 61), but add a greater proportion

of titanium dioxide. This mixture will be sticky, but if you add powder, you can eventually knead it into a manoeuvrable, putty-like consistency.

Cellulose filler
To fill pottery, use a cellulose filler in powdered form. This is the type that you mix with water to fill cracks in a plaster wall, and it is available from DIY stores. Plaster of Paris will work equally well. To prevent water from being drawn from fillers into the body of the pottery, paint the broken edges with PVA adhesive before applying the filler.

After filling porcelain, use a cellulose primer filler over the epoxy putty as a final surface before finishing. This forms a good base for paintwork. As an alternative, you can use fine-surface cellulose filler for small repairs to porcelain, as long as the piece is for display only. Once you have prepared the filler, make sure that you clean your hands and all your tools thoroughly with water or methylated spirits before handling any china, otherwise you may smear traces of filler that will set hard and spoil the surface finish.

Repainting china

Patterned china is the easiest to retouch, especially bold, free designs rather than intricate decoration. Decoration that incorporates fine, straight or regularly spaced line work is very hard to copy and, surprisingly, retouching a white background to the correct shade is actually the most difficult task of all.

Matching crazing

Some glazes may be partly or wholly crazed. If a patch of newly restored paintwork is surrounded by crazing, you should disguise the new work by faking the crazed effect on the retouched area. The simplest method is to lightly draw the lines on to the dry paintwork with an extremely sharp, hard pencil. Sharpen it constantly to keep the thickness of the lines even. If you apply too much pencil, remove it with a fingertip or soft eraser. If the crazing is stained you may have to use coloured inks and a very fine pen.

Seal faked crazing with a coat of clear glaze. An airbrush is ideal for applying this, because a brush can sometimes disturb new pencil. However, you can get a satisfactory result with a paintbrush if you apply the glaze very lightly and carefully.

Retouching worn gilding

Some pieces of china have a gold edging or pattern. This may wear off in places, but can be replaced using metallic powders. Mix the powders together a little at a time until the proportions look right, then add a little clear glaze (too much will give a dull finish). Add a little thinner if necessary and, finally, hardener just before you paint the mixture on to the work with a fine brush. Use light, even strokes and try to apply the gilding in one movement. The effect is likely to be more even if you avoid painting an area twice.

It is often easiest to paint the edges of items like cups or saucers by rotating the piece against the tip of the brush. Support your painting arm on a pile of books to hold it still at a convenient height.

When painting flat areas of gold, it is difficult to conceal brush strokes, and the gold particles have a tendency to separate out from the glaze. Try painting the pattern first with a clear glaze that has a touch of coloured pigment added, which gives you a line to follow. Leave this glaze for a short time until it becomes "tacky" (a test strip on an old tile will indicate when it is ready). Sprinkle dry metallic powder from the tip of a soft brush over this glaze and lightly stipple it down with the same brush. Leave it for a few minutes, then tap any excess

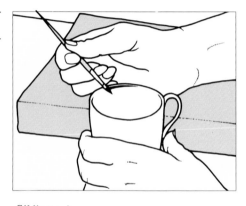

Gilding a rim
You may find it easiest to paint the rims of bowls or cups by rotating the piece against the tip of the brush. Support your painting arm on some firm object to hold it still at a convenient height, and use the other hand to turn the cup.

powder on to the folded card and return it to its container.

When the varnish is dry, dip a piece of tissue in clean water and squeeze it gently over the work to wash away any loose powder. Finally, pick off any remaining powder from the edge of the gilded area with a cocktail stick dampened in water. Leave it overnight to set, then burnish it with a soft cloth. Do not apply a coat of clear glaze over the top, as it will dull the shine on the gilding.

Tools and materials

Airbrush compressor

Paintbrushes

Airbrush

Use good-quality sable paintbrushes, ranging from size 00 down to number 3. You will hardly ever need large brushes. When you buy brushes, make sure that they come to a fine point. You should reserve at least one brush specifically for gilding. If you are using acrylic paint, clean your brushes in water. You will need to use a special thinner to clean brushes when they have been used for glaze. Pieces of clear glass or white ceramic tiles are ideal to use as a palette for mixing colours.

An airbrush is not an essential tool, but it can be used to produce a very effective edge to a repair. They are difficult to use successfully if you have not had any experience and, if you do not intend to do many repairs, you may prefer to stick to brushes. You will need to buy an airbrush that is capable of fine adjustment to enable you to paint very small areas without obliterating the surrounding paintwork. An airbrush is expensive, however, especially if you buy a compressor to power it. It is possible to start off with canned compressed air (as shown here) until you can afford the compressor. If you use an airbrush, wear a vapour mask over your nose and mouth to stop you from breathing in the fine particles of paint that an airbrush produces.

MATERIALS

Glaze
A glaze that can be cured by baking in an oven gives the best results, but has several drawbacks. Heat can darken adhesives, accentuate minor cracks or crazing and encourage fillers to shrink. And worst of all, if the piece has been repaired previously, it could even disintegrate. Also, ceramics must be baked in an oven reserved for this purpose, because even the slightest grease in a domestic oven could ruin paintwork. It is best to use a cold setting glaze.

Cold cure lacquer, available from DIY shops, is a good cold glaze for ceramics. You mix the lacquer with its own hardener, and it cures in 12 hours. For the final coat, you must use the clear variety, but the lacquer is also produced in white; use this as a base for mixing colours.

Coloured pigments
You will need artists' powder pigments to match the groundwork of the china. A wide range of colours is available at artists' suppliers. Buy small quantities, as they are very strong.

Acrylic paints
These paints, mixed with water, are perhaps the easiest medium for painting patterns on china. Once the paint is dry, you must seal and protect your work with a coat of clear glaze.

Metallic paints
If you want to simulate gilding, mix coloured gold and silver powders with glaze. You can buy these powders in artists' suppliers and some model shops.

Gold leaf
You can buy gold leaf, but it is difficult to use and very expensive. Imitation gold leaf is available in various shades. Transfer gold leaf is perhaps the easiest kind to use.

Repairing damaged colour and glaze

The basic procedure for painting china begins with mixing the right colour of the paint and glaze mixture and then using it to retouch the ground colour, before the pattern colours are matched and retouched. A coat of clear glaze is applied to protect the work.

The purpose of painting damaged china is to disguise any repairs as much as possible by concealing the hard edge of the break. Simply applying a thick coat of colour will do just the opposite, however; the line between the new colour and the original glaze will be all too obvious. In order to hide the repair, you must "feather" the edge of the painted area, however small, with a brush until it merges imperceptibly with the surrounding colour. Keep the area of new colour as small as possible. If you have to retouch a large area of groundwork, or reproduce a shaded or speckled glaze, you may find that you get a better effect if you use an airbrush. Once you have mastered the technique, you will get very attractive results.

Whether handpainting or airbrushing, practise first on inexpensive items, and take great care to match colours exactly.

Retouching damaged china

 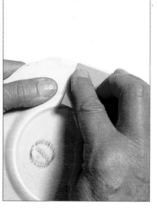 

1 *Start by applying a coat of tinted glaze on to clean china, working from the centre outwards. Load your brush with enough glaze so that it flows naturally, but does not flood the area. Avoid going back over any area twice, as this may leave brush strokes. As you approach the edge of the section you are working on, squeeze excess colour from the brush, leaving it with a flat (rather than pointed) tip. Working reasonably quickly, as most types of paint will begin to dry after only a minute or two, feather the edge with light strokes, dragging the colour out to the brink of the repair. Work in different directions to avoid a definite line.*

2 *While the paint is still wet, perform the same feathering operation again, this time with a clear glaze. If you have painted over a surrounding pattern, use a sharpened cocktail stick moistened with thinners to move the paintwork up to the edge of the pattern. Once set, rub down the first layer of glaze with the finest plastic-backed silicon carbide paper. Use the lightest possible touch, concentrating on losing the edge and the brush strokes. Wipe away any dust with a damp cloth. Now apply another layer of tinted glaze, adjusting the colour as necessary. Keep the number of coats you apply to the minimum that is necessary.*

3 *When you are satisfied with the base colour, and have removed any excess paint, apply a coat of clear glaze over the whole repaired area, feathering out the edge as before with a wide brush dampened in thinners, to blend it with the surrounding glaze. Apply the paint as lightly as possible so that the thinner in the glaze does not disturb the new paint.*

The final coat of glaze needs to be protected while it dries, so that it does not attract specks of dust which will spoil the finish. Use a shoebox or polythene sheet on a frame to cover the piece, or else simply shut it in a clean, dust-free cupboard while the glaze hardens.

Matching colour

The first step in all retouching work is to match the colour accurately. Unfortunately, there is no magic formula that enables you to match the colour of new paintwork to the original. Even a white background will need some colouring, as no ceramic is pure white. If you intend to use acrylic paint as a base, lay a speck of white paint on a tile and add a little colour to it. Repeat this until you find a close match and try a speck on the piece. Use a rag moistened in thinner to clean the china between each test.

An alternative method is to mix white cold cure lacquer and pigments. Place some lacquer on a white tile and thin it if necessary. Lay a

Blending colours
There is no short cut to blending pigments to match the original glaze; the only accurate method is by trial and error. Try sample specks on the piece until you get a good match, wiping them away each time until you find the right colour.

minute speck of pigment on the tile and, before adding any to the glaze, crush it with a palette knife to remove lumps. Mix the pigment into the glaze with a palette knife. Once you are satisfied with the colour and tone of the glaze, add hardener.

Retouching missing patterns

Once you have retouched the background colour, but before adding clear glaze, retouch any area of pattern. Use acrylic paints thinned with water, and match colours as before. A fine-pointed sable brush is the most versatile

tool for this work, but you may need pens or cocktail sticks to copy fine detail.

It is possible to trace a section of pattern from another part of the piece and transfer it to the repaired section by rubbing the back of the tracing with a soft pencil before laying it in place. As you draw over the tracing, the marks will be reproduced on the groundwork.

Repainting patterns

1 *Mark the pattern on the piece with a soft pencil, using a series of dots rather than a line. Dividers will help you to space regular motifs, as shown above.*

2 *Starting at the edge, block in your first colour. If you paint over the next colour, you can remove the excess with a cocktail stick moistened in thinner.*

3 *Fill in the other colours in the same way, following your pre-drawn lines. Once the pattern has dried, seal and protect it with a coat of clear glaze.*

Cleaning and repairing glass

Glassware, like china, can usually be cleaned effectively, but it is not so easy to repair successfully. The nature of the material makes most repairs obvious to the naked eye.

Never put antique glass in a dishwasher; wash it by hand instead. Lay a foam mat in the bottom of a plastic bowl filled with warm water and liquid detergent, and wash one piece at a time. Add a few drops of ammonia if the glass is very dirty or greasy.

Dry glassware carefully, as damp conditions can cause staining. Let the piece drain on a tea-towel, then polish it with a lint-free cloth. Dry the insides of vessels with a hairdryer. Store glass in a dry, ventilated place.

Washing glass

If you cannot wash drinking glasses immediately, leave them to soak on their sides in warm, soapy water. Each glass should be washed individually with a long-handled, soft-headed mop in a large bowl of clean, soapy water. To clean the crevices of cut crystal, use an old, soft toothbrush. Rinse glasses well in clean, hot (not boiling) water for a sparkling finish, and stand them upside-down on a rack or a clean, folded cloth. When they have drained, dry thoroughly with a linen cloth. Glass tables and shelves can be cleaned with a cloth soaked in methylated spirits.

Glass with metal mounts or parts should not be immersed in water. Clean it with swabs of damp cotton wool, keeping the metal dry.

Storing glass

It is best to store glasses the right way up, to avoid damaging the rim, and away from strong smells. Lavender bags, camphor balls and other distinct aromas will contaminate the glass and taint your drinks. Polish glasses with a clean linen cloth before you use them, rather than when you put them away.

Removing stains

Glass which is cloudy or stained should be filled with water and two teaspoons of ammonia, left overnight, then rinsed and washed. A badly stained glass may respond to soaking in a solution of one cup caustic soda to 3½ pints (2 litres) of warm water, but be sure to rinse the glass thoroughly afterwards. To remove hard-water marks from vases, soak them in distilled water or a vinegar and water solution. Never try to remove stains with abrasive cleaning tools or substances.

Alcohol will often leave dark stains on glass-ware. Decanters are the most common casualties, especially if they have been stored with their stoppers in place. Staining may be worse if hard water has left deposits of calcium carbonate. Unfortunately, you cannot remove all stains completely, but an acid treatment is often effective. To remove spirit stains from the inside of a decanter, half fill it with vinegar and cooking salt, then add half a cup of uncooked rice or sand and swill around. Rinse it well in clean water and leave it to drain. Stains can be removed from glass tables and shelves with methylated spirits on a cloth.

Repairing broken glass

To repair broken glass, modify the techniques used for mending china (pages 62–7). Be particularly careful when handling damaged glassware because the broken edges are extremely sharp.

You can use epoxy adhesives effectively on glass, but the colour of the glue will draw attention to the joint. To make the repair less obvious, use a water-clear anaerobic adhesive, which sets by the action of the ultraviolet rays in natural daylight – in bright sunlight it takes ten seconds, and on a dull day about two minutes. The best place to work, therefore, is at a table in front of a shaded window in artificial light. When you have glued the piece, you simply draw back the curtains to expose the glass to daylight and leave it for 24 hours.

To join two pieces of glass, first clean the edges carefully with methylated spirits or white spirit and attach adhesive tape to the body of the item. Put specks of anaerobic adhesive along the edges of the broken pieces, smoothing it out to a thin, even layer with a scalpel. Then bring the joint together, applying just enough pressure to squeeze out any excess adhesive. Tension tape across the join on each side of the glass. Run a knife blade across the joint to check alignment, and adjust any error. Wipe off any excess adhesive with acetone. Having glued a joint, you may find that the two parts slide as you attempt to bring them together, because the edges of broken glass are perfectly smooth. With thick glass, it helps to abrade the edges lightly before gluing. Otherwise, avoid the problem by using as little glue as possible.

Finally, expose the joint to daylight for a short period, then leave it overnight to

Gluing a glass stem
Stand the glass on its rim and glue the two halves of the stem together, making sure that the base is level. Support the base in position with two strands of Plasticine while the glue dries.

continue hardening. Clean up the joint line with a sharp knife. Avoid using abrasives – they could scratch the glass.

Mending coloured glass
Some opaque-coloured glass filters out ultra-violet rays. If your piece is of this type you cannot use an anaerobic glue, because it will not set. As an alternative, use a cyanoacrylate glue, or tint an epoxy adhesive to match the glass (page 61). Always warm the two tubes of epoxy glue on a radiator before mixing them together, to make sure that the glue is liquid.

Repairing a chipped edge

Careless handling can easily lead to minor damage, such as a small chip on the rim of a drinking glass. This makes the glass unusable, since broken glass leaves sharp edges. If you want to use the glass, you will need to grind away the top of the rim to remove the chip. With a display piece, you must decide whether the chipped edge spoils its appearance enough to merit grinding down the rim.

Grinding a rim

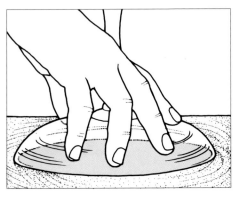

1 *Glue fine wet-and-dry abrasive paper to a flat surface. Dip the rim in water and rub it over the abrasive, using a circular motion.*

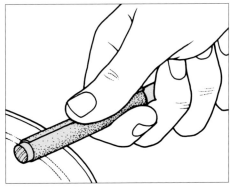

2 *Grind over the sharp edges with wet-and-dry paper wrapped around a pencil or dowel. Polish out the finely scratched edge with a miniature buffing wheel.*

Filling chips, holes and cracks

Fillings in glassware cannot be camouflaged with a layer of paint, and it is therefore impractical to fill any large chips or holes. You can, however, improve the appearance of smaller faults by filling them with a drop of clear anaerobic adhesive.

Back up the holes with clear adhesive tape, add adhesive and leave to harden in daylight. It will take at least 24 hours to set. When the glue has set hard, pare it flush with the surface of the glass by laying a knife blade on the glass, facing away from you, and running it down the joint to cut off excess glue. Polish the repair with chrome polish.

A clean crack in glass can be disguised by running a line of anaerobic adhesive along each side of it. Blow on it to encourage it to flow into the crack. Wipe off any excess with acetone before exposing it to daylight to harden. Use this method also to disguise the air-filled cracks that often occur when two pieces of glass are glued together.

Retouching painted glass

Coloured glassware is attractive and well worth collecting. The technique for painting glass is very similar to that for china (pages 68–71). You need not worry about brush strokes showing, as these paints flow rather like a wood stain. Glass paint is transparent, so if you need to match opaque colours, use acrylic paints instead (page 69).

Use a tile or a tinfoil tray to mix colours in, and keep a small piece of silk and thinner beside you to wipe away any mistakes.

Retouching glass

  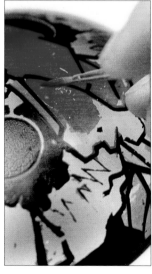

1 *When you think you have the right shade, try a speck of paint on the piece, next to a patch of original colour. Wipe off each attempt with thinner on a scrap of silk until you have a good match.*

2 *Once you are satisfied with your colour match, begin to paint in the edge, using a fine artists' brush. If you go over the edge, wipe off paint with thinner, using a cocktail stick if necessary.*

3 *Finally, take a brush of paint and touch in the middle section, letting it flow out naturally. Leave the piece to dry in a horizontal position, and protect it from any dust or moisture.*

Caring for stained glass

Many older homes have attractive stained glass panels in their front doors and windows. To wash stained glass, make a solution of warm water and a few drops of ammonia, and apply it with a soft brush. Rinse and dry the glass thoroughly. If the window is large, work on a small section at a time so that you can wash off the ammonia quickly. Take care to prevent the ammonia from splashing into your eyes.

Repairing stained glass

1 *Stained glass is held by lead "cames". To remove a piece, cut diagonally into the corners of the lead with a knife, tapping the blade gently with a hammer if necessary. If the panel is freestanding, lay it on a board to keep the frame flat.*

2 *Use a flat-bladed knife to prise back the came, and remove the old glass and putty. Make a thin cardboard template as a guide to cutting the shape. If you are nervous of cutting the glass, give the template to a glazier.*

3 *Press putty into the cames and insert the new glass. Fold the cames back into position and rub them down with a rounded burnishing tool such as a screwdriver handle. Finish the corners with abrasive paper, then solder them in place.*

Caring for glass lustres

A chandelier is the best-known example of an item made of glass lustres. You can also find lustre vases, candlesticks and lamps.

Grimy lustres can be washed in the same way as other glass objects, but either remove the metal parts first, or dry them very carefully afterwards. When dry, polish lustres with acetone or methylated spirits so that they sparkle brilliantly.

The lustres should be able to spin freely so that they catch the light. Examine the metal rings and hooks on which they are suspended. Close up any open rings with a pair of pliers and make wire replacements for any badly repaired metal parts.

Try to match the colour and thickness of the existing wire as closely as possible. Jewellers can supply you with fine silver wire. You can also try various fuse wires, or use a sharp knife to strip down electrical cables to obtain lengths of copper wire.

The fine, tapered jaws of round-nosed pliers will enable you to twist the wire into the correct diameter to make a ring. Crop excess ends with side-cutting pliers. Make sure that you open the rings sideways rather than pull them directly apart, as pulling them apart may destroy the neat circle.

Missing lustres can sometimes be replaced with a close match from an antique shop, but finding a match obviously is not easy. Alternatively, lustres can be made from a clear-casting resin, available from craft shops.

Types of metal

All kinds of decorative and utilitarian objects are made in metal, and metals themselves differ widely in their nature and value – from the expensive silver of engraved salvers to the cheap cast iron of firedogs. You can usually recognize metals by their colour and weight. However, some alloys can be difficult to identify at first glance.

Brass

Brass is a common yellow alloy of copper and zinc. It is easy to recognize unless it is heavily tarnished, when it can be a brown or greeny-black colour. It is used to make a wide range of items, both practical and decorative.

Bronze

Bronze is an alloy of copper and tin that ages to deep brown. It is an ideal casting metal, and is therefore most often found in the form of ornaments and door furniture. Spelter is similar, but lighter and of poorer quality.

Chrome

Chrome is a plating on base metal. When clean, it has a bright, white finish. Chrome is extremely hard and is found as a protective finish on all sorts of objects ranging from teapots and cocktail shakers to tables, chairs and lamps.

Copper

Polished copper is reddish brown in colour, but will tarnish to a dull brown. It is often used to make kettles, jugs and saucepans, which are then coated on the inside to prevent copper poisoning. Copper is a good conductor of heat, and is often found on the bottoms of good-quality steel saucepans.

Gold and platinum

Gold is used mainly to make jewellery. Pure gold is very soft, so it is mixed with other metals to make an alloy. The amount of gold in the alloy is expressed in carats, 24 carats being pure gold. Platinum is much harder, and very resistant to heat and chemicals. It is often used in modern jewellery-making.

Iron

Iron is commonly found in two forms, wrought iron and cast iron. Wrought iron is hammered into a two-dimensional pattern – often scrolls and twists – and the pieces are welded together to form a grid. Cast iron items are made in a mould and are normally in one piece or, at most, several large pieces bolted together. They are fully three-dimensional. Cast iron is brittle and, when broken, the inside is grey and has a coarse texture. Both wrought and cast iron are used to make items that are both decorative and hard-wearing, such as fireplaces and garden furniture.

Lead

Tarnished lead is dull grey, but it looks silvery when cut. Lead is not commonly found; perhaps one of its best-known uses as a household ornament is for antique toy soldiers – both the heavy solid-cast types and the lighter hollow castings.

Pewter

Pewter is basically an alloy of tin, but at various times its composition has changed, with different amounts of lead, copper, antimony and bismuth being added. It normally has a greyish patina with a soft sheen. It has been used for centuries to make tableware, especially mugs.

Silver

Silver can be either solid or plated. Like gold, it is a soft metal, and other metals are mixed with it to make a tougher alloy. The amount of silver in the alloy is indicated by the silver mark. Silver is used to make a variety of household objects, such as cutlery, salvers, candlesticks and jewellery.

Steel

Steel is an extremely tough alloy of iron and carbon that is capable of maintaining a sharp edge, which is why it was mostly used to make tools and weapons. Today stainless steel is used to make knives, as well as saucepans and cutlery.

Tools and materials

You will not need many tools for the day-to-day care and repair of metal objects. A chamois leather is ideal for buffing polished metal, while a soft hairbrush is useful for polishing decorative metalware. A nail-brush is stiff enough to scrub away any dirt and grease without scratching the surface.

For more substantial repairs, you may need a bench vice to hold articles while you remove dents or bend metal back into shape. A plastic- or rubber-faced hammer, or a rubber mallet, may both be used to shape metal without leaving marks in the surface.

A soldering iron is a much more specialized tool, which you will rarely need. If the occasion does arise when you need to solder two pieces of metal together, however, choose a large electric soldering iron with a tapered head. A soldering iron is used to heat solders, metals with low melting-points that harden quickly to form a joint between pieces of metal. A propane torch produces an intensely hot flame which will heat metal quickly for hard soldering. Blow lamps are cheaper and will also do the job, but a torch that is finely adjustable will enable you to produce better results.

MATERIALS

- Rust remover: Use this to treat corroded steel and iron.
- Paint stripper: Removes old lacquer or paint from brass, copper or cast-iron items.
- Paraffin: Use this to dissolve rust on metal and to make up abrasive pastes.
- Washing soda: Use this to remove corrosion from some metals by electro-chemical action.
- Whiting and jewellers' rouge: These fine abrasive powders remove fine scratches.
- Emery paper and cloth: This hard, black grit takes out deep scratches from metal. Emery is too coarse for soft metals like silver or copper.
- Ammonia: Use a mild solution to clean lead.
- Methylated spirits: This will clean grease from any surface, and remove excess epoxy glue.
- Buffing soap: A mixture of fine abrasive and wax for use with a power buff.
- Metal polishes: Liquids, pastes and wadding.
- Lacquer: A clear lacquer based on acrylic resin prevents polished metal from tarnishing.
- Epoxy resin glue: This adhesive produces extremely strong bonds between metal.
- Cyanoacrylate glue: This glue sets hard in seconds, and is useful for joining small parts.
- Wire wool: Use very fine wire wool to clean corrosion from hard metals and to clean up a joint prior to soldering or gluing it.
- Metallic pastes and powders: These will blend in a filling with surrounding metal.

Hardwood stake

Power buff

Stake
Shape the end of a hardwood stake to push out dented metal.

Cloth mop

Power buff and cloth mop
To burnish damaged metals to a high gloss, use a cloth mop or buff which you fix on to a bench-mounted power drill or grinder.

Painted metal

Rust is the enemy of ferrous metals (those that contain iron and steel) and must be kept at bay on painted metals, such as wrought-iron gates, with a rust-inhibiting primer and a sound coat of gloss. Even small chips in the surface paint can allow moisture to seep under the paint film and encourage corrosion. First locate the areas of rust and remove all traces with an emery cloth or a wire brush. Rust re-forms rapidly, so apply rust-inhibiting primer immediately. Non-ferrous metals such as aluminium and copper should be washed down with white spirit, abraded and primed.

Caring for metals

When cleaning metalware, always support it on a pad of soft cloth – if you lay soft metal directly on a table you could damage it. Take extra care when cleaning objects composed of mixed materials, because metal cleaners may damage the other substance and washing or dipping may dissolve the glue fixing it to the metal. For example, bone- or ivory-handled cutlery should not be left to soak in hot water.

Everyday cutlery should be washed in warm, soapy water as soon as possible after use, since food remains and even soaking in water will cause stains and pitting. A spoonful of mustard added to the rinsing water will remove fishy smells on silverware. Pots and pans should be soaked thoroughly to remove burnt food deposits, then washed (not scoured) in hot, soapy water. Leave to drain, then dry carefully, especially untreated cast-iron cookware, which tends to rust.

Protective finishes

Most proprietary metal cleaners will protect against tarnishing to some extent, but an extra finish will provide greater protection. Brassware can be given a coat of varnish or lacquer; chrome will be protected by a layer of Vaseline; untreated iron or steel should be greased or primed and painted with a special paint; silver can be kept in tarnish-retardant bags or in a drawer with a soft lining.

Cleaning metals

Regular cleaning and polishing will prevent rust from forming on metalware. However, if it does develop, use a proprietary cleaner to remove most of the corrosion.

Brass

Unless a piece has been lacquered, washing alone will not restore the metal; you will need metal polish to remove tarnish. If a commercial polish does not remove tarnishing, mix a level tablespoon of salt and a tablespoon of vinegar in ½ pint (¼ litre) of hot water and use extremely fine wire wool to swab the brass with it. It is not necessary to rub hard, as the solution will dissolve the corrosion. When the brass is tarnish-free, wash it in hot, soapy water, rinse and dry it, then apply polish. To treat badly corroded brass that is showing signs of verdigris, immerse it in a dip or use a commercial rust remover.

Bronze

Never use abrasives or metal polishes on bronze; simply wash the piece in warm, soapy water and dry it thoroughly. Bronze intended for display outdoors can be protected with a thin coat of wax polish.

Chrome

Use a soft brush and soapy water to wash grease and dirt from a chrome surface. If there is any slight discoloration, remove it by adding a few drops of ammonia to the water. Do not use abrasives, as they will damage the thin plating. Rinse and dry the metal, then use a cream chrome polish to restore its brilliance.

Chrome does not rust, but if the plating has worn thin, the metal underneath (usually copper, iron or steel) may be corroded. If so, ask a professional to replate the object.

Copper

Copper will corrode from a beautiful reddish-brown when clean to a dull grey-brown and will eventually produce bright green patches of verdigris. Copper is cleaned and polished like brass, but avoid the harshest methods, as these might affect the patina. Chemical dipping is quite safe, but unless tarnishing is very stubborn, do not use wire wool. Instead use a coarse cloth to apply salt-and-vinegar solution, and finish with metal polish on a soft cloth.

Iron and steel

Iron and steel will corrode badly in the presence of moist air, forming a layer of rust. If left unchecked, it will pit the metal and eventually destroy the object. To combat rust, soak lightly corroded pieces in paraffin for several hours before rubbing off the softened rust with fine steel wool. Use a commercial rust remover for badly rusted items. You can protect decorative items by coating them with wax polish, oil, lacquer or primer and paint.

Pewter

Pewter will develop an attractive grey patina in time, but you may prefer to polish the metal to a silvery finish with metal polish. Do not store pewter near oak, as this wood contains an acid which will attack the metal.

Silver

Silver tarnishes quickly on exposure to the air, forming a brown or even purple coating. Tarnishing is accelerated in humid or salty conditions. Wash silver every time you use it and before polishing, because even minute grains of grit or dust can scratch the metal.

Wash items one at a time in hot, soapy water, using a soft cloth to swab the metal. Rinse in hot, clean water and dry thoroughly to prevent stains. A thorough buffing with a soft cloth may be all that is necessary to give silver a deep shine, but if the metal is tarnished, you will have to use a commercial polish.

There are various commercial polishes, but perhaps the best type is a long-term silver polish which provides a chemical barrier to preserve the shine longer than standard polishes. When polishing, white cotton gloves prevent your fingernails from scratching the metal and stop the acid in your skin from tarnishing clean silver. Apply polish with a clean, soft cloth and burnish with another. Decorated silver can be cleaned with a soft nail-brush; use a soft hairbrush to polish it. Wash the silver again to remove all traces of polish, then burnish the piece with a dry cloth or chamois leather.

Using a chemical dip

Chemical action will clean copper, brass and silver without removing metal, so it is particularly useful for silver plate. Do not try to clean different metals in the same dip and never dip inlaid or enamelled pieces.

Lay aluminium foil in the bottom of a plastic bowl or bucket and place the metalware on it. Wearing protective gloves, dissolve half a cup of sodium bicarbonate (baking soda) in 2 pints (1 litre) of very hot water and pour it over the metalware. The solution will bubble violently as the corrosion is transferred chemically from the object to the aluminium. Lift the object out after a couple of minutes. It may still appear tarnished, but if you rinse it under hot water and dry it on a soft cloth you may reveal clean metal. If traces of tarnish remain, wash this off with the solution used for corroded brass. Dip the metal a second time if necessary. Once you have rinsed a silver article, dry and burnish it immediately to avoid water stains. You can dip silver-plated items, but if any base metal is showing through, leave the piece in the dip for only a short time. Wash and dry in the same way as for solid silver.

Chemical dips
Wear gloves and use wooden tongs or a stick to lift an article out of a dip. Do not touch silver with rubber gloves; they may leave black marks.

Repairing damaged metalwork

Most metal cleaners and protective finishes are designed to minimize the effects of minor scratches and knocks, and regular polishing should provide a good sheen and remove rust. Dents in pewter, copper and hollow brass can be removed easily, but it is advisable to take dented gold or silverware to a professional for repair. Small cracks and holes can be fixed with acrylic or epoxy resin adhesive. To disguise the repair, acrylic resin can be mixed with metal (such as brass) filings for a good colour match.

Removing scratches

Fine scratches can often be disguised with a layer of polish. With deeper scratches, use a fine abrasive to grind the metal down below the level of the damage. Metal polish is slightly abrasive, but if the scratch still shows after polishing, mix up a paste of whiting (fine chalk) with methylated spirits, paraffin or white spirit. Using a circular motion, apply it on a cloth wrapped around your fingertip. Wash the piece, and polish again. Badly scratched brass and copper can be cleaned with successively finer grades of emery paper, using oil as a lubricant. Never use coarse abrasives on soft metals like silver and pewter. Even mild abrasion will damage the patina on bronze.

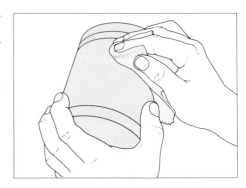

Removing scratches
On most metals, a layer of the appropriate polish will help to disguise scratches. To remove silver scratches, apply methylated spirits mixed with jewellers' rouge (available from jewellers' suppliers).

Filling holes and cracks

You can fill painted cast iron with a proprietary epoxy filler. For self-coloured metals, make a filler by mixing epoxy glue and metallic powders (available from art shops). Thicken this mixture by adding a little kaolin and powdered pigments to vary the colour. When mending holes in thin metal, back them with modelling clay before applying the filler. Leave the filler to set overnight before rubbing it down with fine abrasive paper.

If further camouflage is necessary, try applying the metallic paste sold in art shops as a colourant for picture frames. Rub it on with your fingertip or thin it with white spirit and paint it on with a brush.

Removing dents

Shaping metal is a skilled craft, so valuable items that are badly dented should be taken to a professional. You can press out small dents in soft metals (pewter, copper or brass) easily, however. Avoid using a hammer; it usually increases the damage.

Pushing out dents
Pewter and lead are so soft that you can manipulate them with your fingers alone. Push the dent back and lay the piece on newspaper. Rub the area with your thumb to remove the damage.

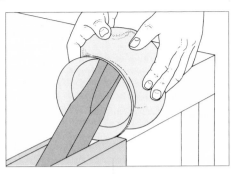

Removing dents
Take a short length of wood and use a rasp and spokeshave to shape the end to fit the damaged item. Hold the wood in a vice (above) and gently press and rub the metal against the shaped end until the dent is pushed out. Rub down with crocus powder, then with whiting, and polish.

Restoring a base
If an article has a dented flat bottom (right), first place it on a hard surface. If the base has a rim, fit a stake inside to support the base. Position another stake on the inside and tap the end with a hammer.

Repairing a crushed object

To repair a crushed article, shape a piece of hardwood to resemble the blade of a paper knife, but carefully round the end and edges. Smooth the tool with abrasive papers and give it a light coating of wax. Next, work it into position. Then slide the blade to and fro,

gradually burnishing the item roughly into shape. When you can ascertain the true shape of the piece, make up another hardwood former that fits snugly into the item. Wax the former and coax the metalware over it by rocking and twisting the piece or tapping it on your palm. Once the former is in place, you can use your fingers to shape the piece and also to smooth out any creases.

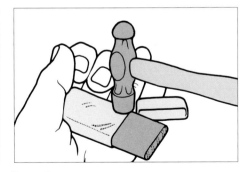

Inserting the first former
Gentle levering and twisting will gradually work the point of the tool inside the crushed metal item.

Removing creases
Hold the item, with the former in place, and tap gently with a lightweight hammer.

Repairing broken metal

Modern glues are safe and easy to use and have made it possible to repair broken metalware which would previously have been abandoned as unmendable. Adhesives are particularly suitable in cases where you cannot use heat – such as when joining low melting-point metals like pewter or lead. Extreme heat will also damage the patina of metalware and inlays or fittings in materials like wood or ivory.

If the joint is going to be put under strain, however, you should use lead solder instead. The same applies if the joint has only a small surface area. You cannot glue thin sheet metal edge to edge, for instance, unless you back up a joint with an additional metal strip. Cyanoacrylate glues are suitable for small repairs, but a two-part epoxy adhesive will produce a stronger joint.

Repairing a broken fire surround
Scrub the joint and the back of the fireplace with warm, soapy water. Use methylated

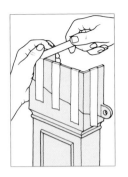

Gluing broken metal
Once you have cleaned and glued the joint, wipe off any excess glue with methylated spirits. Tape the two halves firmly together with adhesive tape to ensure a close, airtight join. Leave in place overnight until the glue has set.

spirits or acetone to degrease the joint. Then stand the fire surround on its head so that you can position the smaller piece of metal on it. Mix up the adhesive and apply it sparingly along one edge. Position the broken piece in place, rocking it gently to seat it properly, and squeeze out excess glue. Tape the broken piece tightly in place. Wipe off any excess glue with methylated spirits. Leave the glue to set overnight. Once set, lay fibreglass matting (obtainable from an auto accessory shop) across the back of the joint to reinforce it.

Repairing metals with soft solder

Particular metals melt at various different temperatures, and the moment at which they liquefy is called the melting-point. Solder is a metal which has a lower melting-point than most metals. Consequently it will flow into a heated joint in another metal of a higher melting-point. Once the solder has cooled, it acts as a bond in the joint.

Soft solder is an alloy of lead and tin. It has such a low melting-point that you can apply heat locally with a soldering iron, thus reducing the likelihood of damaging any surrounding materials like wood or ivory unless they are in direct proximity to the joint.

As long as the metal is clean, a soldered joint will be stronger than one made with adhesive. Solder is therefore preferable if the joint is going to be put under a load or stress.

Before you solder metal you must clean up the joint, and then clean off the oxidization that

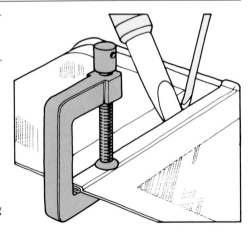

Mending a joint in tinware
Soft solder is an ideal choice to mend the folded joints found in antique metal toys and containers. Clamp the joint, then run solder and iron along it. If heating would damage the paintwork, use an adhesive instead. Before soldering, clean the inside of the joint with fine wire wool on a screwdriver tip to ensure that dust and dirt do not reduce the strength of the new joint.

forms immediately on the surface by using a solvent flux. Some active fluxes will corrode metals unless you can wash them from the joint after cooling. Passive fluxes will not harm the metal, so it is safer to use these whenever possible, even though they are less corrosive and, therefore, less easy to use. In order to soft solder a joint, its surface area must be reasonably large, and the two edges in close contact. The metal you are repairing must be a good conductor of heat. The easiest metals to solder are tin, copper, brass and lead, but you need to be careful not to melt lead. Pewter is even more vulnerable and requires a special low-temperature solder, so it is best to take the piece to a professional.

Repairing metals with hard solder

Hard solders contain silver and brass and are sometimes called silver solder. They are made in a range of strengths, colours and melting-points. All have a higher melting-point than soft solders and require a blowtorch to work them. Brazing is a form of hard soldering using brass. A joint made with hard solder is much stronger, but the higher temperatures involved will ruin any patina on the metal. You will have to remove any combustible material, such as wooden fittings or ivory inlay.

Use a blowtorch to heat up the metal. For small repair work where high temperatures are required, use a small welding or brazing kit which runs off cylinders of butane gas and oxygen. The metal must be made hot before the solder will flow. To maintain the heat, build a wall of firebricks around the work. After cleaning and fluxing, set the work up, wiring the parts together if necessary. Heat larger pieces first with a broad flame, otherwise they may distort. Heat the joint in the centre until it is red hot. Dip the solder rod in the flux and

Soldering a hollow candlestick
Join the two broken halves with a spacer of brass sheet which fits tightly inside the candlestick. Place a piece of solder against the joint and heat it; the solder will flow into the joint when the right temperature is reached. Wire the two halves together while the candlestick cools.

touch it on the joint. Draw the rod along the joint, preceded by the flame. With small joints, place a piece of solder against the joint and then heat it.

When the object has cooled, clean the joint. Chip away the hardened flux until it lies flush and finish with a file and abrasive.

If a valuable piece of metal is in need of repair, it is wise to seek professional advice, as you may damage the original solder while you are heating the metal.

FLUX

The key to a good joint is to clean the parts thoroughly and apply enough heat to make the solder flow. If the clean metal oxidizes when heated, this will stop the solder from flowing and bonding to the surface. To prevent this from happening, you should use one of the two different types of flux available.

"Active" flux is an acid which chemically cleans the surface of the metal. It is usually supplied as a liquid, and you apply it with a small brush. This type of flux is corrosive and must be washed off with water once the joint is soldered, to prevent corrosion from setting into the metal around the joint. However, it is easier to use than the non-corrosive "passive" types of flux, and it is effective in primitive oxidization.

The most common passive flux comes in the form of a resin paste. Passive fluxes are generally used when it is not possible to rinse the joint. These fluxes do not actively remove oxides, but merely protect the surface from the air, so you must clean the metal thoroughly before applying them. Clean it to a bright finish using a file, emery cloth or wire wool. Once the surface has been cleaned, do not touch it with your fingers, as they will leave grease on the metal.

How to sharpen knives and scissors

Kitchen knives should be sharpened regularly, especially those with carbon steel blades, which blunt more quickly than stainless steel. Five types of sharpener are available from hardware stores and DIY shops – an oilstone, a sharpening steel, a hand sharpener, an electric sharpener and a fine slipstone. On each type of sharpener, the blade is sharpened gradually, at an angle of 30°, working first one side, then the other. When using an electric sharpener, follow the manufacturer's instructions and take care not to over-sharpen the knife. Saw-edged blades such as bread knives need to be sharpened with specialist tools. If you try to sharpen them with a regular sharpener, you will ruin the blade.

Blunt scissors may be caused by a loose screw joint between the blades. To cure this, place the scissors with the head of the screw on a metal surface and hit the other end with a hammer. If the scissors are still blunt, you will have to use a slipstone. Never sharpen table cutlery or scissors with rounded ends designed to be used by children.

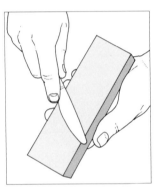

Using an oilstone
Place the stone on a flat surface at hand level and cover it with a light oil. Draw one side of the blade away from you along the stone, then turn the blade and pull it back along the stone towards you. Repeat several times until the blade feels sharp.

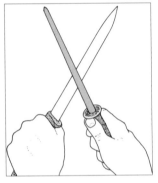

Using a sharpening steel
Hold the blade edge away from you and cross the knife and steel at right angles near the handles. Holding the blade at no more than 30° to the steel, draw it across first on one side, then on the other, and repeat about ten times.

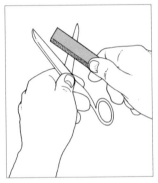

Using a slipstone
Draw the slipstone along the face of the blunt scissor blade, working at right angles to the blade. If the edge of the blade is damaged, lightly oil the slipstone and run it over the inner face of the blade to smooth out any chips or cracks.

Caring for plastics

Plastic furniture and surfaces should be cleaned carefully with a damp cloth to prevent particles of grit from scratching the finish. Use neat washing-up liquid to remove any stubborn patches, then rinse off and dry carefully. Plastic laminates can be wiped down in the same way, but should be rinsed well to avoid streaking. Cream cleansers are best on plastic baths to avoid scratching, and plastic lampshades can be washed in a warm water and detergent solution. To remove stains on tableware, use denture cleaner or a bicarbonate of soda paste. Do not use abrasives of any kind. Wipe up spills immediately to prevent further damage. Clean soft plastics with a detergent solution rather than cream cleaners, as creams will leave the surface feeling sticky.

Mending broken plastic
Cracked and broken plastic tableware will attract germs, so it should be thrown away, never mended. Plastic furniture and toys, however, can be repaired successfully with the

appropriate adhesive. Contact adhesive is ideal for ABS plastic (utensils, tool handles), rigid PVC (shower units, furniture) or decorative laminates (table tops). It is applied to both surfaces, left to dry, then pressed together. Clear adhesive is suitable for polystyrene (bathroom units, furniture) and flexible PVC (blinds, shower curtains). Epoxy adhesives are the most expensive and provide the strongest bond. They should be used for thermo-setting plastics (handles, switches), nylon (curtain rails) and acetal (taps).

Treating persistent stains
Stubborn stains, such as ink stains, can be removed by rubbing a little toothpaste, denture cleaner or sodium bicarbonate (baking soda) on the stain with your finger. Rub it off after a couple of minutes. Washing-up liquid will also remove certain stains.

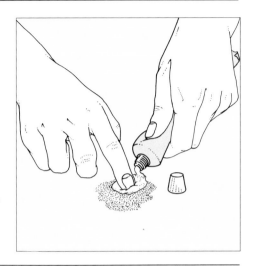

Caring for leather

Leather needs regular care and attention, or it soon becomes hard and powdery. Before cleaning leather upholstery, test for colour fastness by rubbing a small hidden area with soap and a damp cloth. If the colour comes off on your cloth, the leather is untreated and needs to be cleaned carefully. The best way to protect treated leather is to rub in hide food regularly, or to polish it with a wax or cream. Dark leather can be kept in good condition if you rub in castor oil or neat's foot oil once or twice a year. Use white petroleum jelly for pale leather, as either castor oil or neat's foot oil will cause it to discolour.

Renovating leather
Restore faded leather by touching it up with a leather stain or coloured lacquer. Work saddle soap thoroughly into stiff, dry leather until it regains its suppleness.

Cleaning untreated leather
Sponge off grease marks with a little white spirit on a soft cloth, then use soap and a slightly damp cloth. To remove bad stains, squeeze on a little rubber solution and leave to dry for 24 hours. The solution should absorb the stain and remove it.

Removing stubborn dirt
Saddle soap will remove ingrained dirt from most leather. Rub a damp sponge over the soap to produce a lather, then work the lathered sponge over the leather in a circular motion. Wipe the piece with a clean, damp sponge and leave to dry.

Cleaning treated leather
Wash with warm water and pure soap, taking care not to make the leather too wet. To remove stubborn stains, rub the leather gently with a soft nail-brush. If the mark persists, use a mixture of three parts castor oil and two parts surgical spirit. Leave for 24 hours, then wipe off with castor oil.

Chapter Three

Walls and Ceilings

Walls and ceilings form the backdrop to a room, providing the surface for the decoration, and any skimping on preparation or bad repairs will show. To get a good finish on the decoration, the walls and ceilings need to be smooth and well prepared. Repairing damaged surfaces does not always involve stripping the entire area; if done with care, patching damaged plaster or replacing tiles, for example, can be just as effective.

Tools and materials

Cheap tools produce poor results. However tempting it is to save money, this is always a false economy, because good-quality equipment lasts longer, even improving with age, is more satisfying to use and, most important, promotes a finer finish. When you have finished using them, clean your tools thoroughly and store them in a cool, dry, well-ventilated place. Shavehooks and scrapers are cleaned with wire wool, then wiped with petroleum jelly or a lightly oiled rag. Sharpen blunt shavehooks with a file or grindstone.

Paint scrapers are useful for removing old paint, in conjunction with paint-stripping solution. Old wallpaper can also be stripped after it has been liberally soaked in warm water or stripping solution. A simple upward motion is all that is needed. Shavehooks are used for removing flaking and softened paint from wooden mouldings. Gas blowlamps can strip off layers of paint, but should be used with care because of the fire risk. Hot-air strippers are far safer.

To repair cracks and dents, a filling knife, filler and tray are all that are needed. Most surfaces need abrading before receiving paint. Some surfaces clog the abrasive, so wet-and-dry types are produced, which can be used wet and wiped down. When using abrasives on wood, work in line with the grain. Abrasive papers are available in grades from coarse to fine and are graded according to the grit size: 40 is very coarse, 100 is medium and 200 is very fine, for finishing.

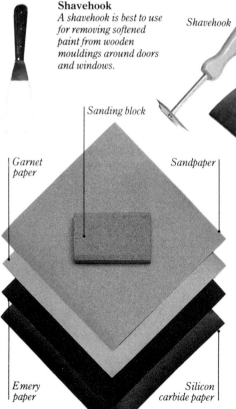

Filling knife
Used to spread fillers in wood or plaster, this has a flexible blade, so that filler can be pushed into holes. Blade widths range from 1–4in (25–100mm).

Filling knife

Shavehook
A shavehook is best to use for removing softened paint from wooden mouldings around doors and windows.

Shavehook

Large scraper

Sanding block

Abrasive paper
Glasspaper or sandpaper is used to finish timber roughly. It wears quickly but is inexpensive. Garnet paper, a hard, sharp abrasive, is made from the semi-precious red stone and is ideal for wood finishing. Emery paper is black and available with paper or cloth backing. It is used mainly to clean and polish metal. Silicon carbide paper, often called "wet-and-dry" paper, can be used wet to prevent it from clogging when rubbing down painted surfaces.

Garnet paper

Sandpaper

Emery paper

Silicon carbide paper

Large scraper
This is the most versatile scraper and can be used to remove old, softened paint and dampened wallpaper. Scrapers with wide blades are suitable for large areas; narrow blades are useful for window frames.

Sanding block
This is a cork or wooden block around which you wrap a sheet of abrasive paper. You can buy a sanding block or make one from a piece of wood.

Orbital sander

Belt sander

Power sanders
Finishing or orbital sanders are the most widely used type. A strip of abrasive, moving at high speed in a series of tiny orbits, gives a fine finish on wood and painted surfaces. Belt sanders are powerful machines that can be used to sand wood and metal quickly. They are more expensive than orbital sanders, but sand in a straight line. Disc sanders or sanding disc attachments for a power tool can be useful, but care must be taken not to scratch the surface.

USING LADDERS

Always set up a safe working platform before attempting to decorate ceilings and stairwells. In most houses, you can make your own working platform by using a combination of ladders and boards. If the stairwell is particularly high, however, a narrow scaffold tower, hired locally, may be the best solution. When using step ladders, always ensure that they are fully open and that the shelf is pushed well down. When climbing ladders to reach the platform, remember to empty your pockets of scissors and knives.

A variety of convertible step ladders are now available, which will either slide or swing out into a straight ladder, for using against the wall. Ensure, however, that the connections will not allow the ladder to slip when extended and check for loose screws and jammed parts.

If you are buying a new ladder, the aluminium types are generally lighter and cheaper than the old wooden sort. Always ensure that the ladder reaches at least 3ft (1m) above the highest level at which you wish to stand and never stand above the third highest rung. Face the ladder as you climb and do not lean over too far either side while working. For larger areas, use a working platform.

Ceilings and walls
Arrange a strong working platform across the room where you are working. Use two step ladders, some trestles or heavy tea chests, and a plank or a series of boards which span the complete room from wall to wall. In this way, the platform will only need to be moved once for each wall. Make sure that you can reach easily, as stretching is

dangerous. A single plank spanning more than 5ft (1.5m) will need additional support.

Stairs and stairwells
The exact arrangement of ladders, steps, boards and boxes will depend on your staircase, but the same basic system can be adapted for most stair shapes. Put a step ladder on the top landing and lean a straight ladder against the head wall with its foot firmly lodged against a stair riser, then link them with boards. If you need to span gaps of over 5ft (1.5m), use two planks doubled up and secured together with nails or strong tape. Wrap cloth around the tops of the ladder to prevent it from slipping and protect the wall. For the lower levels, put a step ladder in the hall and form a platform with planks resting on a ladder step and a stair.

Renewing wall coverings

You will need to repair and prepare the wall surfaces in a room before renewing the decoration. Careful preparation ensures that the effort you put into papering or painting is not wasted. If the existing decoration is a strong colour or has a pattern likely to show through, it should be removed. Wallpapers should be stripped and the plasterwork underneath filled and prepared for new paper; paintwork should be washed down or stripped, and any holes filled and sanded prior to repainting. Covering old paint or plaster with lining paper gives a good surface as well as helping to conceal strong colours.

Stripping old wallpaper

Any existing wall covering should be stripped off to leave bare walls, since joins, peeling, blistering and a strong pattern in the old paper may show through the new paint or paper. Fresh adhesive may also soften the old covering and pull it away from the wall, together with the new decoration.

Take time and care when stripping wallpaper. Try not to scrape too vigorously, or lumps will be gouged from the plaster, leaving more holes to fill in later. Be patient with stubborn areas and continue soaking and scraping until the paper loosens. Standard wallpapers are removed by sponging with warm water until the paper is soft enough to

scrape off. Easy-strip papers are simply peeled off, leaving behind their backing paper.

When all the old paper has been removed, wash down the walls with hot water to remove any traces of old paste and to loosen any final nibs of paper, then fill any holes or cracks (page 93). When a wall covering comes away easily – assuming it is not an easy-strip type – it indicates a flaking, dusty or damp surface. Scrape away any flaking paint, then check and treat the cause of any dampness in the wall (pages 214–19) and apply a coat of oil-based primer-sealer to provide a sound surface for the new wall covering. If preparing over sound paintwork, wash down the wall first. Take care not to get the wall too wet, and allow plenty of time for it to dry off before applying the new paint or paper.

Stripping normal wallpaper

1 *Use a large brush or a sponge to remove the wallpaper with warm water. Thicker papers may need an extra soaking: sponge the room once, and the water will start to loosen the old paste. The paper should then scrape off easily. Soap powder or liquid detergent added to the water will speed up the soaking process.*

2 *Once the paper has softened, scrape it off using a scraper. Keep the scraper as flat as possible, to avoid gouging holes in the plaster. A handful of wallpaper paste added to the water will both thicken it enough to give it more time to soak through the paper and prevent water from running down the wall.*

Stripping vinyl wallpaper

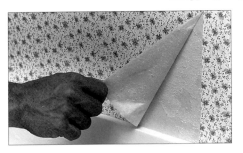

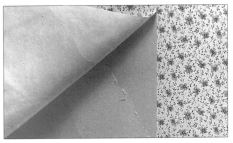

1 *Easy-strip vinyl wall coverings, now widely available, can be removed simply by releasing the bottom edge of the paper with your fingernail or a stripping knife, and pulling each length straight off the wall. Pull carefully upwards, not outwards, to avoid ripping the backing in uneven strips.*

2 *A layer of thin white paper will remain on the wall as each length is removed. This is the backing paper and can remain in position to act as a lining paper for the new wall covering. If, however, the backing paper comes away in places, it must be removed completely, rather than patched.*

Washable wallpapers

Wallpapers intended to withstand the condensation of a kitchen or bathroom are more difficult to remove, as they are washable and so do not respond to soaking. The best method of removing papers like this is by using a steam stripper to loosen the paper, which you can then peel off by hand. Steam strippers are simple to operate and can be hired from most DIY hire shops.

Stripping difficult papers

1 *Washable and overpainted papers are made to withstand water, so soaking the surface will have little effect. First score the surface using a wire brush, a serrated scraper or a sharp implement; this will break down the surface and allow the water to infiltrate and loosen the old paste.*

2 *If the job proves hard going, try hiring a steam stripper; it is simple to use and creates less mess than soaking and scraping. Steam generated by the machine passes through a plate held close to the wall, loosening the paper so that it can be scraped off immediately with a hand scraper.*

Preparing walls

More preparation is needed if a wall is to be painted than if it is to be concealed with wallpaper. Even a small hairline crack will show through paint if it is not filled and smoothed first. Where an otherwise sound wall is a network of small cracks, cover it with lining paper or wallpaper for overpainting.

Sound surfaces
The wall surface should be as smooth and even as possible, so fill all cracks and holes. A new plaster wall should be left to dry for several weeks before sealing with a primer or a thin coat of emulsion prior to painting, and fresh plasterboard should be given a coat of plasterboard primer-sealer. A previously painted wall must be washed from the bottom up with diluted sugar soap, then rinsed.

Preparing ceilings

Remove any light fittings that may impede the work, not forgetting to turn off the mains first and to seal any exposed wires afterwards. Then assess the condition of the existing paint and plasterwork. If it is sound, wash down the surface with diluted sugar soap and rinse thoroughly with clean water, taking care not to allow any drips to percolate fixed light fittings.

If the paint is discoloured by nicotine stains, apply a coat of aluminium sealer paint. Dried water stains, caused by a leaking roof or pipes, will show through emulsion, so these need to be coated with an oil-based primer-sealer. Kitchen ceilings are often coated with accumulated grease, which will prevent the paint from sticking if it is not removed. Likewise, soot or dust deposited on the ceilings above coal fires must be cleaned off to prevent it from discolouring subsequent layers

of paint. Fill any superficial cracks with cellulose filler. If distemper remains in an old house, scrape off the flakes and either wash off the rest or coat the ceiling with primer-sealer before repainting. If paint dust has accumulated, seal the ceiling with a coat of stabilizing primer.

Papered ceilings
Loose ceiling paper should be stripped off, but any which is firmly attached can be left and painted over. When removing paper, always wash off any remaining adhesive. If existing paper bubbles when washed, make a small slit when it is dry and restick the edges.

Remember that a ceiling may have been papered because it is badly cracked though structurally sound or, in the case of a plasterboard ceiling, because the joints are conspicuous. Do not remove ceiling paper unnecessarily; stripping and repapering a ceiling is time-consuming work.

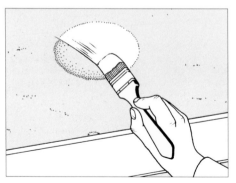

Nicotine stains
Cover nicotine stains with a coat of aluminium sealer paint to prevent their showing through the next layer.

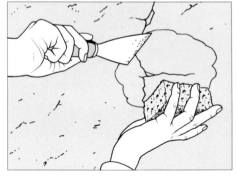

Distemper
On an old ceiling, distemper can be removed with a scraper. Use a sponge to catch the flakes.

Filling cracks and holes

Time spent filling cracks and holes will be well rewarded in the final result. Standard interior-grade cellulose fillers are suitable for most inside plaster or wooden surfaces. They come as ready-to-use paste in tubs or tubes, or as a powder to be mixed with water to a creamy consistency. Most small holes can be simply built up with filler and smoothed off. Corners in walls can be easily chipped. Apply thin layers of filler and, when the surface is slightly raised, allow it to harden and sand it down. Small, superficial chips in otherwise good paintwork can be filled with a fine surface filler worked into the surface and spread with a broad filling knife, then sanded to produce a smooth finish. Badly crazed plasterboard ceilings can be covered with thick textured paint, which conceals the cracks and stretches with the normal movement of the ceiling.

To avoid waste when preparing paste, try not to make up more than you can apply within the setting time marked on the packet (usually about 30 minutes). Unlike cellulose filler, resin-based fillers will not shrink as they dry and harden, so can be applied flush with the surface, instead of left proud, and will produce a smooth surface with less abrasion.

Applying filler

1 Score the crack with the side of a filling knife to widen the cavity for the filler, and brush away any debris from inside and around the crack.

2 Moisten the crack with a water-soaked brush. Prepare the filler and pack it tightly into the crack with a filling knife.

3 Push in the filler by drawing the filling knife across at right angles. If the crack is deep, allow the filler to dry and apply another layer.

4 Smooth off the filling while it is still soft. If it will not lie flush, leave it to harden and rub down with abrasive paper for a smooth finish.

Repairing damaged plaster

Contrary to popular belief, applying plaster successfully is not a difficult skill to master, nor is it a closely guarded secret, known only to the professional. In fact, all that is really needed is the patience and time to practise the techniques first. You cannot expect to become an expert overnight, but master the basics and you will be able to plaster as well as a professional. In many cases, small cracks, holes and dents can be repaired with small quantities of plaster or pieces of plasterboard.

Modern gypsum-based plasters have helped to remove much of the labour of home plastering. They are quick-setting and can be applied more easily and smoothly than the cement-based types.

Fixing plasterboard requires less skill. It can be used to "dry-line" a solid wall, to cover a previously plastered wall, or to create a non-load-bearing partition wall. Some types of board have a special fine finish intended for receiving paint or wallpaper, while others are designed to be a base for a layer of plaster. Plasterboard can improve the insulation and, like plaster, leaves a perfect finish for decorating. Remember that you cannot attach shelves or heavy fixtures to a wall made only of plasterboard and wooden uprights.

Tools and materials

The only specialist tools needed for plastering are a hawk, a trowel and a float, and for plasterboard, 1⅕in (30mm) nails and hessian scrim. For preparing the surface, you will also need a bolster chisel and a club hammer to remove the old plaster, battens for marking out the area and "screed beads".

Plastering tools
For mixing up plaster, you will need a clean bucket and a batten; use an old paintbrush to dampen the wall before you start. A hawk about 12in (30cm) square is used to carry small quantities of plaster to the wall. The most important tool for applying plaster is a trowel with a rectangular steel blade, roughly 10 × 5in (25 × 12cm). Use a planed length of softwood, about 3 × 1in (75 × 25mm) and 5ft (1.5m) long, for levelling the floating coat. Drive three or four nails into a wooden float for "devilling" or scoring surfaces.

Plasterboard tools
You will need a sharp knife and a pad saw to cut the boards, a "foot-lifter" to raise them, 1⅕in (30mm) galvanized nails to secure them and a sponge and fine hessian scrim for finishing.

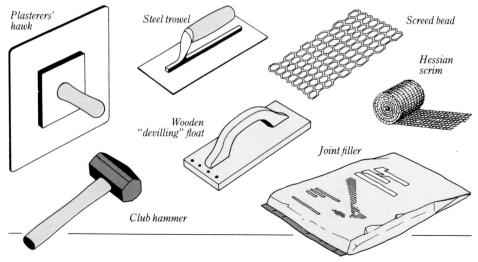

Plasterers' hawk

Steel trowel

Screed bead

Hessian scrim

Wooden "devilling" float

Joint filler

Club hammer

Types of plaster

Two main types of plaster are in common use today, one based on a mineral called gypsum, the other made from cement. Cement-based plaster can be used on internal walls but it may take days to dry out and, if the mix is not measured out accurately, it may not adhere well to the masonry beneath. Gypsum-based plasters are quick-setting. They are sold pre-mixed, so all you have to do is add water. Those that contain lightweight aggregates, such as vermiculite, are also easier to work.

Coats of plaster
Walls are usually plastered in two layers. The first, known as the backing, browning or floating coat, is applied thickly to mask any unevenness in the surface. The second

(finishing) coat is applied thinly and is smoothed over to give a perfectly flat surface for decorating. Key the floating coat before applying the finishing coat. Seal the plaster with a coat of primer if it is to be painted.

The most widely used gypsum plaster is made in various grades to suit walls of differing absorbency. High-suction surfaces such as brickwork absorb moisture rapidly and need a base coat of browning plaster. Engineering bricks, concrete, dense blockwork and plasterboard, which are less absorbent, low-suction surfaces, are sealed with a bonding plaster. A finishing coat is used in both cases.

To test the absorbency of the wall, splash some water on to the bare masonry. If it soaks in immediately, the wall is high-suction; if it runs off, the wall is low-suction. If in doubt, treat it with PVA bonding agent to make it a low-suction surface.

Types of plasterboard

Plasterboard is a layer of gypsum plaster sandwiched between two layers of heavy paper. The paper extends over the long edges of the boards, but not over the short ends. There are two main types of plasterboard: baseboard, which has grey paper on both faces and is intended for plastering over; and wallboard or dry lining board, which has one ivory-coloured paper face for painting or papering and one grey paper face, like base-board, which can be plastered.

The most popular types of wallboard come in two thicknesses – 3⁄8in (9.5mm) and 1⁄2in (12.7mm) – and have either square or tapered edges. Tapered edges allow the joints to be reinforced unobtrusively with tape and joint finish, when fixed ivory side out. The standard board size is 7ft 10in × 4ft (2.4 × 1.2m), but a number of other sizes are available, which are useful for matching unusual stud spacings.

Baseboards are used mainly on ceilings to replace areas of old lath and plaster. Other types of composite wallboard are available for special jobs. These include insulating plasterboard, vapour-check plasterboard, and thermal wallboard, another insulating board.

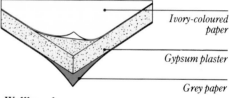

Ivory-coloured paper

Gypsum plaster

Grey paper

Wallboard
The white paper face on wallboard can be painted or papered without plaster. The grey face can be coated with a thin layer of plaster.

CARE OF PLASTERBOARD

Handle and store plasterboard with care. Full-size panels are heavy and brittle and should be carried vertically by one person only. Do not carry plasterboard flat (parallel with the ground) between two people, as the panels are likely to break under their own weight. The gypsum core is dense, soft and crumbles easily.

Be particularly careful if you are transporting plasterboard by car. Secure it to a padded roof-rack by crossing ropes over it in several directions, and make sure that you do not pull the ropes too tight. If you tie sheets of plasterboard only across the middle, they can easily lift at one end and split or snap off completely. If you need to store plasterboard for any length of time, make sure that you stack it on dry, flat surfaces to prevent the boards from cracking.

Preparing the surface

Before you begin any plastering job or repair, it is important to prepare the background thoroughly. Hack off the old plaster with a bolster chisel and club hammer, rake out the loose plaster and dust it off, then repoint any crumbling pointing with mortar. Smooth surfaces, such as concrete and timber, need keying before the plaster will hold. On concrete, hack a series of criss-cross lines in the surface with a cold chisel and apply a coat of PVA bonding agent. On timber, nail on a piece of expanded metal mesh, cut to fit the shape of the lintel.

Applying the plaster

The success of any plastering job depends on the consistency of the plaster and its smooth application. The first essential is to mix the powder with water until the plaster resembles thick porridge without any lumps. Cleanliness is all-important, since any dirt or chunks of hardened plaster could spoil the finish. To improve the workability of the plaster and to feel at ease with a hawk and trowel, it is worth practising the loading and applying technique several times. This involves scooping a mound of plaster on to the hawk, playing it between the hawk and trowel, then spreading it on the surface. When you feel confident with the technique, scrape off and discard the plaster, then apply the floating coat.

Mixing the plaster
The first time you mix plaster, tackle just a bucketful. When the water has soaked into the dry plaster, stir the mix slowly but thoroughly with a batten until it is smooth and fairly stiff. Tip the bucket on to your spot board, then chop and knead the plaster, using a clean plasterers' trowel. If the mix seems too wet, sprinkle on some more plaster and mix again. For larger quantities, use a bath-sized trough.

Working the plaster

1 *Place the trowel on the hawk with its blade at right angles to a neat mound of plaster. Push the trowel against the mound while tilting the hawk towards you. Push the trowel up to take off the plaster, then tip it over to drop the plaster on the hawk from a few inches.*

2 *Take about half the hawkful of plaster on to your trowel. Rest the right-hand edge of the trowel blade against the right-hand edge of the area you are replastering (if it is straight) and tilt the blade up until its face is at about 30° to the surface of the wall.*

3 *Using even pressure, push the trowel upwards and tilt the blade more steeply as you press the plaster on to the wall in a sweeping, squeezing motion. Scoop up the rest of the plaster from the hawk and repeat the movement. Repeat for the rest of the space.*

Replacing plasterboard

Plasterboard should be nailed to timber framing (for a stud partition wall) or to timber battens (for dry-lining a solid wall), so that the vertical and horizontal joints between boards can meet over solid timber. To minimize cutting, try to obtain boards of the correct height and width. Some boards are intended to match the standard stud spacing of 2ft (60cm) or 1½ft (45cm). In rooms with high ceilings, try to use boards 8ft (2.4m) long; you may have to use two panels, one above the other.

On a solid wall, remove the skirtings and architraves and then position the battens to coincide with the board edges. If the wall is flat, stick the boards directly to the surface. You may need to cut the boards to match the position of the stud framework on a partition wall. With both types, trim the sheet to allow a ½in (12mm) gap at the foot of the wall, to aid fitting. The boards can then be fixed, the joints covered and the skirting board added.

Cutting boards to size
Unless you are fortunate enough to find boards that are the exact height of your room and that fit into the bay widths precisely, you will have to use cut pieces. Scribe along the cutting line with a sharp knife to cut through the paper.

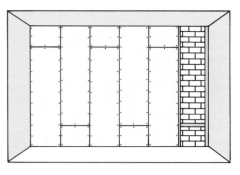

Covering high walls
Where possible, use boards of the correct length and trim off ½in (12mm) at the bottom. If the walls are too high, you can arrange the boards in two tiers and stagger the joints.

Stand the board on its edge, with the cut line vertical, and grip the top end of the waste piece. Then slap this section with your other hand, while pulling it back slightly with your first hand. This should break the core and leave the paper intact on the other side. Fold the board to 90°, then run a knife down the fold to cut the paper and free the offcut. To fit around obstacles, however, use a pad saw. Ensure that the board is well supported as you cut, or it may break in the wrong place. At external corners, arrange for a paper-covered board edge to overlap a cut one.

Cutting a straight edge
Break the core of the board, then bend it and slice through the paper with a sharp craft knife.

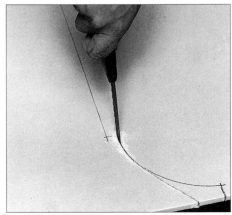

Cutting a curved edge
Use a pad saw to cut around awkward shapes such as alcoves and fireplaces.

Securing the plasterboards

1 *Manoeuvre the cut-to-size board into position against the wall. It needs to fit tightly up against the ceiling and to finish below the skirting height, so use a "foot-lifter", made from offcuts of timber, to lever it up and leave both hands free to drive in the fixing nails. Subsequent boards should be fixed in the same way, each pushed closely against its neighbour to form neat butt joints.*

2 *Insert galvanized 1¹⁄₅in (30mm)-long plasterboard nails at 6in (15cm) intervals and ½in (12mm) from the board edge to fix the board to the battens. Hammer them in until the head just grips the surface of the paper, then tap in another 1–2mm so that the hammer head just dimples the board surface without bursting it. You can fill the dimple with plaster later for an invisible fixing, if it seems necessary.*

Finishing off

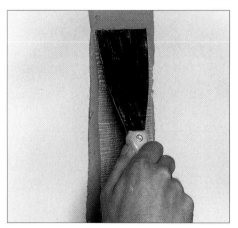

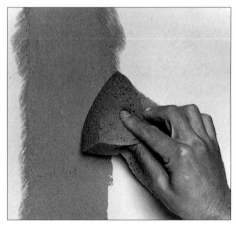

1 *Disguise the joint by applying a narrow band of joint filler along the joint, then press lengths of fine hessian scrim into each joint from floor to ceiling. Draw a filling knife downwards to bed the scrim smoothly and evenly in the band of plaster. With tapered-edge boards, apply more filler until the joins and surface stand flush.*

2 *Moisten a jointing sponge and wipe off the surplus. When the filler has set, apply a thin layer of joint finish with a trowel and feather the edges with the jointing sponge. With square-edged baseboard, apply a skim coat of "board finish", then a finishing coat. Allow at least 24 hours for the finishing coat to dry. Finally, replace the skirting board.*

Patching plasterboard

Since there is a cavity behind each piece of plasterboard, holes have to be patched rather than filled. For small holes, cut a piece of plasterboard slightly larger than the gap in both directions and secure it in place with plaster or nails. The plastered area is then finished with a skim coat.

For holes larger than 3in (75mm), cut out a rectangle of plasterboard back to the studs on each side, then cut a new piece to match the gap and nail it to the studs on each side with plasterboard nails. To support the top and bottom edges of the patch, tape scrim around the joins, or use a trowel to force some finishing plaster into the gaps before smoothing a skim coat over the patch.

Patching small holes
Bore a hole through the centre of the patch and insert a knotted piece of string. Dab fresh plaster on the patch as shown. Pull the string to wedge the patch against the back of the board. Press more plaster into the hole and leave it to harden. Cut the string, then dampen and fill the hole with plaster until it lies flush.

Filling holes in plaster

Plastered walls which are basically sound but damaged in patches can be repaired without replastering. Interior filler or finishing plaster can be used, but a plaster that dries in two stages leaves the best finish and will remain workable for up to two hours. Before filling holes, consider the extent of the repair. If a solid wall sounds hollow when tapped, the plaster needs to be entirely replaced.

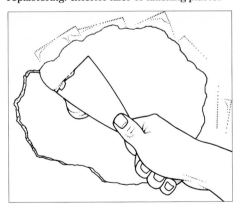

Repairing holes in solid walls
Score around the edges of the hole with an old nail. Brush out the dust and moisten the surface with a small brush. If you are using dry filler or plaster, mix it up to a stiff consistency, then push it into the hole with a plasterers' trowel and allow it to harden. Add a second layer and, when this has set, sand the repair flush with the surface, or use a broad-bladed scraper to remove the excess plaster.

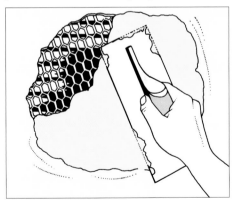

Repairing holes in lath and plaster
Cut away the loose plaster and brush out the dust. If the laths are damaged, bridge the gap with a small piece of expanded metal mesh wedged into the hole. Fill the hole to just below the surface, cross-hatch with a knife edge to provide a key for the second layer, and leave it to harden for 30 minutes. Mix more plaster, wet the patch and fill it completely. Add a finishing coat and sand when dry.

Repairing chipped plaster

Plastered corners are particularly prone to damage. To ensure a straight line and a true angle at the corner, it is best to fit a batten first to one side of the corner, then to the other, while you fill the damaged area with plaster. If, however, the corner already has a reinforcing angle bead, simply patch the hole between the edges of the damaged area and the nosing of the beading on each face of the corner, using the centre strip as a guide, and level off against the angle.

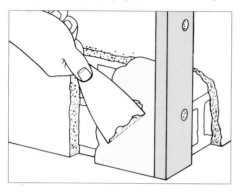

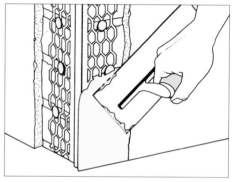

Using a batten
Pin a batten to one side of the corner, its edge flush with the other side. Fill the hole on one side, using a trowel or filling knife, so that the plaster lies flush with the batten. When this has set, remove the batten and fix it over the filled patch. Repeat the process on the other side and sand the corner.

Patching a reinforced corner
If an angled "screed bead" was inserted when the wall was plastered, patch the hole by filling over the damaged area. Draw the trowel or knife upwards and smooth off against each face of the screed bead. Use a corner trowel, if one is available, to round off the edge. When the filler is dry, sand the corner.

Replacing polystyrene ceiling cove

Ceiling cove, fixed to the angle between the wall and the ceiling, will complement any ceiling. It helps to take the squareness out of a room and lends it a finished look. Moreover, the normal seasonal movement of a house may cause cracks to form at the junction of the ceiling and the wall, usually the weakest point of the house structure. These cracks, although harmless, are unsightly and can be permanently concealed beneath ceiling cove. There are three types of cove: plaster, polystyrene and cotton-fibre. Polystyrene cove is supplied in 3¼ft (1m) lengths, with special corner pieces for both external and internal corners. If you do not use such pieces, a cornice mitre box will help you to cut the cove at the correct angle.

Preparing the work area
Start by ensuring that the area to be covered is dry, clean and free from flaking paint and wallpaper, then snap a chalked stringline on the wall as a horizontal guide line for the base of the coving. If you need to remove only a small strip of wallpaper from a papered wall, use a sharp knife and scrape it off dry – do not use water, since it may loosen the remaining paper.

Securing the cove in place
Brush a purpose-made adhesive on to the back of a corner piece and stick it in position. However, if either the wall or ceiling is uneven, use a thick, buttery, ceramic-tile adhesive, to ensure that the cove grips firmly. Fix corner pieces first, then straight pieces working out from the corners. Continue fixing straight pieces along the wall, butting up the edges. To cut a length to fit, use a sharp knife against a steel straight-edge.

Fixing polystyrene cove

1 *Clean the angle between the ceiling and the wall. Snap a horizontal chalked stringline on the wall for the lower guide line and trace the top line on the ceiling by holding a corner piece in position. Spread adhesive on the piece and fix it in place, following the guide lines.*

2 *Apply adhesive to straight lengths and push the first carefully into position against the corner piece to form a neat butt joint. Continue working out from the corners, then use a sharp knife to cut smaller lengths to fit.*

Replacing plaster ceiling cove

Prepare the wall and ceiling as for polystyrene cove. Go around the room, cutting lengths to fit, and tap nails above and below each piece for temporary support. Ornate corner pieces are available; however, if these are not used, the end of the cove has to be mitred to form a neat joint at internal and external corners. To ensure that you cut precisely the right angle, use a special mitre box or a paper template.

Use a fine-tooth saw to cut the cove and a saw or sharp knife when mitring corners. Rough edges can be smoothed with sandpaper.

Mix up plaster-cove adhesive, layer it thickly on to the back of the cove and press the length into place. Use any emerging excess adhesive to fill gaps at the edges or between lengths and clean away the rest with a wet brush before it starts to dry. Continue to hang the cove, butting up the lengths and following your chalked guide lines. When the adhesive has set – usually after 24 hours – the cove can be painted with emulsion.

Mitring plaster cove

1 *Use the template supplied with the cove to mark off a corner mitre, cut it with a sharp knife and smooth off the edge with abrasive paper.*

2 *Spread a thick layer of adhesive on to the coving, push it into position and tap in a support nail. Fill any gaps with adhesive and wipe away the excess.*

Replacing tiling

Tiles are resistant to water, heat and most household chemicals. They are hard-wearing, easy to clean and demand little maintenance. Although time-consuming, the relaying of tiles requires no special skill, particularly with modern adhesives and lightweight tiles.

Beyond the wide range of ceramics, tiles are now produced in a variety of materials. Cork, brick, mirrored glass, vinyl, polystyrene and steel tiles offer new textures and can be fitted in much the same way as ceramic. Heat- and frost-resistant and other special-purpose tiles have broadened their practical value.

Tools and materials

For a good result, the correct tiling tools are essential; they cannot be improvised. Always ensure that you have the correct adhesive and grouting for the type of tile and situation, and in sufficient quantities. A flexible waterproof sealant is useful to fill gaps around baths or sinks (page 105). Plastic spacer lugs or match-sticks are needed for ceramic wall tiles that are not already self-spacing.

Ceramic wall and floor tiles
The essential tools for ceramic tiling include a trowel or spatula for applying adhesive to the wall or floor, and a notched plastic spreader which is drawn through the adhesive to leave a series of ridged lines on which to bed the tiles. Many types of tile cutter are available, some incorporating a measuring gauge for marking an accurate cutting line. For fitting around pipes and other awkward areas, tile clippers, pincers or a tile saw should be used. A tile file is available for smoothing rough edges. Use a rubber grouter or sponge for filling the joints with grout, and a large sponge for wiping the tiles clean. With wall tiles, you will need a hammer, screwdriver and spirit level if the support battens also need to be replaced.

Adhesives
Always choose waterproof adhesive in damp situations, such as shower cubicles and sink splashbacks, where ceramic tiles are likely to be soaked regularly with water. There is no need to change adhesives half-way through a job, so continue with waterproof adhesive if this proves more convenient. Thin-bed adhesive, which is spread about ⅛in (3mm) thick, is normally used in preference to the thick-bed type, which is more difficult to use.

Grouting
Cement grout is supplied as powder to be mixed with water into a creamy paste. For colour add a powdered pigment, or use a ready-mixed coloured grout. Waterproof grout should be used to fill between tiles fixed with waterproof adhesive. Use it also for tiled kitchen work surfaces, as the tiles will be washed regularly.

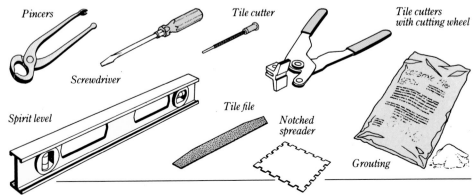

Pincers

Tile cutter

Tile cutters with cutting wheel

Screwdriver

Spirit level

Tile file

Notched spreader

Grouting

Preparing the surface

A bolster chisel and club hammer, or a small kango hammer with a chasing tool, are used for removing existing tiles. They are all usually obtainable from a tool hire shop, if you do not want to buy them. If necessary, reline the surface to be tiled with plaster or plasterboard on walls and ceilings.

All surfaces must be sound, level and dry. Rub down shiny surfaces to key them for the tile adhesive. If a layer of old ceramic tiles is flat, firmly fixed and well keyed, new ceramic tiles can be applied on top.

It is difficult to align tiles unless the wall is perfectly flat. Hold a long, flat piece of wood against the surface vertically, horizontally and diagonally: if it "see-saws", the wall is uneven and will need to be levelled before tiling.

Replacing whole tiles

If you are retiling a large area, apply the tiles in horizontal rows from the bottom up, working in areas of 10ft^2 (1m^2). When the tiles have been in position for 24 hours, the borders can be filled with tiles cut to size. If plastic spacers have been used, they can be removed at this stage and kept for reuse.

Laying tiles
Smooth a layer of adhesive on the wall and draw a notched spreader over to create uniform ridge lines. Lay the tiles in horizontal strips, inserting plastic spacers to ensure uniform grouting lines.

Cutting ceramic tiles

There are various tile-cutting gadgets available, some incorporating a measuring and marking gauge. A regular tile cutter has a sharp tungsten-carbide tip which scores through the glaze so that the tile can be snapped in half along the score line. Another type of tile cutter contains a small cutting wheel to score the glaze, and jaws to hold the tile. When the handles are squeezed, the jaws close and break the tile.

Where a specially shaped tile is needed, make a cardboard template of the shape you want and then transfer it to the tile. To cut out an L-shape, a pattern of the shape is traced on to the tile. The tile is then scored deeply and evenly along the cutting line and criss-cross shapes are scored through the waste portion of the tile to break up the glaze. These can then be chipped away with tile clippers or ordinary pincers. A tile saw is useful for awkward shapes, and will almost certainly be needed if slivers of tile less than ½in (12mm) have to be cut, although these should not be necessary if the job is well planned.

Using a tile cutter
Place the tile on a flat surface, decorative side up, and score a single line through the glaze, using a try square as a guide. Place two matchsticks under the tile, one at each end and in line with the scored line. Press down on either side of the tile until it breaks cleanly. Smooth any rough edges with a tile file.

Replacing ceramic tile accessories

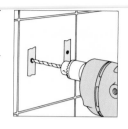

Screw fittings
If you need to drill new screw holes, do not attempt to drill straight into a tile, since the bit may slide around. Stick masking tape over the hole position and drill through it.

Tile accessories, such as towel rings, soap dishes and toothbrush holders, are fixed to the wall either by screws or with glue. They are vulnerable and most often in need of repair or replacement. With screw fittings, simply remove the screws and replace the accessory. Those with a ceramic base the size of one or two tiles are fixed using standard tile adhesive. They are replaced in the same way as broken tiles. When removing the broken tile or accessory, work from the centre of the tile outwards and take great care not to damage the surrounding tiles. Select a replacement that is exactly the size of the old one and which is either the same colour or a harmonious match. Allow plenty of time for the adhesive to set before you next use the accessory.

Replacing a ceramic soap dish

1 *Using a hammer and chisel, break up and chip out the damaged soap dish, making sure that you remove all the old grouting and adhesive from the cavity.*

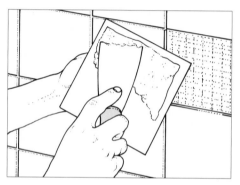

2 *Use an adhesive spreader to apply the tile adhesive over the back of the replacement dish, keeping it about ½in (12mm) clear of the edges.*

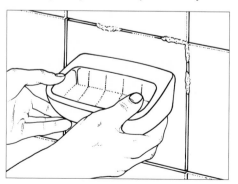

3 *Press the dish firmly into position, making sure that it lies flush with the surrounding tiles. Wipe away any excess adhesive.*

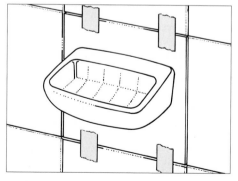

4 *Hold the new fixture in position with masking tape until the adhesive has set. After two days, remove the tape and fill the joints with grouting.*

Regrouting ceramic tiles

The grouting around tiles may need to be renewed from time to time, especially around showers or basins. Grouting is often sold ready-mixed, but it is more economical to use powdered grout to which you add water and mix it to a creamy consistency. Coloured grout is also available, either ready-mixed, as a dye to be added to the powder, or as a paint to be applied over old grouting.

Applying the grouting

1 *Spread the grouting on to the surface of the tiles and, using a damp sponge, work it well into the cracks between the tiles.*

2 *When the area is covered, draw a small, rounded stick into each joint to press the grouting tightly home. Take care not to press too deeply.*

Renewing sealant

Silicon rubber sealant is used around baths, basins and sinks to prevent water from seeping behind. In theory, it is flexible and so will keep the gap permanently sealed despite any movement, but you may find that, after a while, it shrinks slightly and needs to be renewed. Renew it as soon as it becomes necessary, to avoid problems of damp.

Replacing sealant
Squeeze the tube with consistent pressure so that the sealant is produced in a steady line. Draw the nozzle along the join between the edge of the bath or sink and the tiles, and smooth it with your finger. Allow it to dry completely before using the bath or sink.

Replacing panelling

Panelling provides a simple way of levelling an irregular wall surface and requires little attention. Insulating material and new wiring can be concealed behind it. Panelling can be made of individual boards or of sheet material designed to imitate boards; individual boards are easy to transport, but using sheet materials involves less work.

Two basic board types are available: tongue-and-groove, where the boards interlock, and shiplap, where each board rests over a lip on the previous one. Sheet panelling varies greatly in cost and quality. Cheap boards often consist of a photographic reproduction of wooden panelling printed on to a thin vinyl sheet, attached to standard hardboard.

Apart from the panelling itself, you will probably need to attach new supporting battens to the wall. These can be unplaned as they will be concealed under the panelling. If the battens are for an exterior wall, it is worth getting the timber treated with preservative so that it will not rot. If the panelling is intended to increase insulation, you should consider putting glass fibre, mineral wool or expanded polystyrene between the boards and the wall.

Preparing a wall for panelling

Panelling will hide the wall completely, so you should make sure that it is well prepared and free of problems such as damp. Internal walls usually give no damp problems, but external walls must be perfectly dry. Do not worry if there is condensation on the wall.

Examine porous walls for damage to the pointing. Rake out and replace all loose and crumbling mortar and brickwork, and treat the whole wall with a silicone water repellent. This will prevent water from getting in, yet still allow the wall to "breathe". It is a good idea to fix a polythene sheet over the wall surface before attaching the battens, which will stop condensation from forming.

You will also need to remove the skirting board (pages 116–17) and any picture rail that might obstruct the panelling to allow for the supporting battens. If you are going to use insulation material under the panelling, this should be inserted after the battens are in position, not before.

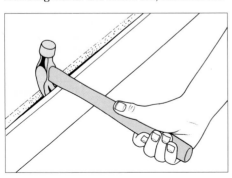

Removing skirting boards
If you want to remove the skirting boards, be careful not to damage them. Loosen a section of the skirting with an old chisel, and then slip the claw of a hammer under the board to lever it away. Pull out any nails in the skirting from the back – if you take them out from the front you will damage the face of the board.

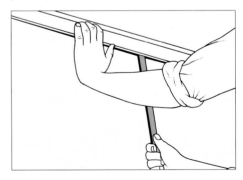

Removing picture rails
You need only take these away if they stand proud of the battens and obstruct the panelling. Make a cut in the rail close to one of the nails and break the rail away. It will be easier if you use a length of steel pushed under the rail to lever it up. This method causes least damage to the surrounding plaster.

Tools and materials

Use a circular saw with a fine blade, or alternatively a cross-cut hand saw, for cutting sheet materials. If you are using a hand saw, one with eight teeth to 1in (25mm) is best. For cutting individual boards and battens, use a tenon saw. You will also need a pad saw or else a power jigsaw for cutting holes. Other equipment includes claw and pin hammers for pinning the boards to the battens and removing skirting, a nail punch for driving the pins below the surface, a drill, a steel tape measure, a spirit level and a try square.

If you decide to fix the panelling with adhesive instead of pins, you will need a mastic gun and adhesive cartridges, available from DIY shops. Panel clips are very useful for fixing tongue-and-groove boards invisibly.

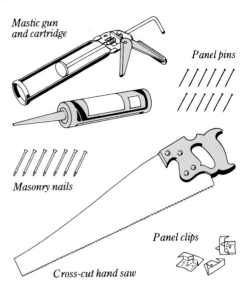

Mastic gun and cartridge

Panel pins

Masonry nails

Panel clips

Cross-cut hand saw

Types of panelling

Board panelling is available in two forms: tongue-and-groove boards and shiplap boards. Tongue-and-groove boards are usually available in whitewood (spruce), knotty pine (deal, Scots pine and red Baltic pine) and often in a good range of more unusual decorative species. They usually come with chamfered edges to form a decorative "V" joint and with either a flat or a decorative face – channelled or scalloped, for example. The standard thickness is ½in (12mm), although ¾in (19mm) and ⅓in (9.5mm)-thick boards are readily available.

Shiplap boards are similar to tongue-and-groove boards, except that the top edge of each board fits under a rebate in the edge of the previous board. When fixed horizontally, the water will run down the face of the boards without penetrating the surface. Shiplap boards are usually available only in deal.

Sheet panelling
Wallboards, thin plywood or hardboard sheets, come with a variety of surfaces. The best quality sheets have a veneer of real wood, which may also be grooved to simulate tongue-and-groove boards. Cheaper varieties have a photographic image of a wooden surface printed on paper or plastic and bonded on to plywood. Both types come in sheets that are sufficiently large to cover most walls from floor to ceiling without horizontal joins.

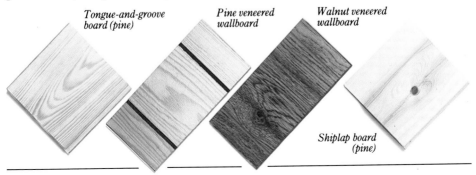

Tongue-and-groove board (pine)

Pine veneered wallboard

Walnut veneered wallboard

Shiplap board (pine)

Replacing board panelling

At least a week before you start, take the panelling into the room where you are going to fit it, to allow the timber's moisture content to adjust to the room. This is particularly important if there is a big difference between storage and room conditions. If the wood has been stored outdoors and is then brought into a centrally heated room, it will shrink and, if you put up the panelling too soon, unsightly gaps can open up between the boards. There are two main ways of fixing boards. The traditional method is to drive pins through the boards into the battens. Always sink the pins with a nail punch, so that they lie below the surface. Take care not to let the hammer slip and bruise the wood. Fill nail holes with a matching stopper. As an alternative, clip systems are now available that provide invisible fixings for tongue-and-groove boards.

Cut your final board so that a gap of about ¼in (6mm) is left between it and the wall to allow for expansion. If you do not leave a gap, the panelling may bow if it expands. You can hide the gap later by fitting a length of beading or a piece of decorative moulding.

Sockets and switches
Surround the unit as closely as possible with short pieces of batten secured with panel adhesive. Pin the panelling in place, making sure that the top edges of the socket are flush with the boards.

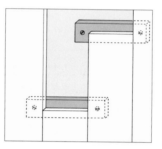

Joining boards
If necessary, short lengths of board can be butt-jointed, provided that the join is positioned over a batten. For a neat finish, cut the ends to a perfect right angle using a set square and mitre box.

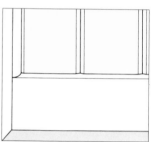

Finishing off
A strip of beading or moulding pinned down the side of board panelling will provide a neat edge, hiding the expansion gap and helping to conceal any irregularities in the wall.

Replacing sheet panelling

For sheet panelling you need horizontal battens with additional vertical battens placed so that their centre lines correspond to the edges of the sheets. If, however, you are fitting this type of panelling on to a partition wall, the simplest method is to remove any wallpaper and stick the sheets directly on to the wall. If you prefer to use battens, you should find the timber uprights in the wall and nail the battens to these. The plasterboard itself cannot give adequate support for the battens.

If the walls are square, you can stick the panels on to the wall using panel adhesive and a mastic gun. Alternatively, fix horizontal battens at 16in (40cm) intervals. You will also need one vertical batten for each joint in the panelling. It is difficult to butt the sheets perfectly together. A good solution is to make a feature of the joint, either by hiding it with beading, or by leaving a slight decorative gap. Remember to allow for the width of the gap when putting up the vertical battens.

If you have left small gaps between each sheet, you can either cover these with a wood or plastic strip, or leave them as they are. As an alternative to creating exact butt joints at the corners, you can leave a narrow gap to allow for variations in the width of the wall and finish off the corners with beading. You can also put beading at the top for a neat join between the panelling and the ceiling.

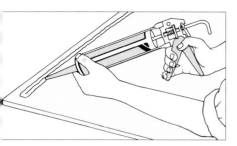

Gluing sheet panelling to the wall
Panel adhesive will take up any small variations in the wall surface. Apply ribbons of adhesive on the back of the sheet at about 16in (40cm) intervals. Press the sheet on to the wall, working quickly from bottom to top. If the adhesive is losing its effect by the time you put the board up to the wall, try cutting up the boards.

Gluing sheet panelling to battens
If the wall is very uneven, it is best to use battens. Pack the battens with pieces of hardboard to allow for the unevenness in the wall. Apply the adhesive liberally to the relevant battens and, working quickly, press the sheet on to it, making sure that the panelling is in contact with all the battens.

Replacing panelled ceilings

All ceiling panels – whether sheet or board – will need to be attached to battens; do not glue panelling to ceilings. Fix the battens to the joists at 24in (60cm) intervals. Run them at right angles to the ceiling joists, so that you have regular fixing points.

Decorate the new panels before putting them up. If you are putting up the panelling in a bathroom or kitchen, seal both sides of the wood so that it does not absorb moisture.

Start working from one wall and use the same techniques as for wall panelling. Clips are easiest to use because you can put them in position before offering the panels up to them. If you use pins, make start holes in the wood first. If you are using cut pieces of board, arrange the joins over the batten centres. Getting an exact fit around the perimeter of a ceiling is not easy. Cover gaps with beading or moulding secured with panel adhesive.

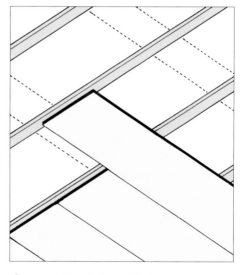

Supporting ceiling panelling
For ceiling panelling, attach supporting battens at right angles to the ceiling joists.

FINISHING OFF SHEET PANELLING

There are two basic problems when you are panelling up to a corner with sheet material – measuring and finishing off the corner. With external corners you have to overlap slightly and sand one sheet back to create a butt joint, or you can leave a narrow gap and finish off the corners with beading.

The greatest problem with sheet materials is cutting holes of the right shape to fit around obstructions such as electrical fittings. The safest way is to make an accurate template in thin cardboard. Transfer the pattern to your sheet when you are sure it is accurate. If you are in any doubt, cut the holes small and enlarge them to fit.

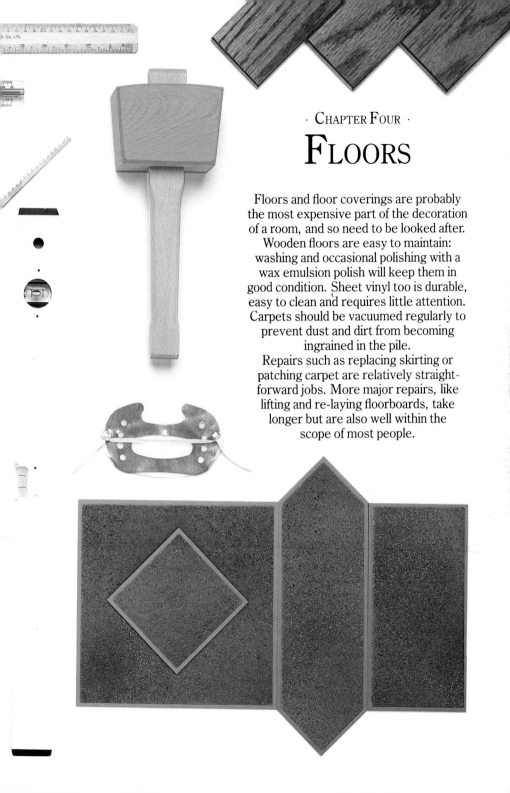

· Chapter Four ·

Floors

Floors and floor coverings are probably the most expensive part of the decoration of a room, and so need to be looked after. Wooden floors are easy to maintain: washing and occasional polishing with a wax emulsion polish will keep them in good condition. Sheet vinyl too is durable, easy to clean and requires little attention. Carpets should be vacuumed regularly to prevent dust and dirt from becoming ingrained in the pile.

Repairs such as replacing skirting or patching carpet are relatively straight-forward jobs. More major repairs, like lifting and re-laying floorboards, take longer but are also well within the scope of most people.

Tools and materials

For most jobs you will need at least one hammer and one saw. In addition, you will require a number of other items, depending, of course, on the job you are doing. For sanding wooden floorboards, you will need to hire special equipment (page 120).

For cutting along the tongue before lifting floorboards you will need a circular power saw. A hand saw designed specifically for floorboards is also available. It has a blade with a curved end to make it easier to start the cut. A circular saw with a tungsten-carbide blade should be used for cutting chipboard, which blunts normal blades quickly. A power jigsaw is useful if you want to cut across floorboards, but you can use a pad saw. You will need a drill to make starting holes before using these saws. Most need a hole about ½in (12mm) in diameter. For intricate cuts – for example,

when you are laying flooring around curved obstructions – use a coping saw, and use a tenon saw for straightforward trimming.

A pair of pincers is useful for removing old carpet tacks and nails. You will need a medium-weight or a lighter pin-type hammer for most flooring work. Use a nail punch for hammering down nails, to ensure that they lie below the surface. This is particularly important if the floor is to be sanded. Some form of lever is needed for taking up floorboards. A bolster chisel is good for this, and you may also find a strong length of steel useful. Use a block plane when filling gaps between floorboards with thin strips of wood. A mallet and chisel can be used to chip away wood from the underside of a new floorboard, so that it matches older surrounding boards, and for jobs like taking out damaged blocks in a parquet floor.

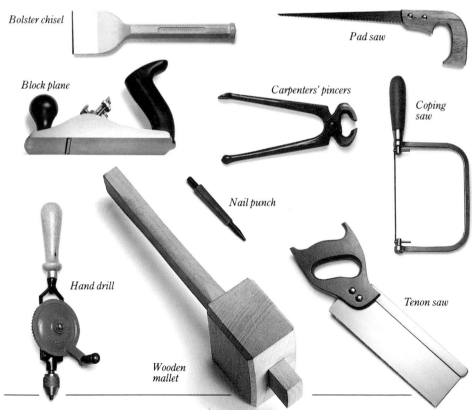

Bolster chisel

Pad saw

Block plane

Carpenters' pincers

Coping saw

Nail punch

Hand drill

Tenon saw

Wooden mallet

Care and repair of floors

Old floorboards and joists become loose and worn and may need securing, replacing or even re-laying. You may be able to renovate the surface of an existing floor, but if you are thinking of sanding a floor, the boards will need to be in good condition. If, however, you are thinking of laying carpet, vinyl or woodblock flooring, then a new sub-floor, such as chipboard or hardboard, will provide a good flat surface underneath. Damaged skirting can be repaired by cutting out the broken section and fixing a new piece in its place.

Filling gaps between boards

If there are only a few gaps between the boards you can pack them using papier mâché or wood filler, provided that the gaps are very narrow. A better method is to use wood strips, planed along their length so that one side tapers. Apply PVA glue to each side and tap the strip down so that it wedges into the gap. When the glue has dried, plane the wood level. The same technique is used to repair a split panel in a table top (page 28).

Filling with strips of wood
After you have allowed the adhesive to dry, plane the strip down to the existing floor level.

Securing loose floorboards and joists

It is worth lifting loose floorboards to see if the joists beneath are also moving. Sometimes, particularly in old houses, joist ends work loose where they are built into the walls. If this has happened, they must be made firm.

There are two ways to secure joists. One is to pack the hole with pieces of slate secured with mortar and wedge the joist firmly in place. An alternative method is to use a joist hanger. This is a special galvanized steel joist support. There are different sorts of joist hanger: with one type you screw the hanger firmly to the wall; another design must be built into the mortar joints in the wall.

If the joist ends have rotted, either replace the affected joists or call in a flooring specialist to make the repairs. Secure loose floorboards by renailing them to the joists with 2½in (63mm) cut floor brads or lost-head nails, or by screwing them down with 2in (50mm) gauge 10 countersunk-head wood screws.

Fixing loose joists
You can pack loose joists with pieces of slate secured with mortar.

Using joist hangers
Built into or screwed to the wall, a joist hanger provides firm support.

Renailing loose boards
Insert the nails slightly to one side of the original nail holes. Make sure that they go into the centre of each joist and use two nails at each joist position.

Removing boards by cutting

If you want to lift only a short length of floor-board or release a long board that is trapped under the skirting, it may be necessary to cut across the boards before levering them up. This may also be a helpful method for taking up tongue-and-groove boards.

The first thing to do is to locate the joists which support the floorboards. For obvious reasons, avoid cutting through the joists supporting the floor – cut alongside one of them. To find a joist, look along the length of the floorboards for a line of nails across the floor; these nails attach the board to a joist. Joists are usually 2–3in (50–75mm) wide and will extend roughly 1–1½in (25–40mm) each side of the nails. With square-edged boards, insert a thin knife blade through the gap between the boards and slide it along the length to help you find the joists.

Drill a hole through the board to one side of the joist and mark a cutting line across the width of the board. Cut through the board with a power jigsaw or hand pad saw and lift it out. When cutting, angle the blade of the saw towards the centre of the joist. This will create a chamfered edge, so that the board is supported when you replace it.

Removing tongue-and-groove boards
The main difficulty is lifting the first board. Once this is done, you can lever the others up fairly easily. First cut through the tongue by sawing along the length of the board. Use a circular saw, set to cut about ½in (12mm) deep. Retract the guard, tilt the saw forward and lower the blade between two boards. The saw will leave a small gap the width of the blade between the boards which will have to be filled later. Alternatively, use a floorboard saw, which has a curved blade, so that you can start the cut easily.

Cutting and lifting floorboards

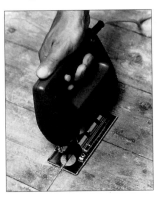

1 *Drill a hole about ½in (12mm) in diameter to take the saw blade at a position close to the joist and draw a line along the joist.*

2 *Cut along the line, tilting the top of the saw slightly towards the centre of the joist to create a chamfered edge.*

3 *Lift up the board, using a bolster chisel as a lever. The chamfered edge will help to support the board when it is replaced.*

Removing and re-laying floorboards

Floorboards can have either square or tongue-and-groove edges, which are harder to lift up. Before you begin to lift either type, look for screwed-down boards. These are easy to lift and will tell you what type of board makes up your floor. If there are damaged areas or many gaps between the boards, it is best to lift the whole floor and re-lay it, putting in new boards where necessary.

Re-laying boards is straightforward; the main problem is getting them as close together as possible. To do this, hammer a pair of wooden wedges between the boards and a piece of wood to press together the floorboards before nailing them down permanently.

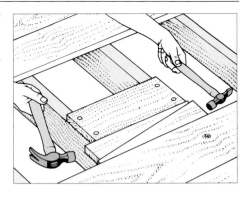

Re-laying floorboards
Lay four or five adjacent boards in position and nail a length of wood to the joists a short distance from them. Hammer a pair of wedges between the boards and the wood to tighten the boards. Nail the boards in place, then remove the wedges and piece of wood.

Removing square-edged boards

1 *Insert a bolster chisel or other strong metal lever into the gaps between the boards. Use it to prise up each board, starting close to a convenient board end.*

2 *Lift up the board until you can insert another chisel or lever on the opposite side, then work both levers along the board. Be careful not to trap your fingers.*

3 *To help loosen the board, start with a chisel, then place a strong metal lever underneath. Press down on the free end of the board to force it up along its length.*

Fitting new boards

New boards will need to be fitted to replace old, split or rotten boards. If you have re-laid a floor, you will probably be left with a narrow gap at the end; this will have to be filled with a new board. You may have to cut new boards along their length to make them fit a long, narrow gap in a floor – such as when filling a gap left after re-laying. A bench-mounted circular saw is useful for making these long, straight cuts.

The new boards may not be exactly the same thickness as those that make up the rest of the floor. If they are slightly too thin, use pieces of wood as packing between the boards and the joists so that they lie flush with the rest of the floor. If the new boards are too thick, use a chisel to chip away the wood and make them thinner at the joist positions.

You can fix most of the boards with 2½in (63mm) cut floor brads or lost-head nails. Screw down any boards that may have to be lifted in the future, as this will make them easier to remove.

Removing skirting

Damaged skirting will have to be removed or replaced. You will also need to remove skirting when putting up new plasterboard or panelling (pages 97–8, 106–9).

To remove a section of skirting, insert the end of a bolster chisel or other strong metal lever between the wall and the skirting and lever the skirting outwards slowly and carefully, taking care not to split the wood. Place a wooden wedge into the gap created

and continue levering, using a succession of wedges as you work along the skirting. When it is free, place the new section alongside it and mark the length.

Cutting new skirting

Inside and outside corners should be mitred; you will find it easiest to use a mitre box to make accurate cuts. Special care needs to be taken in measuring and marking the necessary cuts to get an accurate angle, especially if the walls are not absolutely square. Use a tenon saw to make the cuts.

Removing damaged skirting

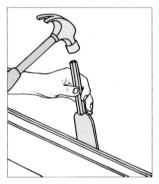

1 *Insert the end of a thin chisel or other metal lever between the wall and the skirting and lever slowly and carefully outwards.*

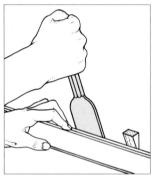

2 *When the gap between the wall and skirting is large enough, slide wooden wedges in the space to keep the skirting out from the wall.*

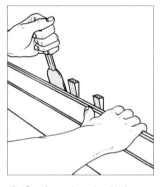

3 *Continue along the skirting, inserting more wedges as you go, until the skirting is loose enough to pull away from the wall.*

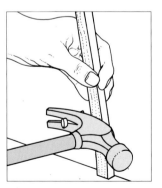

4 *Using a claw hammer, remove all nails from the wall. Protect the surface of the wall with a wooden block behind the hammer's head.*

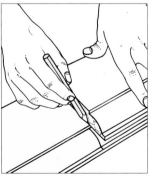

5 *Place the new section of skirting against the old one and measure the length. Mark the position of any corner angles.*

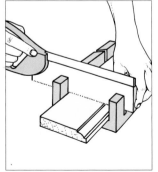

6 *Use a mitre box and tenon saw for the corner angles, then nail the new section in place. Use a nail punch to sink the nail heads.*

Replacing skirting

If you need to attach replacement skirting, you should use the method that was employed when the original boards were fitted. If the wall is made of solid bricks, the skirting boards may be attached directly to the wall with masonry pins or nailed to wooden blocks. These are fixed to the wall with screws and wallplugs set into the mortar joints between the bricks. Pins should be long enough to penetrate the wall by ¾in (19mm). With hollow partition walls, fix the skirtings to the wall's internal uprights.

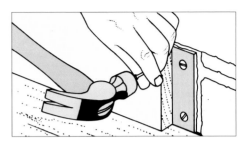

Masonry walls
Attach new blocks to the wall if there are no timber "plugs" already set into the mortar joints. Nail the skirting to the blocks.

Cutting to fit an uneven floor

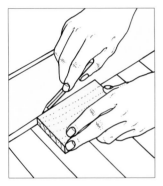

1 *Measure the widest gap between the skirting and the floor and cut a wooden block slightly thicker. Holding a pencil on the block, slide it along the floor to mark the edge of the skirting.*

2 *Using either an electrical circular saw or jigsaw, or a hand panel or rip saw, cut along the pencil line, holding the saw at an angle so that the front of the skirting is deeper than the back.*

3 *If the wall is a partition type, fix the skirting with nails that pass through the plasterboard to the uprights of the frame. Push the skirting firmly against the floor and wall as you nail it in place.*

Hiding gaps under skirting

It is possible to use papier mâché or wood filler to seal gaps between boards and skirting, but they usually go on opening and closing as the room temperature varies. The best method is to nail moulding around the skirting to hide the gaps but still allow for some movement.

Fitting moulding
Press the moulding on to the floor and nail it to the skirting only, so that the floor can still move.

Laying hardboard

Hardboard creates the ideal sub-floor for many floor coverings. Use standard hardboard, ⅛in (3.2mm) thick, or ³⁄₁₆in (4.8mm) hardboard for very uneven floors. Use oil-tempered hardboard in kitchens and bathrooms. Before laying, condition the boards. Separate them and stand them on edge for 72 hours in the room where you are going to put them down. In kitchens and bathrooms they should be sprinkled with water. Fill any deep holes in the floor with papier mâché.

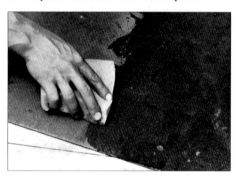

Conditioning hardboard
In new homes, kitchens, and bathrooms sprinkle the rough sides of the hardboard sheets with about 1pt (600ml) water per sheet and stack the boards flat, back to back, in the room where they are to be laid. You will need to leave standard board for 48 hours and tempered board for 72 hours.

Fixing hardboard sheets
Cut each sheet in half to provide more expansion joints and some in half again (the number will depend on the room size) to give staggered joins. Fix the boards smooth side down with ring-shank nails, hardboard pins or staples about 4in (100mm) apart around the edges and 6in (15cm) apart over the rest of the board.

Laying chipboard

Chipboard comes with either straight or tongue-and-groove edges and in ¾in (19mm) and ⅞in (22mm) thicknesses. For most purposes, ¾in (19mm) chipboard is adequate, but use ⅞in (22mm) chipboard for joists spaced further than 18in (45cm) apart. For a smooth, strong floor, tongue-and-groove edged panels are best. These normally come in sheets measuring 8 × 2ft (2.4 × 0.6m).

If you use square-edged boards, nail and glue 2 × 3in (50 × 75mm) timber between the joists so that all the edges are supported. This will cut down flexing. With tongue-and-groove chipboard there is no need for cross timbers. The edges of each panel should come half-way across the supporting joists. Fix the panels with 2½in (63mm) lost-head wire nails. Leave screwed-down access panels over cables and pipes. Chipboard blunts saw blades, so if you

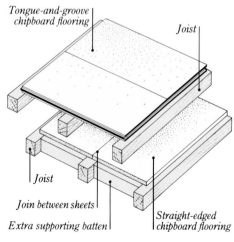

Tongue-and-groove chipboard flooring

Joist

Joist

Join between sheets

Extra supporting batten

Straight-edged chipboard flooring

are going to cut many panels use a circular saw with a tungsten-carbide tipped blade, or a hard-point handsaw. An electric jigsaw is best for intricate cuts.

Repairing chipboard

Chipboard floors require few repairs, but they can give problems when you have to lift a panel to gain access to cables, pipes, or joists beneath the floor. Sometimes a chipboard floor will flex as you walk across it, especially along the joins between adjacent panels. The best solution to this problem is to rest all the unsupported edges on lengths of 2 × 3in (50 × 75mm) timber, glued and nailed into position between the joists.

Chipboard is a strong material, but it is sometimes softened and weakened as a result of damp from a water leak. The only cure for this is to replace the affected section of the floor. Only in rare cases will a whole panel of chipboard be affected, so the best method is to cut out the weakened area with a circular saw. It is then a simple matter to lever up the board. If you do need to take up a whole panel, punch down the fixing nails and prise it up. Repair the floor by fitting a new piece of chipboard, cut slightly larger than the original, if it was removed with a circular saw. Support it if necessary on cross timbers placed between the joists and screw it down with chipboard screws. You can fill gaps around a replacement panel with a layer of wood filler.

Replacing a panel

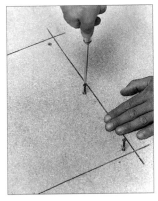

1 *Select the area you want to remove and pencil cutting lines on the surface, running the lines alongside the nails. Use a circular power saw and set the blade to cut ³⁄₄in (19mm) deep (or ⁷⁄₈in – 22mm – with thicker board) so that you do not saw through the joists.*

2 *Hold the saw firmly and keep your feet clear as you cut. To remove a tongue-and-groove panel, saw around the join with adjacent panels to free the board, then use a slim nail punch to drive the fixing nails as deeply as possible below the surface, and lever up the board.*

3 *A circular saw may leave a wide saw cut around the panel, so cut the new piece slightly larger than the original. Fit cross timbers between the joists to support the edges and fix the new panel using 1½in (38mm) chipboard screws at intervals of about 12in (30cm).*

SUB-FLOORS

Hardboard, chipboard and plywood all form good sub-floors for use under carpet, vinyl, tiles and all the different hardwood coverings – parquet, mosaic panels and woodstrip flooring. They can be used to cover worn floorboards that would otherwise need to be replaced or re-laid.

Tips for laying
• Condition hardboard for use in damp rooms, such as bathrooms and kitchens, by sprinkling the rough sides with water.
• Leave standard hardboard in the room where it is to be laid for 48 hours and tempered board for 72 hours before laying it.

• Cut hardboard sheets in half so that they are easier to handle and to provide expansion joints.
• Use pieces cut in half again at the edges of alternate rows to give staggered joins.
• Lay the first sheet in the centre of the floor and work towards the edges of the room.

Sanding floorboards

Floorboards that have been sanded, sealed and polished have a warmth, colour and subtlety of texture. They are hard-wearing, so are ideal for living rooms, passages and other areas which receive a lot of use.

Sanded and other hardwood floors are easy to maintain by washing and occasional polishing with a wax emulsion polish. If the finish deteriorates, rub the surface in line with the grain with medium or fine wire wool soaked in white spirit to remove the old polish, then reseal the floor. Treat minor scratches with paraffin wax applied on a small cloth. You may be able to disguise large scratches using a wax repair crayon of the type used on furniture, otherwise sand the affected area and reseal it. Sweep the floor regularly, to prevent loose dirt from scratching the polish.

Tools and materials

The main item you need for sanding floorboards is an industrial drum floor sander, which will enable you to sand the main part of the floor. You will also need a smaller hand sander for the edges. Both can be hired from tool-hire shops, which will also supply abrasives. One day's hire should give you plenty of time to prepare a large room. You will also need a dust mask, a nail punch and hammer, pincers for pulling out protruding tacks and nails, and a hand scraper for corners.

Floor sander
This has a large, revolving drum that takes the abrasive paper and is driven by a powerful electric motor. The machine has a vacuum action and a bag to remove most of the dust. The drum may be 8in (20cm) or 12in (30cm) wide. The smaller model is easier to handle and is suitable for all but the largest rooms. If the floor is in reasonable condition you should start by using medium-grade abrasive paper and finish with fine grade. Coarse-grade is available for very uneven surfaces and an extra-coarse grade will probably be needed if there is a build-up of wax polish on the floor.

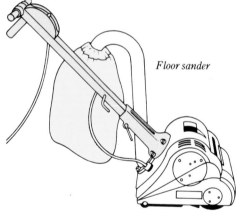

Floor sander

Hand sanders
The floor sander is too large to go right up to the edges of the floor, so you also need a hand sanding machine. A belt sander is ideal, because it does not produce swirl marks on the wood surface. If you use a disc-type sander, take care not to score the surface. Both types of hand sanders should be fitted with a vacuum bag. A sanding attachment on an electric drill is not powerful enough.

Belt hand sander

Dust mask

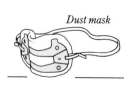

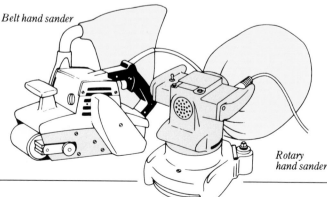

Rotary hand sander

Sanding a floor

Make sure that all the boards are securely fixed. Look for split, damaged, or badly patched boards and replace them. If there are a lot of gaps between the boards, take them up and re-lay them. Pull out any protruding carpet tacks and nails using pincers. Then deal with the nails that fix the boards to the joists. If they protrude, they will tear the sanding belt, so drive them well below the surface using a nail punch or alternatively another large nail that has had its tip filed off.

After you have prepared the floor, sand the main area with a large floor sander. Start with medium or coarse abrasive on the machine's drum to strip away the surface, before changing to a finer grade to get a smoother finish. You will not be able to get right up to the edges of the room with the large sander, so use a hand sander for these areas. With both machines, work in a direction parallel to the boards. Even a hand sander cannot get right into the corners of a room, so you will have to finish off these small areas, together with places where there are other obstructions, using a simple hand scraper.

Although sanders have dust-collecting bags, these are not capable of picking up all the dust when you have finished sanding. Vacuum the floor thoroughly and clean it carefully with a damp cloth. Leave the surface to dry completely before sealing it.

Using sanding machines

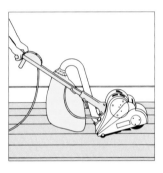

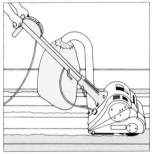

1 *Before you switch on a large belt sander, tilt it back so that the drum is raised off the floor. Switch it on and lower the spinning drum on to the floor. The sander will move forwards and you will have to restrain it so that it travels slowly – but not too much, or it will continue to sand the same small area of floor and start to gouge out a depression.*

2 *Work the machine forwards and backwards in the same direction as the floorboards. Overlap each pass by about 3in (75mm). If the floor is very uneven make the first few passes at 45° to the boards, working parallel to the boards when you switch to finer paper. Never sand at right angles to the boards – it will not even out the surface.*

3 *When you have sanded the main floor area, tackle the edges with the hand sander. Finally, using a hand scraper, finish off the corners and other confined areas which you cannot reach with the hand sander.*
When using either a floor sander or a hand sander, make sure that you keep the cable out of the way by running it over your shoulder.

Sealing floorboards

When you have sanded a floor, you need to seal it so that it will resist wear and can be kept clean easily. Floorboard seals come in two types. Polyurethane-based seals form a clear, gloss or matt coat over the wood surface.

Oleo-resinous types soak into the wood and give a scratch-resistant, lustre surface. Both types usually darken the floor colour slightly; to change the colour of the boards more radically, apply a stain before sealing the floor, or a stain and seal in one. When the floor is perfectly clean and dry, apply the coats of seal. Allow to dry for 12 hours between each coat.

Care and repair of floor coverings

Sheet vinyl is a durable and easy to clean floor covering, particularly suited to kitchens and bathrooms. Once laid, it needs little attention, except sweeping and occasional washing and polishing. Abrasive cleaner may damage the surface, so use mild detergent to remove any spills before they stain. If a glossy vinyl fades, it can be recoated with a wipe-over liquid coating.

Hardwood floors, such as parquet or mosaic blocks, are also hard-wearing and easy to maintain. Rubbing the surface with a dry mop will improve the sheen; otherwise they just need washing, occasional polishing with a wax emulsion polish and regular sweeping, to get rid of abrasive dirt. Any scratches or damages to the finish are treated in the same way as for sanded floors (pages 120–1).

Preparing the floor

Before laying carpet or any other floor covering, you should check that the floor is smooth, dry, clean and firm. Timber floors may need to be repaired or replaced and a new sub-floor laid (pages 112–19). Cement screed and concrete floors may be concealed beneath other surfaces, so ensure that the floor is dry and level. If the floor is uneven, apply screed. First fill any dents with mortar and remove grease with wire wool and white spirit. Apply priming liquid to non-absorbent surfaces and dampen absorbent surfaces.

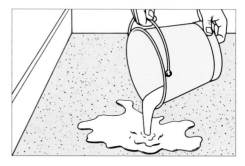

Applying screeding compound
Mix the screed and pour it on the floor. It sets quickly and can be covered by carpet after 24 hours.

Minor repairs

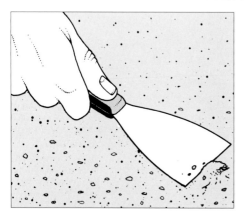

1 *To ensure that the surface is level, you will probably need to remove the existing floor covering. Take up the covering and scrape away flaking or crumbling sections with a paint scraper.*

2 *Vacuum the floor to remove dust and fill any indentations with cement mortar or filler. Apply a coating of diluted PVA bonding agent before filling to improve adhesion.*

Dealing with damp

If damp is not detected and treated at an early stage, it will spread rapidly and ruin any newly laid carpet. If you have noticed "tide-marks", or if you suspect that the room may be damp, test the area to see if the problem is caused by superficial condensation or rising damp (page 219). Before treating a floor for rising damp (pages 216–18), ensure that the surface is clean and free of dust.

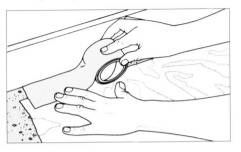

Testing for rising damp
Tape a square of polythene over the affected area of the floor, taking care to seal the edges. If moisture forms on the surface of the plastic, the cause is condensation, and the cure is better heating and ventilation. If droplets form on the underside, you have rising damp, which must be cured.

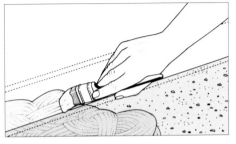

Curing rising damp
If the surface is dusty, vacuum the floor then apply a coat of diluted PVA bonding agent and fill any indentations. Remove the skirtings and paint the floor with a damp-proof membrane. Take the membrane up the wall a short way to link with the damp course, then replace the skirtings.

Patching carpet

If the carpet has a woven (as opposed to foam) backing, the back of the damaged section must be coated with a band of latex carpet adhesive along the cutting line, to prevent it from fraying. When the adhesive is dry, the old patch is cut out from above. This is then used as a template for matching size, pattern and pile. The adhesive treatment is repeated before cutting the new piece, and carpet tape is fixed around the edge of the hole on the back of the carpet, to hold the new patch in place.

Carpets and matting can be prevented from fraying by binding the edges with tape and rubber contact adhesive. Tap along both sides with a hammer to make sure that it bonds well.

Patching hessian-backed carpet

1 *Spread adhesive on the back of the carpet around the damaged area. Place a cutting board under the carpet and cut through the backing.*

2 *Cut a new piece to fit, matching the pattern and pile direction. Fix strips of carpet tape around the hole and press the new patch in place.*

Repairing a parquet floor

Parquet blocks are assembled in a basket-weave pattern. They look rather like mosaic blocks, but unlike mosaic, they usually have tongue-and-groove edges so that they interlock and form a very flat, good-quality floor. The blocks are laid loose, held in place by the interlocking tongues and grooves. Parquet floors do not require sanding, but they do need a good underlay, either hardboard or special coarse paper impregnated with bitumen and covered with cork chips.

To remove a damaged area, chisel out a central block. Once this is removed, you can lift out any other affected pieces. Scrape the floor surface clean, then stick new matching blocks into place using flooring adhesive. The new blocks may be slightly thicker than the surrounding floor, especially if the original floor has become worn. Plane them down to the right level once the adhesive has dried.

Chiselling out a parquet block
Use a mallet and chisel to chip out a damaged parquet block. Starting at the centre of the piece, chisel out the wood until you can remove the whole block. You will need to cut off the tongue of the new block before you will be able to fit it in place.

Patching tears in sheet vinyl

Any large areas of damaged vinyl should be patched with an offcut. The new patch should be cut larger than the tear and adjusted to match the pattern. Having chosen a suitable line of pattern for the edge of the patch, use a sharp knife to cut through both pieces of vinyl. The old piece is then removed and the patch coated with adhesive and pressed into place.

Fitting a new patch
Check that the new patch matches the old vinyl before gluing it in place. Use vinyl repair adhesive to "weld" the edges of the tear at the surface. Wipe off any surplus adhesive before it sets. Use a seam roller to ensure that the edges lie flat.

Replacing binder bars

A threshold strip fastened on to the edge of vinyl or carpet in a doorway will protect the material from scuffing and will neatly cover the join between two rooms if the floor coverings are different. It will also help to hide a bad join between two sheets of vinyl. Binder bars have evenly spaced, pre-drilled holes and are fixed with screws. They are available in aluminium, but a strip of hardwood could be used instead.

Screwing down the binder bar
Cut the binder bar to size, taking a little off each end to ensure that the fixing points remain evenly spaced. Then screw it in the door threshold over the join between the two floor coverings. Tighten the screws regularly, to avoid accidents.

Repairing vinyl tiles

Most vinyl tiles are self-adhesive; others are stuck to the floor with a special adhesive. The adhesive holding a tile in place can be softened by heating the tile with a torch or warm iron, taking care not to damage the surrounding tiles. Remove the tile by lifting one corner and peeling it away. If this does not work, chip out the damaged tile with a mallet and chisel,

working from the centre outwards. Before sticking the new tile in position, try it in place to make sure that it fits, matching the pattern and trimming if necessary. Warm it to make it flexible, stick it in place and weight it down until the adhesive sets.

Vinyl tiles tend to curl up at the edges. This can be cured by using an electric iron to soften the adhesive, applying fresh adhesive and weighting down the tile until the new adhesive is completely dry.

Replacing a damaged tile

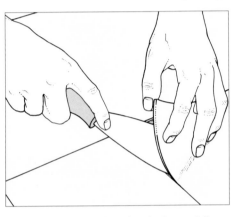

1 *Using a torch or hot iron, heat the damaged tile to soften the adhesive. Carefully lift a corner with a filling knife and peel the tile away.*

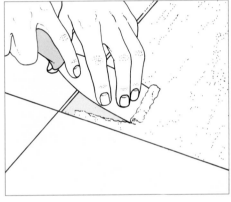

2 *Scrape off the old adhesive and clean all debris from the hole. Try the new tile in position, checking that the pattern matches, and trim it to fit if necessary.*

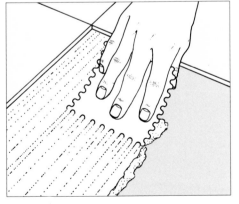

3 *If the tile is not self-adhesive, apply an even layer of vinyl-tile adhesive over the sub-floor with an adhesive spreader, avoiding the surrounding tiles.*

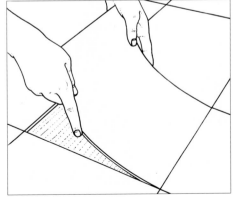

4 *Warm the new tile with an iron to make it flexible and press it in position. Put a board across and weight the tile in place until the glue sets.*

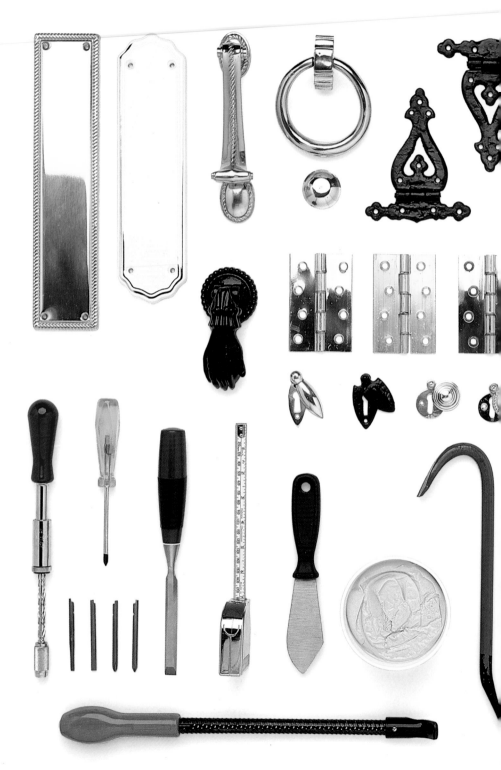

· CHAPTER FIVE ·

DOORS AND WINDOWS

Doors are made in a variety of styles and materials, for a range of functions. Most are made of wood and hung on hinges, but sliding or folding doors, useful if space is limited, may be made from a lighter material such as plastic, or consist of a framework faced with sheets of hardboard or plywood. Strong hardwood or aluminium doors are for external use. There are two basic types of window: fixed panes, which do not open, and opening panes, usually either sashes or hinged casements. They provide light and, in the case of opening panes, ventilation.

Doors

Doors come in different materials (wood, metal, glass and plastic), and in a range of styles (hinged, sliding and folding). They are designed for a variety of uses – for example, internal and external doors are made to different specifications. Most doors are made from wood and hung on hinges. The two most common wooden types are panelled and flush doors. Panelled doors have a framework of solid wood with the space between filled with solid wood, plywood, or glass. Flush doors have a much lighter framework which is covered on both sides with facing sheets of hardboard or plywood.

Tools and materials

When replacing doors, accurate measuring and marking up is essential; flexible steel tapes are the most versatile. A spirit level or plumb bob is essential for checking that the doors hang vertically at the hinge side. Use a sharp knife to mark the position of the hinges and a bevel-edge chisel to chip out the wood. You will need both single slot and cross-head screwdrivers for fixing hinges and door fittings.

A panel saw is the most useful all-round hand saw for trimming the bottoms of doors, as you will need to cut both across and along the grain. A small block plane is best to use for trimming small amounts. A drill will only be necessary if you need to fix a loose frame.

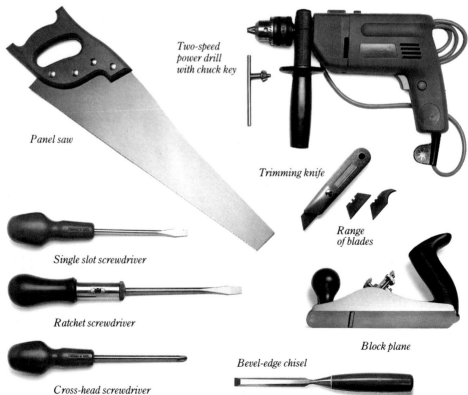

Panel saw

Two-speed power drill with chuck key

Trimming knife

Range of blades

Single slot screwdriver

Ratchet screwdriver

Block plane

Cross-head screwdriver

Bevel-edge chisel

Types of door

For exterior use, strong, hardwood panelled doors are best on older houses, while aluminium glazed doors blend in well with modern homes. Indoors, many homes have flush doors, although panelled doors often look more attractive. Fire doors, usually flush doors with a fireproof core, are often required in flats and tall buildings. Bi-folding and sliding doors may be used to divide rooms.

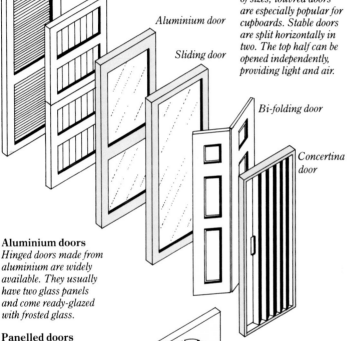

Louvred door

Stable door

Aluminium door

Sliding door

Bi-folding door

Concertina door

Louvred and stable doors
Available in a wide range of sizes, louvred doors are especially popular for cupboards. Stable doors are split horizontally in two. The top half can be opened independently, providing light and air.

Sliding and folding doors
Any door can be made to slide by using rollers and tracks. Bi-folding doors are hinged so that only half of the door projects when open. The flexible slats of concertina doors fold together when the door is open.

Flush doors
Lighter than panelled doors, these vary greatly in cost, depending on the quality of the facing material and the internal core. Hardboard facing is suitable only for indoors, while plywood can be used inside or outside. Some flush doors have a moulded facing to make them look panelled. Others have an opening to take a pane of glass. In flush fire doors the core is always made up of fireproof material.

Aluminium doors
Hinged doors made from aluminium are widely available. They usually have two glass panels and come ready-glazed with frosted glass.

Panelled doors
These are available in a wide range of designs. Outdoors where strength and security are important, choose a door with a hardwood frame and protect it with a preservative stain. Use safety glass if the panels take single, large panes, and bevel-edge glass for smaller panes. Indoors, panelled doors with softwood frames are adequate. These can be made of redwood or Douglas fir.

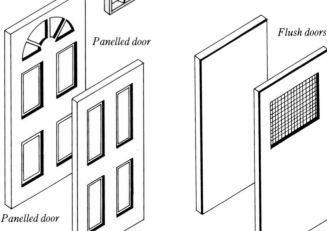

Panelled door

Flush doors

Panelled door

Door furniture

Door fittings allow a door to fulfil its function as a means of entry and exit. If it is to work properly, it needs the correct accessories. They are available from DIY, furnishing and specialist shops, where the range is usually on display. Alternatively, you may prefer to consult several manufacturers' catalogues to make your choice. Always check that your measurements are correct and that both the size and material of all the fittings are compatible with each other. Remember that the door fittings should be fixed into place after the door surface has been painted, stained or varnished. Apply oil to metal catches and hinges from time to time, and if nylon fittings squeak, loosen the screw heads a fraction.

The range of door and furniture fittings is huge. Your choice of materials for knobs,

knockers, handles and other fittings is largely an aesthetic decision, although the size and type will be determined by the door's function. Newly painted or varnished doors may show up scratches and wear on old door furniture, so to set off new decoration to advantage it may be worth the relatively small expense of a new set of door furniture. Shiny brass or gold-plated fittings usually look best on gloss-painted or varnished doors, particularly front doors, while wood, china or plastic lend themselves to interior and cupboard doors. Use modern-style fittings in a new home and traditional styles in an older house. If your choice is governed by price, note that synthetic and plated materials now provide good imitations. However, brass, gold-plate, zinc and aluminium hinges supply stronger support for heavy doors.

Knobs, knockers and handles

Knobs, knockers, letterboxes, key plates and covers, bell pulls and door numbers fixed on to front doors are primarily decorative but retain a practical function. The range of designs and materials for both front doors and internal doors is huge, and co-ordinating sets of furniture are available. When replacing door handles, it is often advisable to take the old one with you to check the size.

Turning handles
Turning or bolt-through handles, which operate a spring latch, come as round or lever handles. The choice of shapes and sizes is wide, and most come in a range of metals, including brass, chrome, gold plate and stainless steel, but wood, glass, porcelain and plastic will also stand up well to wear. Some have matching escutcheons.

Plastic lever handle and escutcheon

Brass lever latch handle

Pull handles
Used in conjunction with an independent catch, pull handles may be round or long, and are available in the same range of metals as turning handles.

Satin chromium-plated pull handle

Chromium-plated pull handle

Stainless steel pull handle

Stainless steel knob

Plastic pull handle

Plastic knob

Door handles

There are two types of door handle: a turning handle that forms an integral part of a catch, and a static handle, used on doors with independent catches. Turning door handles come in two forms – levers and knobs. Both operate by rotating a square metal spindle, which passes through the door and the catch. If the door is very thin, you may need to cut the spindle to fit.

A knob set
On one side of a knob set sits a knob attached to a rosette, which is nailed to the face of the door. A long, square-shaped spindle fits into the knob through the rosette, and passes through a hole in the door and the catch. On the other side of the door, a knob, attached to a rosette, slides over the spindle and is secured to the door face.

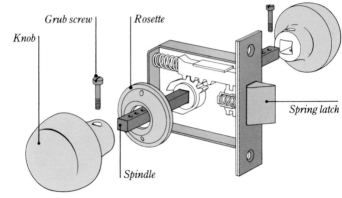

Grub screw | Rosette | Knob | Spring latch | Spindle

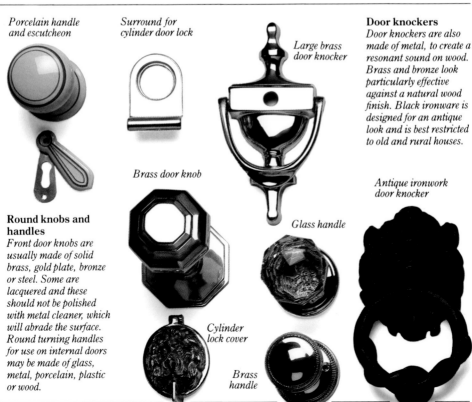

Porcelain handle and escutcheon

Surround for cylinder door lock

Brass door knob

Large brass door knocker

Door knockers
Door knockers are also made of metal, to create a resonant sound on wood. Brass and bronze look particularly effective against a natural wood finish. Black ironware is designed for an antique look and is best restricted to old and rural houses.

Antique ironwork door knocker

Round knobs and handles
Front door knobs are usually made of solid brass, gold plate, bronze or steel. Some are lacquered and these should not be polished with metal cleaner, which will abrade the surface. Round turning handles for use on internal doors may be made of glass, metal, porcelain, plastic or wood.

Glass handle

Cylinder lock cover

Brass handle

Door hinges

Hinges must be strong enough to support the weight of the door and must allow it to open wide enough. The best qualities are metal, but plastic types are adequate for small doors. Various hinges are designed for specific types of door and it is important to choose a suitable type in the correct size. You will generally need a 3in (75mm) size for internal flush doors, a 4in (100mm) size for panelled and external doors and smaller sizes for cupboards and cabinets. You will have to decide how wide you would like the door to open. The standard hinge opens to 95°, but 110° types are available for wider opening, and 170° hinges will allow the door to lie flat against the adjoining surface. If you want the door to remain shut without a catch to hold it, you will need a sprung hinge. The lift-off hinge is designed specifically for use on cabinets. It allows the door to be removed

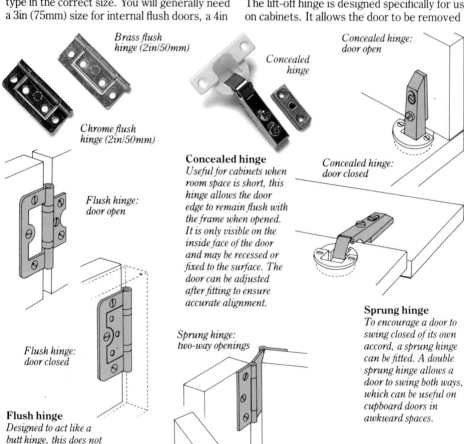

Brass flush hinge (2in/50mm)

Chrome flush hinge (2in/50mm)

Concealed hinge

Concealed hinge: door open

Concealed hinge: door closed

Flush hinge: door open

Flush hinge: door closed

Concealed hinge
Useful for cabinets when room space is short, this hinge allows the door edge to remain flush with the frame when opened. It is only visible on the inside face of the door and may be recessed or fixed to the surface. The door can be adjusted after fitting to ensure accurate alignment.

Sprung hinge: two-way openings

Sprung hinge
To encourage a door to swing closed of its own accord, a sprung hinge can be fitted. A double sprung hinge allows a door to swing both ways, which can be useful on cupboard doors in awkward spaces.

Flush hinge
Designed to act like a butt hinge, this does not need to be recessed, as one half of the hinge closes within the other. For use on lightweight doors, it is screwed to the door edge and frame. It is available in 1½in (38mm) to 4in (100mm) sizes.

Brass cylinder hinge

Cylinder hinge
Even less obtrusive than the concealed cabinet hinge, the two halves of cylinder hinges fit into wide holes drilled in the edge of the door and the frame.

easily for cleaning or painting, and is available in a butt or cranked shape.

It is also important to check that the hinge will allow the door to open the way you intend. If you want the door to open towards you with the hinge on the right, you should ask for a right-hand hinge; if you want it to open towards you with the hinge on the left, ask for a left-hand hinge. Most internal room and furniture doors need two hinges; heavy doors benefit from a third fitted half-way up the door.

Butt hinge
The standard hinge for most doors and windows, butt hinges are especially suitable for solid timber doors. They are available in 1in (25mm) to 4in (100mm) sizes. The hinge is either recessed into the door or into both the door and the frame. The pins on both hinges must be perfectly aligned with each other and with the door edge for the hinge to work efficiently.

Brass butt hinge (3in/75mm)

Steel butt hinge (3in/75mm)

Steel rising butt hinge (3in/75mm)

Plastic rising butt hinge (3in/75mm)

Rising butt hinge
Designed for doors that need to rise over carpets, the rising butt hinge is open-ended. It is available in the same sizes and is fitted using the same method as the butt hinge.

Door catches

Ball or roller catches are suitable for a light internal or cupboard door. The catch consists of a spring-loaded ball or roller inside a cylinder. When the door is closed, the ball or roller fits into a recess in the strike plate fixed to the door frame. There are two types of French window catch: an espagnolette bolt consists of two bolts which extend the length of the door and slot into recesses at the head and sill of the frame. The bolts are operated by a central handle. Brass French window catches are fitted to the top and bottom of the door. They consist of bolts which slot through a key plate into the door frame and sill. Magnetic catches are used on furniture. There are various types and shapes available, but all consist of a nickel-coated plate, which is fixed to the door, and a cased magnet, which is fixed to the cupboard or cabinet.

Brass roller catch

Magnetic catch for sliding door

Small brass roller catch

Nylon roller catch

Plastic magnetic catch

Brass French window catch

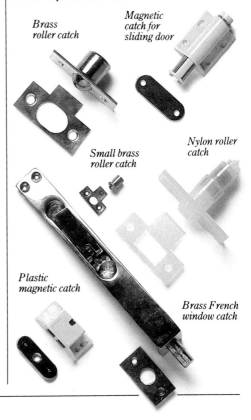

Repairing doors

Most repairs, other than replacing door fittings, will involve removing and rehanging the door. Rehanging is basically a straightforward job, provided you use levers and wedges to hold the door in position in the frame while fitting the hinges. The hinge side of the door and frame should be vertical. If you need to cut a door to fit, measure it carefully before cutting and check that your measurements are accurate by holding the door in place. When planing a door, work with the grain, checking that the edge is straight.

Measuring and cutting doors

Before buying a door, measure the width of the door frame and check it at several points. Then measure the height. The door should be ¼in (6mm) less than the width of the frame, with a ⅛in (3mm) gap at the top and sufficient space at the bottom to clear the floor covering when the door opens. If you cannot get a door of exactly the right size, remove some wood from a larger door to make it fit. Use a set square to check that the frame is square at the corners.

The hinge side of the frame should be vertical. If it is not, the door frame should be removed and refixed, or replaced if necessary before you attempt to hang the door.

Do not rely on measurements alone when marking a door for cutting. Check them by positioning the door in the frame with supporting wedges underneath, then mark the outline of the frame on the door. Flush doors are more difficult to cut to size because they often have only a very thin wooden frame. The best solution is to cut equal amounts from either side of the door.

Planing a door
Use a plane to trim a small amount from a door. On the top and bottom, plane inwards from the edges so that you do not split the timber. The edge of the door should be square, except on the opening edge, where the outside is fractionally narrower than the inside to allow for opening.

Sawing a door
If there is a lot of timber to remove, use a saw. A circular saw is less tiring to use than a hand saw and has a rebate fence, which helps you to cut accurately. Cut just inside the line so that you can finish off with a plane. Try to remove equal amounts from both sides or from the top and the bottom.

Fitting a door handle

Fitting a knob set
Cut the spindle to the correct length so that the handle fits snugly against the door. Check the length by sliding on the knob and, if it fits, attach the knob to the spindle with grub screws.

There are two types of handle that can be fitted to doors where a mortise lock has been installed. One sort, usually called a knob set, is secured by small grub screws to a square spindle that passes through the centre of the lock. The other type is screwed to the door itself and fits over the spindle.

The only problem with the second type of door handle is that some doors are too thin to give a proper fixing for the screw and accommodate the mortise lock. With doors that are too thin, the solution is to fit a piece of wood to each side of the door, to which you can attach the handle. Either glue it in place or screw it to the door beyond the line of the lock.

Little extra work is required to fit the handles once the mortise lock has been installed. The spindle must be cut to the right length to leave the handle in the correct position. Then simply slide the knob on to the spindle and insert the grub screws to secure it.

Fitting hinges

With a new door and frame, the hinge positions should be about 6in (15cm) from the top and about 8in (20cm) from the bottom. A third hinge will be needed for heavy doors, which you should place centrally, equidistant from the other two hinges. When rehanging an existing door or using a frame that is already fitted, it may be simpler to use the existing hinge positions. If, however, you do need to change the hinge positions, the old screw holes will need to be filled with dowels (page 137) and a new hinge rebate marked and chiselled out using a bevel-edge chisel.

For light internal doors use 3in (75mm) hinges. Use two 4in (100mm) hinges for other internal doors, and three 4in (100mm) hinges for heavy external and bathroom doors.

Cutting hinge rebates

1 *Use a hinge itself to trace the dimensions and hole positions and a try square to draw the lines. Cut recesses in the door and frame long enough for the inside face of the hinge to be flush with the door and the hinge pin just clear of the door.*

2 *To make the recesses, first cut along the lines with a sharp knife, then use a sharp chisel and mallet to remove the wood. Hold the chisel bevelled face down to produce a flat-bottomed recess. Take off small amounts of wood at a time.*

3 *Unless you are using the existing frame positions, fit the hinges to the door. Drill small pilot holes and fit the hinges with countersunk screws of the same material as the hinges. Hold the door in place and mark the hinge positions on the frame.*

Curing squeaking and sticking doors

Squeaking doors have two main causes. The hinges may need oiling, or part of the door may be catching on the frame as it opens. If neither of these things seems to be happening, the door may be warped. Squeaky hinges can usually be cured with a little household oil. But if they are very dry and stiff, you should remove them, apply a more penetrating oil, and work them free before replacing them. Stiff hinges put a strain on the fixing screws.

If part of a door is catching on the frame, it may be that the hinges are recessed too far into either the door or the frame. If this is the case, remove the door and pack the recesses with cardboard.

Squeaks are often caused by protrusions on the hinge side of a door. Sand down any small high spots in the woodwork.

A door that sticks probably either has too much paint or has swollen because of moisture in the atmosphere (this is particularly likely if it is an outside or kitchen or bathroom door). In either case the solution is to plane off the swollen area.

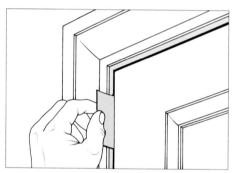

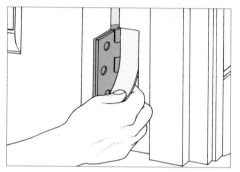

Finding where a door is sticking
If you are not sure exactly which part of a door is sticking, close it on to a strip of carbon paper. This will rub on the door or frame where the door is sticking, and will leave a mark to show you which area needs to be planed down.

Refitting door hinges
If the hinges are recessed too far into the rebates, pack them out to the correct position. Use thin pieces of cardboard and build these up until the door hangs straight. It should then open and close easily without squeaking or sticking in the frame.

Repairing loose doors and frames

Door frames, especially internal ones, are often only loosely attached to the wall. If a door frame is loose, drill new, deeper holes into the masonry with a masonry drill bit and refix the frame to the wall.

Doors rattle when they have shrunk and become too small for the frame. There are two solutions. Fitting foam draught excluder around the frame (page 193) is a simple task and will probably cure the problem as well as keep out draughts. If this does not work, move the striking plate of the catch or lock.

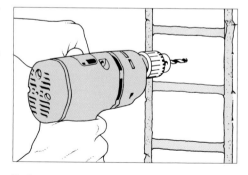

Refixing a loose door frame
Drill new holes and insert wallplugs. Put back the frame, attaching it with long screws that pass deep into the masonry to give a firm fixing.

Curing a sagging door

A door will sag either because its hinges have got loose or because the joints of the door itself have worked loose. If the hinges are loose, you may be able to solve the problem by simply tightening the screws or fitting larger ones. If the original hinges are too small, they can become distorted. Replace them with larger hinges or add a third hinge in the centre.

Refitting hinges
If the joints of the door have worked loose, you can strengthen them with glue and dowels. Remove the old screws, drill larger holes, and fill these with glued dowels. When the glue has dried, drill small pilot holes in the dowels, then reattach the hinge using new, larger screws.

Dealing with a warped door

If the door has warped on the hinge side, you may be able to cure it by fitting a third hinge. But warping is more common on the other side, preventing the door from closing properly. Where this has happened, insert thin slivers of wood to force it into place. If the middle of the door prevents it from closing, fit temporary bolts to the top and bottom of the door and insert a sliver of wood at the centre.

Bending back a warped door
If a door has warped and will no longer close properly, inserting thin strips of wood between the door and the frame will force the door back at the top or bottom. If you leave the door like this or repeat the process often enough, it will eventually be pulled back permanently into its original shape.

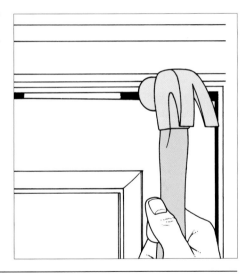

Hanging folding doors

Bi-folding doors normally come with fitting instructions. Once you have trimmed them to the right size, fitting is straightforward. They have a track that fits along the inside top of the door frame. Pivot pins are inserted into holes drilled into the top corners of the doors. One rotates, the other slides along the track.

A concertina door has a track that fits all the way around the frame. The width of the door frame is not as important for this type of door as it is for others. If the door is already assembled, fitting is very easy. You simply fix the door into the track. With some designs, the door has to be assembled first and, to finish off, a pelmet may be fitted to hide the working parts at the top of the frame. This has to be cut to the right length for the door.

Hanging a sliding door

Sliding doors are usually lighter than hinged doors and easier to lift into position. There are various types of sliding mechanism, and exact instructions for fitting are generally supplied with the door itself. But the basic principle usually involves fitting a wooden batten to the wall and attaching the track from which the door is suspended.

First prepare the door opening. The door stop can be removed by levering it up with a chisel. This may damage the paint and reveal nails underneath which hold the door frame in place. Punch these below the wood surface and use filler to give a smooth finish before repainting. If you are replacing a hinged door, fill the hinge recesses. Use thin pieces of wood glued into place and finish off with filler. The architrave should also be removed from the side on which the door is to be fitted.

If you are using the existing door, you will have to reduce the size of the original opening so that the sliding door overlaps slightly when it is fitted. Fix thin lengths of wood, cut to the right width, to the frame.

Fix a batten to the wall to support the track. With hollow partition walls, the batten must be fixed to the internal uprights. Find these by tapping the wall – once you have found one, the next should be about 16in (40cm) away. The batten should be at least as long as the track and longer if this is necessary to fix it to the uprights. If you are going to fit a pelmet, allow space to attach this to the ends of the batten. The thickness of the batten should allow the door to clear the frame at both sides.

Hanging a hinged door

The most common type, the hinged door, is easy to hang provided that you can find a satisfactory method of holding it in place in the frame while you are inserting the screws in the hinges. It is useful to have some assistance when doing this, but if you are hanging a heavy door on your own, you will need a way of moving it by small amounts without lifting it bodily. Wooden wedges under the door will

Hanging a hinged door

1 *After you have fitted the hinges to the door, lift it into place in the frame to check that it hangs properly. Wooden wedges and a lever will enable you to make small adjustments.*

2 *Once the door is in the correct position, insert one screw into each hinge. This is done to check that the door fits and that you have drilled the holes in the correct position in the frame.*

Hanging a sliding door

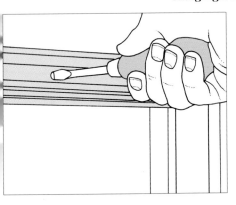

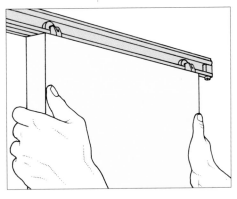

1 *The instructions will tell you at what height to fit the track – there should be enough space at the bottom to keep the door well clear of the floor.*

2 *Make sure that the track is horizontal, then fix the plates and bolts to the top of the door, secure the guide to the floor and hang the door on the track.*

help, but it is also useful to put some sort of lever under the door and over a block of wood. Applying pressure with your foot will then lift the door until the hinges are in the right position, and will hold it in place while you fix the screws.

When you are hanging double doors or French windows, both sides of the frame must be vertical. Most double doors come in standard sizes, so it is best to use doors and frames that match in size. Otherwise, the method for hanging double doors is the same as that for hanging single doors. It is easier if you glaze the doors after you have hung them – they are much easier and lighter to handle without any glass.

3 *At this stage, if the door does not fit properly, you may have to deepen or enlarge the recesses. Be careful not to deepen the recesses too much or the door will bind. If you do cut them too deep, pack them with card.*

4 *When the door fits, insert the remaining screws. Use wood filler for any gaps that you have chiselled out unintentionally. On external doors, fit a weatherboard along the bottom edge to throw off rainwater.*

Care and repair of wood-frame screens

Screens are useful for keeping small insects, such as flies and mosquitoes, out of the house or larder. They need to be made of fine mesh so that the insects are unable to crawl through. Black enamelled steel wire and galvanized steel wire are now almost obsolete, as they are prone to rust. They have been replaced by metal screening materials which are more rustproof, such as bronze, copper, plastic, aluminium and a louvre type of either brass or aluminium, and non-metal materials such as fibreglass and plastic. Another type of aluminium screening that is readily available has an enamel finish for added strength and durability.

Maintenance of screens and frames

Modern screens will last for many years if they are properly cared for. All types of screening will attract dirt and should be cleaned from time to time. Wire screening is also prone to corrosion, especially in areas near the sea where there is salt in the air. Small holes and tears are unavoidable but can easily be patched without involving the replacement of the whole screen. Make sure that you patch any holes as soon as they appear, otherwise they will tear further and you will be faced with a larger repair than was originally necessary, and you may even have to replace the whole screen. If you do replace a damaged screen, do not throw it out, as the mesh can be used for repairs. Store it somewhere dry so that it will not rust or deteriorate.

Protect all wooden frames with a coat of paint. This will prevent moisture from being absorbed which could cause the wood to swell, distort or, in exceptionally damp conditions, rot. It will also improve the appearance of the screen. Coat aluminium frames with wax to prevent oxidation and clean them occasionally.

Repairing small holes and tears in metal and plastic screens

A small hole in metal screening can be sealed with quick-drying waterproof glue. You will need to use an acetone-type glue for plastic screening. Another way of mending small holes is by weaving or darning the area with strands from a scrap piece of screening or fine fuse wire. Keep the wire as taut and the gaps between strands as small as you can.

Patching a large hole

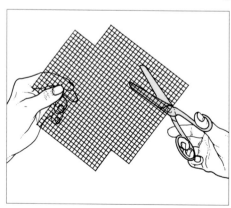

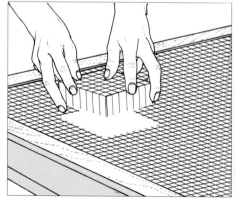

1 *Cut a piece of screening from scrap material which is larger than the hole in the screen, with enough spare all around to fray the edges. Bend the frayed wires back at right angles to the patch.*

2 *Carefully push the wires through the holes in the mesh screening around the hole until the patch lies flush. Bend the wires back towards the centre of the patch to hold the patch. Glue plastic ends in place.*

Cleaning screens

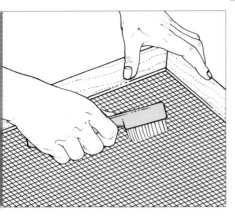 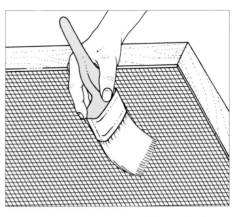

1 *Keep screens in good repair by brushing them with a soft wire brush. This will loosen rust and dirt, which can then be removed using a vacuum cleaner and a round brush attachment.*

2 *Once all dirt has been cleaned off, use a brush or a piece of carpet to apply thinned screen enamel, paint or varnish to both sides of the screen. This will protect the screen.*

Types of joint reinforcement

Joints at the corners of wood-frame screens can be reinforced with metal plates, which can be L-shaped, T-shaped or rectangular, corrugated or chevron-shaped fasteners, wood screws or dowels (see also reinforcing joints in furniture, pages 24–5). If the joints in a screen loosen, take them apart, reglue them and reinforce them in one of the ways shown here to make the repair permanent. Mitred joints are best reinforced with either corrugated or chevron-shaped mitre joint fasteners, which are positioned at right angles to the join. Hardwood dowels can be used to reinforce butt or tenon joints. Drill a hole into the joint in the same way as for a wood screw and cut a length of dowel slightly shorter than the hole. Cut a groove along the length of the dowel to allow excess glue to escape and glue it in place. When the glue has set, fill the hole with wood filler and sand it flush. Finally, paint the frame to protect it. Inspect the frames regularly to check that no screws are missing or loose and that the joints are firm.

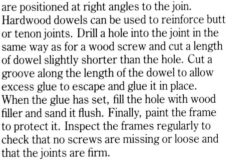

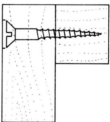 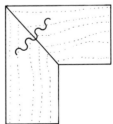

Corner plate
Butt joints can be reinforced with a metal corner plate screwed to the frame.

Rectangular plate
This shape of metal plate can be used to reinforce the corners or to hold the centre rail in place.

Wood screw
Long wood screws will hold the joints in place. Countersink holes and fill with wood filler.

Mitred joints
Reinforce a mitred joint using a corrugated or chevron-shaped mitre joint fastener.

Replacing wood-frame screens

Screens can be damaged by hard balls such as cricket balls or baseballs, or simply weaken and rust with age. If a metal screen begins to rust, replace it straight away to prevent it from staining the surrounding areas. When replacing a wood-frame screen, remove the moulding carefully so that you can use it again to secure the new screen, and make sure that your new piece of screening is larger than the area to be covered; the excess at the edges will give you something to grip when pulling the screen taut across the frame.

To get the screening material taut, you will need to bend or bow the frame. To do this, place 2in (50mm) square blocks of wood under either end and clamp the centre of the frame.

Fitting a screen

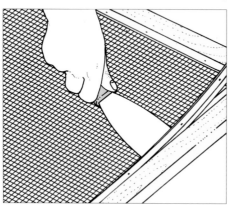

1 *Place the frame on a workbench and ease off the old pieces of moulding with a scraping knife. Work from the centre of each side towards the edges.*

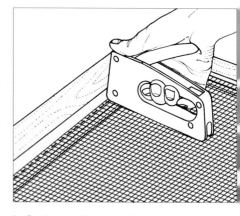

2 *Cut the screening material to size and staple or tack it to one end of the frame. If the material is plastic, fold over 1½in (40mm) all around.*

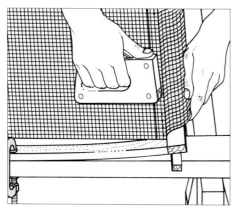

3 *Clamp the frame to the workbench to bend it slightly, and pull the screening material taut across it. Staple or tack down the second end and then remove the clamps and blocks.*

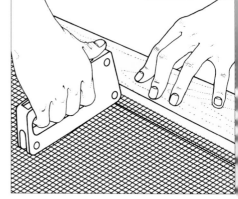

4 *Pull the screening material tight to the sides of the frame and fasten it in place using staples or tacks. Work from the centre of each side to the corners, leaving the centre rail till last.*

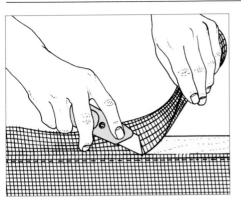

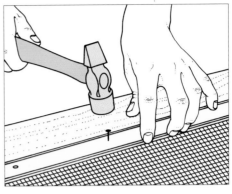

5 *Fasten the screening to the centre rail and trim off any excess material with a heavy-duty craft knife for metal, or a razor blade for plastic. Take care not to cut too close to the staples or tacks.*

6 *Replace the old moulding if possible, or buy new moulding. Tack it in place, sink the nail heads and fill the holes. To finish off, prime and repaint the complete frame.*

Replacing half a screen

If the screen contains a centre rail and only half is damaged, you can replace this section only rather than the whole screen, as long as you use a matching screening material. However, you will not be able to get the screening taut by bowing the frame for this repair. Instead, cut your piece of screening much longer than you need. Begin by securing the screening to the centre rail, then place the excess material over the end of the frame and between two pieces of wood (these should be roughly the same thickness as the frame so that the screening material is not pulled up or down). Nail the pieces to the workbench to clamp the screening in place. Hammering two wedges between the end of the frame and the clamp will pull the screening material taut.

Fixing half a screen

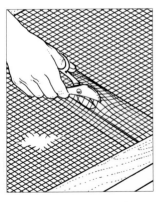

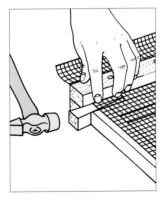

1 *Remove the moulding and trim away the damaged section from the centre rail, leaving the good half intact, attached to the centre rail.*

2 *Fasten the new screening to the centre rail and unroll it. Clamp it just beyond the frame and nail the clamp to the workbench.*

3 *Drive wedges between clamp and frame to tension the material. Attach it to the frame and finish as for the full-length screen.*

Windows

Windows perform three important functions: they let in light, they enable you to look out and they provide ventilation. To fulfil these functions, not all the panes need to be openable, and many windows are made up of a combination of fixed panes or "lights", which you cannot open, and opening panes. These opening panes are usually either sashes, which slide up and down or from side to side,

or casements, which are hinged at one side. For improved insulation, there are double-glazed equivalents of most types of window. You can fit some designs yourself, while others are installed by the manufacturer.

The type of glass used also varies. Standard "float" glass is the most common type, but there are various kinds of toughened glass, as well as patterned and tinted glass.

Tools and materials

There are only a few specialized tools for glazing. If you intend to cut glass yourself, you will need a glass cutter and possibly some glaziers' pliers.

Use glaziers' pliers to snap off small pieces of glass from the edge of a pane, or to remove a long, narrow strip of glass after you have scored it with a glass cutter. A hacking knife is useful for removing broken glass and old putty from a window frame. When replacing a window frame, use a countersink drill bit, so that you can conceal the screw heads. You will also need wood filler to fill the holes.

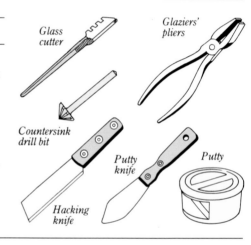

Glass cutter

Glaziers' pliers

Countersink drill bit

Putty knife

Putty

Hacking knife

Types of window

Casement windows usually consist of a fixed light, a side-opening casement and a smaller, top-opening pane called a ventlight. Larger windows can have more than one casement. The panes may be joined together in a curved shape to create a bow window, or in a rectangular or angled shape to make a bay.

Sash windows are very common in older buildings. They consist of two sliding sashes, one in front of the other. Each sash is counter-balanced by a hidden weight or a spring-balance system.

Pivoting windows are usually made from wood and have a single pane that pivots about a central point on the frame. Their main advantage is that you can clean both sides of

the glass from the inside. Traditional French windows consist of a pair of full-length glazed and hinged wooden doors opening outwards. The centre edges of the windows are rebated.

Replacement windows
If you have to replace a window there are two alternatives: an exact copy of the original window, or a double-glazed replacement window. Many double-glazing firms will provide only made-to-measure windows which they install for you, but replacement windows that you fit yourself are also available. These come in four different materials: timber, which you can stain or paint; aluminium, available in silver-grey, in anodized colour finishes, or with a factory-applied acrylic colour; unplasticized polyvinyl chloride (UPVC), usually in white; and steel, either galvanized or in a white finish.

Types of window

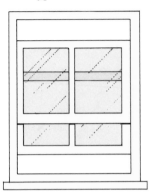

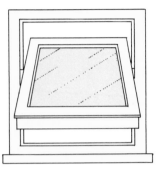

Casement windows
Most widely available with wooden frames, these windows come in a large number of standard sizes. There are also casement windows that have steel frames within an overall wooden surround. These have a thinner section, and therefore provide poorer thermal insulation than window frames that are made completely of wood.

Sash windows
These windows are elegant, easy to clean and allow good control over ventilation. Their main disadvantages are that the sash cords can break and the windows can rattle and stick. Modern sash windows use spiral spring balances rather than weights and are therefore more reliable. They also often have double-glazed panes.

Pivoting windows
Because they are easy to clean from the inside, pivoting windows are very convenient, especially on upper floors. But they have one safety drawback: they are very easy to push open, and therefore should not be fitted where a small child could open them and crawl through.

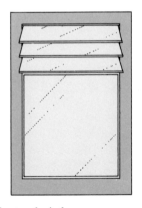

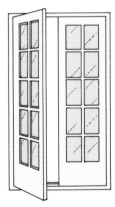

Louvred windows
These windows consist of thin, horizontal slats of glass that are usually set in a metal frame. They are connected to a mechanism that enables you to open all the louvres with a single pull of a lever. Louvred panels often come as part of modern windows and may be the only part to open.

Sliding windows
Some modern windows slide horizontally. This is a design that is particularly popular for full-length patio windows, which are available in a wide range of materials including wood, aluminium and UPVC. Modern sliding windows usually have double-glazed panes.

French windows
Glazed double doors are known as French windows. They are normally fastened with top and bottom bolts operated by a single handle, or espagnolette bolts which extend the length of the door and slide into recesses at the top and bottom of the frame. The door's inner edges overlap.

Double glazing

Windows are responsible for about 10 per cent of the heat loss from houses, while another 15 per cent is lost through gaps around windows and doors. As well as making a room feel uncomfortable, cold windows can cause condensation, which is produced when the warm, moist air inside the house meets the colder inner surface of the glass or the metal frame. Condensation looks unsightly and can lead to paint damage and rot.

Double glazing offers a solution to these problems. It is simply a way of fitting two panes of glass into a window instead of one. The second pane adds something to the heat saving, but it is mainly the air gap between the panes that gives the benefits. To be effective, this air gap should be at least ½in (12mm) wide. A gap of ¾in (19mm) is better still, but a larger gap will not give any further improvement. If you want your double glazing to act as a sound-proofing measure, the gap between the panes should be much larger – between 4in (100mm) and 8in (20cm).

Types of double glazing

There are three main types of double glazing: sealed units, secondary panes, and secondary sashes and casements. Sealed units consist of pairs of glass panes hermetically sealed together in the factory, which replace the conventional glass panes. Secondary panes are sheets of glass or plastic fitted to the inside of the windows. Secondary sashes are framed windows fitted in front of the existing ones.

Most double-glazing systems are designed for use with ¹⁄₁₆in (4mm) glass. Toughened glass should be used for double-glazing very large panes. As a cheaper alternative, use clear plastic sheets over the panes.

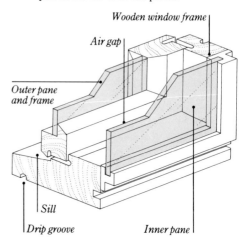

Sealed units
Sealed units have two big advantages: they are unobtrusive and, unlike other types of double glazing, they do not cause condensation. Some units are gas-filled and have heat-reflecting qualities: manufacturers make additional heat-saving claims for these types of unit.

You can fit complete replacement windows with sealed units, but it is more economical to replace the existing panes with sealed units. The units come in a range of glass types in standard sizes, or they can be made to measure. Units with a stepped profile are available for windows with unusually deep rebates.

Secondary panes
The simplest form of secondary pane is a thin plastic sheet stretched over the window frame and attached by two-sided adhesive tape. There is a variety of more sophisticated designs in which the secondary pane is surrounded by a plastic frame and attached to the window with clips, plastic strips, or other fasteners.

None of these panes can be opened easily for normal ventilation, although they can all be removed for cleaning or summer storage. But if the system allows you to fit the pane to an opening casement, both the original window and the secondary pane will open at the same time.

Types of glass

Most glass sold today is "float" glass, so-called because the method of manufacture involves floating the glass out of the furnace on molten tin. This gives a good surface finish and a distortion-free appearance. In addition, there are various types of safety glass.

When choosing which type of glass to use, first decide whether the area you are going to glaze is a high-risk one. Glazing within 2½ft (75cm) of the floor, doors or windows that might be mistaken for holes in the wall, and large expanses of glass that could get broken accidentally, all constitute a high risk. Another important factor is the likely wind loading on the glass. The greater the exposure to wind, the thicker the glass required. In areas that are not high-risk, avoid ⅛in (3mm) glass except for very small panes. Use ⅙in (4mm) glass for windows up to 3¼ft (1m) wide, and ⅕in (5mm) or ¼in (6mm) for anything larger.

In a high-risk area you should not glaze an area larger than 2ft^2 (0.2m^2) with ⅙in (4mm) glass, 8½ft^2 (0.8m^2) with ⅕in (5mm) glass, 19⅓ft^2 (1.8m^2) with ¼in (6mm) glass, and 35½ft^2 (3.3m^2) with ⅖in (10mm) glass. For larger panes, use toughened glass, which undergoes a special heat treatment that makes it four to five times stronger than float glass and impossible to cut, or laminated glass, which is strengthened by a thin layer of plastic sandwiched between two layers of glass.

The wire grid in wired glass does not make the glass stronger but, like the plastic in laminated glass, it holds the pieces together if it is broken. Patterned glass can provide privacy as well as decoration. There is a wide choice of designs and some patterned glass is also tinted. In Georgian panes, glass bullions give an old-fashioned appearance. Other decorative effects can be achieved with stained and engraved glass. To prevent rooms from becoming too hot in summer, use plain or tinted solar-control glass.

Types of window fastening

On most casement windows there are two types of fastener. The cockspur handle is attached to the window and engages with a metal stop screwed to the frame to hold the window closed. The casement stay at the bottom holds the window open. Both are easily fitted with screws.

Sash windows are secured by a simple fitch fastener, or a Brighton catch, which has a threaded bolt and is more secure. These are simply screwed to the rails of the sashes.

The traditional catch for French windows is the espagnolette bolt, which stretches the entire height of the closing door and shoots into holes in the top jamb and bottom sill.

These fasteners are not lockable. For more security, fit locking devices (page 228).

Cockspur handle
This holds the casement window tightly closed against the frame.

Fitch fastener
Simply rotating this catch allows you to open the sash window.

Brighton fastener
The sash window fastener is opened by unscrewing the bolt.

Repairing damaged windows

Window repairs fall into two main areas: replacing a pane and repairing the frame. Cracked panes can be repaired temporarily with clear waterproofing tape stuck over both sides of the crack, but the pane will need to be replaced. When handling pieces of glass, always wear stout gloves. If you need to store a piece of glass temporarily, make sure that you can see it by sticking a cross of masking tape over it to prevent it from being broken.

Removing broken glass

Before starting to remove any glass, lay newspaper on the floor and on the ground outside to catch any falling pieces of glass. Wear thick gloves to protect your hands and stout shoes to protect your feet. A pair of goggles is also useful, to protect your eyes from flying fragments of glass.

Start by removing the large pieces of glass. Take care, because they may break up as you handle them. Then gently pull or knock out the smaller pieces. If you have to break the glass in the frame, put strips of adhesive tape over it to hold the fragments together and cover it with a cloth. The remaining pieces and old putty can be removed with an old chisel or a glaziers' hacking knife. Pull out any glazing sprigs or clips that were used to hold the glass in place. Keep the clips from a metal window frame and mark their positions, but discard the sprigs.

Removing putty
Use a glaziers' hacking knife to remove small pieces of glass and old putty from the frame, wearing thick gardening gloves for protection. When prising off beading, begin in the middle of the length.

Cutting glass

Glass merchants will normally cut glass to size for you and this is always best. But if you have to cut it yourself, you will need a glass cutter, a firm, soft surface (such as a table covered with a blanket), and a straight-edge.

If you are cutting glass for a replacement window pane, check the width and the height of the window at several places. The size of the glass should be ⅛in (3mm) *less* than the smallest measurement. If the window is so badly out of true that you need an irregularly shaped piece of glass, either remove the window and take it to the glass merchant or make a paper template of the shape.

Making a straight cut
Pull the glass cutter towards you using firm, consistent pressure. Break the glass over a wooden rule or straight-edge placed under the scored line.

Replacing a window pane

For most types of window, you will need putty; 2lb (1kg) of putty will be enough for about 11½ft (3.5m) of frame. When applying putty, hold a ball of it in your hand and squeeze it out between thumb and forefinger. There are different types of putty for metal and wooden windows, while solar control glass needs a special non-setting compound. You will also need glazing sprigs (for wooden windows) or clips (for metal frames) to hold the glass in place. Modern double-glazed windows have gaskets to hold the glass in position. Replacing panels in louvred windows is simply a matter of sliding in a piece of glass of the correct size. To cut down the security risk, you can glue the pieces into place.

After you have removed the old pane, prepare the frame. Clean out the rebate that holds the glass and apply primer to wooden frames and a rust inhibitor to steel frames.

Once the pane is in place, finish off the second layer of putty with a paintbrush moistened in water. Remove any excess putty with a knife and allow it to dry before cleaning any finger marks from the glass with white spirit or methylated spirits. Leave the putty for

POINTS TO REMEMBER

- Always wear stout gloves when handling pieces of glass.
- When measuring a window for a new pane, take measurements at several points along the frame, as it may not be perfectly square, and you will need to have the glass cut accordingly.
- The larger the size of the pane, the thicker the glass you should use.
- When glazing a window, leave the putty for about two weeks before painting over it.
- Allow the putty to dry before cleaning finger marks from the glass, as even a slight pressure might dislodge the pane.

about two weeks before painting it. When painting it, make sure that the edges are sealed by overlapping the paint on to the glass, otherwise the putty will dry out and crack.

Replacing a leaded light
The glass in leaded-light windows is held in place by strips of lead which are soldered at the corners. Make a cardboard template of irregular shapes and ask a glazier to cut them, rather than attempting this yourself (page 75). To remove a pane, break the joints and bend back the lead. When you have cleaned out the strips of lead and inserted a new piece of glass, bend the lead back and solder the joints.

Applying putty and fitting the glass

1 *After preparing the frame, apply a ⅛in (3mm) or ⅙in (4mm) layer of putty to the rebate. Push the glass in gently on top of the putty, pressing it only at the edges, not in the middle. To get the correct clearance all around, support the glass on matchsticks at the bottom.*

2 *Next, put in the glazing sprigs or clips every 6in (15cm) and remove the matchsticks. Use a glaziers' hacking knife or small hammer to do this and slide it along the surface of the glass. If you are using metal clips, put them back into their original holes.*

3 *Finally, apply a second layer of putty to the outside and smooth it off to the correct angle (about 45°) using a putty knife. When smoothing putty, always use firm, steady pressure and smooth strokes. If the knife sticks, moisten it with a little water.*

Glazing a door

Fitting wooden glazing beading or quadrant moulding is a good idea if you are glazing a hardwood door. It is also a useful method for a window frame that you want to finish with a clear preservative wood stain. Glazing beading comes in strips, which you can cut into mitred lengths. Check all the measurements if you are glazing an old door or window – it may not be exactly square. A mitre box will help you to get the corner angles exactly right.

Interior doors can be glazed in this way without any putty. Exterior doors should have a thin layer of putty on both sides of the glass to keep out the damp. Use coloured putty if your door is made of hardwood.

Removing an old frame

First unscrew and remove all the opening parts and take out the glass from the fixed lights. Cut through the nails or the screws with a pad saw fitted with a hack-saw blade. With a metal frame, find the lugs that secure the frame in the mortar joints on each side. Cut through these or chisel away the mortar around them. Once they are free, the whole frame can be tapped out a little at a time from the inside, using a heavy hammer. When you have taken out the frame, clean up the sides of the opening and fill the holes left by the protruding "horns" of old wooden window frames.

Cutting out the frame

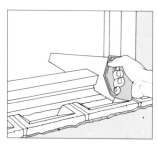 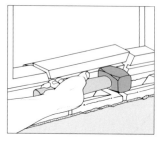 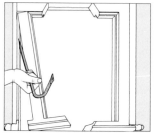

1 *Make angled cuts through the horizontal parts of the frame and remove the middle sections. Do not damage the window ledge or reveal.*

2 *Remove the loosened horizontal sections of the frame, using a heavy hammer to tap them out if you cannot pull them out.*

3 *Take out the side parts, using a lever against the brickwork. A crowbar is best, but a club hammer is also useful.*

Replacing a window frame

In most cases you will be able to keep the existing internal window ledge and fit the new frame against it. Conceal the screw heads by using a countersink drill bit. You may be able to use the original outside sill, although most replacement windows come with a new sill.

Before fitting, give the frame an extra coat of primer if you are going to paint it, or wood preservative if you are going to varnish or stain it. Wooden windows come with protruding horns. Cut these off before putting the frame roughly in position. Measure carefully for replacement frames and fit frames that are no more than 1/5in (5mm) smaller than the existing opening. When fitting new steel frames, cut slots in the mortar joints to take the fixing lugs, and apply fresh mortar.

To get the frame in position, knock in wooden wedges along the top, bottom and sides. You will have to experiment with wedges of different sizes, constantly checking with a spirit level that the window is straight. Then you can mark the fixing holes.

Fixing the frame

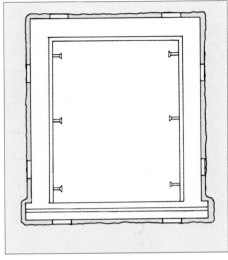

1 *Wedge the frame in place and check that it is square in the opening. When it fits properly, number all the wedges, mark their positions and numbers on the frame and the bricks, and remove them. Then take out the frame and drill holes for the screws at evenly spaced intervals through the frame.*

2 *Next, put a layer of mortar at the bottom of the opening with the correct thickness for the sill to rest on and replace the frame and wedges. With the frame in position, drill holes in the wall through those in the frame, so that they line up. Test the depth of each hole with a screw. Remove the frame.*

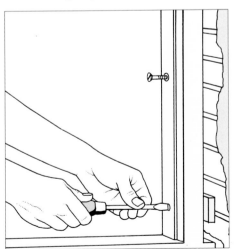

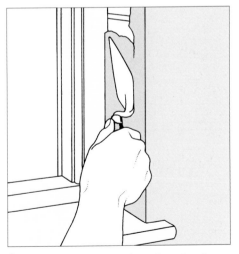

3 *Fit frame plugs and secure the frame with zinc-plated screws. For a neat finish, countersink the holes slightly and fill the hole over the screw head with external wood filler. Apply fresh mortar around the frame to fill the remaining gaps.*

4 *When the mortar has set, it may have shrunk a little. Fill the gap around the window with mastic. If the gap is larger than 1/2in (12mm), insert wooden quadrant moulding to cover the mastic. Fit the windows and glass.*

Freeing a sticking window

Windows can stick because of an excessive build-up of paint or because damp has made them swell. Stripping or planing the frames is the best cure for this. Loose joints, another common cause of sticking windows, may be solved by regluing the joints and clamping them together. Loose hinges can make casement windows stick. Curing loose hinges may be a matter of tightening the fixing screws. If they continue to work loose, drill out the holes, glue in pieces of dowel and insert larger screws (page 137). Sticking sash windows can be caused by loose sash cords. If this is the case, you will need to remove the window and tighten the cord to cure the problem.

Stripping and planing
If the problem is too much paint, remove the paint using stripper or a hot-air gun, then rub down the frame with coarse abrasive paper. If this does not give enough clearance or if there is swelling, plane down the window. If it is not obvious where the window is sticking, insert a piece of carbon paper between the window and the frame to indicate the place.

Preventing window rattle

Casement windows rattle if the catch does not hold them tightly. The solution is to fit draught excluder around the window frame. If the window is distorted, straighten it by closing it on to a thin sliver of wood which forces it in the opposite direction to the way it is twisted, following the same method used for curing warped doors (page 137). Repeat the process, gradually increasing the thickness of the pieces of wood until the frame has been reshaped.

Rattling sash windows are caused by wear creating too much space around each sash. Fit the type of draught excluder that has a nylon pile so that the sash slides along it.

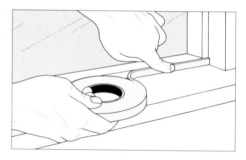

Fitting draught excluder
The simplest type of draught excluder to fit is self-adhesive foam strip, though this needs replacing regularly. It comes in different thicknesses to cope with different sizes of gap. If the gap is uneven, put one layer on top of another where the gap is at its largest.

Adjusting a spiral balance

Modern sash windows are balanced by a mechanism that consists of a spiral rod inside a metal or plastic tube secured to the inside of the frame. Spiral balance mechanisms are usually more reliable than sash cords, although the spring can lose its tension and need adjusting. If the mechanism has to be replaced, remove the sash and attach a new balance first to the sash and then to the window frame.

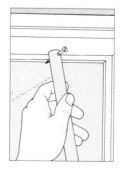

Spiral-balance repairs
Pull the sash down and unscrew the tube from the frame. Twist the tube clockwise to tighten the spring. After a few turns, re-secure the tube. If this does not work, replace the mechanism: tension the spring with the sash in its middle position, then re-secure the tube.

Removing a sash cord

Fitting a new sash cord involves removing the window from its frame; this is a fairly big job and one which damages the paintwork. It is therefore sensible to replace all the sash cords in the window at the same time – if one cord has broken, the others will probably soon need renewing. Use rot-proof, man-made sash cord rather than the traditional waxed hemp, as this will last for longer. If the window is a large one, it will be very heavy and you will probably need someone to help you when it comes to taking it out of the frame.

The job involves removing both sashes, cutting new cords to exactly the right length, and reassembling the window with the new cords in place. Use an old chisel or filling knife to prise off the beading around the window. Cut the cords just above the window, holding on to the ends so that you can let the weights fall gently into their boxes. Turn the lower sash partly sideways, raise it enough to clear the window ledge and lift it from the frame. Remove the panel in the side of the frame to gain access to the sash cord and weights.

When replacing the cords and windows, start with the outer sash. To get the new sash cord over the pulley, tie a thin piece of string to the cord and attach a small lead weight or screw to this. When you pass the weight over the pulley, it will fall, taking the string and cord with it. Make sure that the cords lie properly in their grooves and that the position of the weight is correct. Replace the parting bead and ensure that the window slides up and down as it should. Put back the inner sash in the same way and refit the staff beads. Nail them in position with oval-head nails and drive these beneath the surface of the wood with a nail punch. When both sashes are replaced, you will probably have to paint the window frame. Be careful not to get paint on the sash cords, as it will look untidy and might prevent them from working smoothly.

Replacing a sash cord

  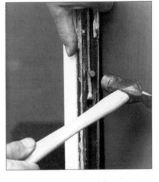

1 *Carefully prise off the beading around the edge of the window with a screwdriver or old chisel. Cut any unbroken cords in the sash nearest to you and let the weights fall down into their boxes. Then remove the inner sash. To take out the other sash, first prise out the parting beads that separate the two sashes. To give access to the sash weights, there is a small panel in the side of the frame, which is usually held in place by a screw.*

2 *Remove the panel and pull out the weights and the remaining lengths of cord. Untie the weights from the old cords and remove the cord from the sides of the sashes, where it will be nailed in place. It is important to get the length of the new cords exactly right; do this either by using an undamaged cord from the same sash, or by ensuring that the weight is just clear of the bottom of the box when the window is fully up.*

3 *Pass the sash cord over the pulley, tie it to the weight, cut it to the right length and temporarily knot the free end to stop it going over the pulley. When you have repeated the process for the other cord, hold the sash up to the frame and nail the free ends of the cords on to the window with galvanized clout nails 10in (25cm) from the top of the frame. Check that the window slides up and down freely, then replace the inner sash.*

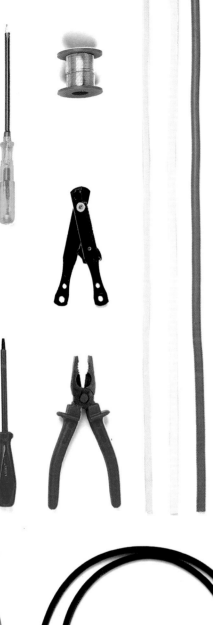

CHAPTER SIX

ELECTRICITY

Electricity can kill. It is therefore essential to take great care in its everyday use and to carry out all electrical work in the home to the highest possible standard. Never tackle any electrical job unless you know exactly how to go about it and understand fully what you are doing. If you are not sure about something, do not hesitate to employ a qualified electrician.

Before you start any electrical job, get to know the basic principles of how household electricity works. Find out how electricity arrives in your home and how the wiring beneath the floorboards and behind the wall coverings makes up the various different electrical circuits. These diagrams are important even if you do not want to replace the fixed wiring, because they show you why you should connect wires in sockets, switches and plugs in a particular way. Once you know how the system works, you will be much less likely to make dangerous mistakes.

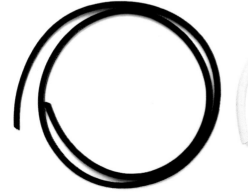

Tools and materials

For everyday electrical repairs and the occasional emergency, there are several inexpensive items that you should keep together, perhaps near the fusebox. The most important items are a torch, a pair of pliers (ideally with insulated handles), a knife or wire strippers, small and medium insulated screwdrivers, a roll of PVC insulating tape, fuse wire or cartridge fuses to replace circuit fuses, and spare 3 amp and 13 amp plug fuses. A screwdriver with a built-in bulb for circuit testing is useful.

For larger-scale repair or extension work, you will need additional equipment. The most useful items are a floorboard saw for removing floorboards, a bolster chisel and club hammer for recessing cable in solid walls, and a measuring tape.

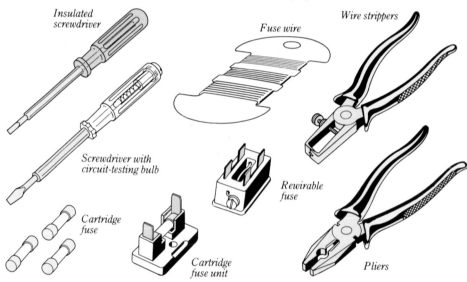

Insulated screwdriver

Fuse wire

Wire strippers

Screwdriver with circuit-testing bulb

Cartridge fuse

Cartridge fuse unit

Rewirable fuse

Pliers

POINTS TO REMEMBER	COLOUR CODING FOR WIRES
• When working on the fixed wiring, turn off the house's mains switch first, remove the fuse that protects the circuit you are working on and put it safely in your pocket so that you do not lose it. • Double-check that the circuit is dead by plugging in an appliance that you know works or using a mains tester. • Always unplug any portable appliance from the mains before attempting to repair it. • Use good-quality materials that conform to British Standards specifications and that are marked as such. • Use cables, flexes and plugs of the correct rating for the circuits in your home and appliances they serve. • For appliances up to 700 watts use a 3 amp fuse, for others use a 13 amp fuse.	Cable usually contains three solid wires, two insulated with coloured PVC (red for live and black for neutral) and a third, the earth wire for the circuit, which is not insulated, just left as bare metal. Flexes also usually contain three wires, all of which have colour-coded insulation; the live wire is brown, the neutral is blue and the earth is striped green and yellow (old flex uses red, black and green respectively for the three cores). In this section the wires have been colour-coded as yellow for live, grey for neutral and black and white for earth. When doing any electrical or wiring job, make sure that you connect the correct wires to the correct terminals, using the colour coding system. Remember that the colour coding may vary from country to country.

Electrical repairs

The fixed wiring of a household electrical circuit connects the sockets, ceiling lights and switches to the mains supply. It should be made up of cable of the correct rating, and the switches and sockets should be mounted on proper backplates or mounting boxes. There are separate circuits for power, lighting and powerful appliances such as cookers.

Two single cables run from the meter to the main fusebox or "consumer unit". The fusebox distributes the electrical current to the various circuits in the home and allows you to turn off all or part of the electrical system for repair or extension work. Each circuit in the home is also protected by passing through a circuit fuse. If there is a fault, or if the circuit is overloaded, the fuse blows. This has the double effect of warning you that there is a fault and of cutting off the power to the circuit, making it safe for you to carry out repairs.

When carrying out a repair or replacing an electrical fitting, make sure that you always work on a "dead" circuit. Switch off the mains switch and remove the fuse which protects the circuit you are working on. Double-check that the circuit is dead by plugging in an appliance which you know works.

Plugs and flexes should be checked regularly for wear or damage. Fix loose connections straight away before they become dangerous. If a flex becomes frayed or worn, patch it temporarily with insulating tape and replace it as soon as possible. Always use a fuse with the correct amperage – if you use a higher amperage, it will cause the circuit to overload, overheat and start a fire.

Mending a fuse

If a fuse blows, there is a fault somewhere in the circuit. You must make sure that the fault has been put right before replacing or mending the fuse and switching on again. There are two basic types of fuse. Cartridge fuses are used in plugs and in many modern fuseboxes. To change this type, all you have to do is remove the old fuse and insert a new one of the correct rating. Older fuseboxes have traditional rewirable fuses. To repair this type, you remove the old wire and replace it with new wire of the correct rating, attaching this to the fuse's two terminals.

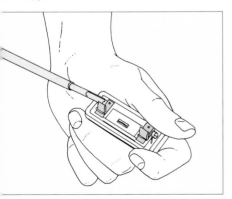

Rewirable fuse
These have a screw terminal at either end. A hole in the body allows you to see if the wire is broken. Remove the old fuse wire, thread the new wire through the fuse body and attach each end to a terminal.

Cartridge fuse
To change a cartridge fuse, remove the fuse carrier and take out the old fuse. Replace it with a new cartridge, which simply clips into place between the two metal holders in the fuse carrier.

Fitting a plug

Always replace a plug if its body is cracked or broken. With portable appliances, fit a resilient rubber plug. When wiring a plug, make sure that the core insulation reaches right up to the terminals, that there are no stray strands of metal conductor loose in the plug, and that the flex is anchored by the cord grip so that it does not pull out.

Wires from some non-metal appliances such as fans may not have an earth core. If this is the case, connect the live and neutral cores to the terminals.

TIPS FOR CARE OF PLUGS AND FLEXES

● Check all your plugs and flexes regularly, at least once a year, to ensure that they are not damaged, loose or worn.
● Remake loose connections and replace any damaged flex; do not patch up worn flexes.
● Keep flexes as short as possible.
● Keep flexes away from heat sources such as electric cookers and fires.
● Make sure that each appliance has flex of the correct rating and that each plug is fitted with the correct fuse.
● Two-core flex must only be used with double-insulated appliances and light fittings that have no metal parts.

Connecting a plug

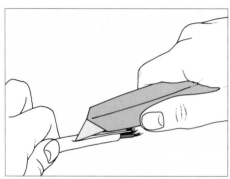

1 *Using a knife or a pair of wire strippers, strip the outer casing from the flex, removing enough for the individual cores to reach the terminals.*

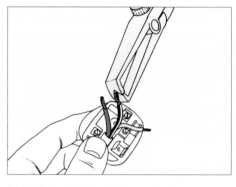

2 *Strip about ¼–½in (6–12mm) of casing from each of the cores to bare the metal conductor in the centre. Twist the wires slightly to keep them together.*

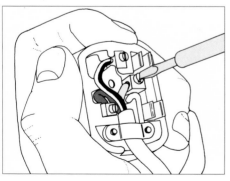

3 *Connect the three cores to the plug terminals. The brown core goes to the live terminal, the blue to the neutral and the green-and-yellow to the earth.*

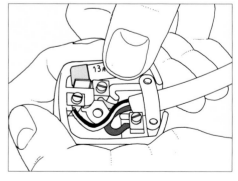

4 *Fit a fuse of the correct rating for the appliance, screw down the cord grip and fit the outer casing, screwing it firmly in place.*

Repairing a table lamp

When a table lamp flickers or does not work, the first thing to check is the bulb and replace it if necessary. Unplug the lamp, check the plug and flex and make sure that all connections are firm. A frayed or damaged flex will need to be replaced with a new one.

If the problem is not with the bulb, plug or flex, it may be in the switch. If you need to replace the switch, first examine the old switch closely before you disconnect the wires and connect the new switch in the same way.

Rewiring a table lamp

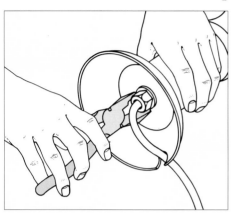

1 *Prise off the protective felt cover on the base of the lamp to expose the wiring. Most lamps contain a lead weight in the base which will need to be removed. Use pliers to undo the nut which secures the threaded tube to the base.*

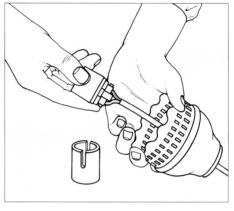

2 *Partially pull the tube out from the top of the lamp and turn the socket anti-clockwise to unscrew it. Remove the outer shell of the switch socket and then the cardboard insulating sleeve. This will expose the screw terminals.*

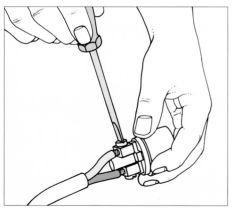

3 *Unscrew the two wires on the terminals, after noting exactly how they are connected. Examine the switch and, if you are replacing the switch or socket, fit the wires on to the new switch in the same way as they were attached to the old one.*

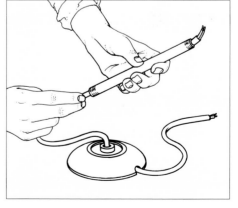

4 *If you are replacing the wire and plug, feed the new wire through the lamp base and threaded tube. Connect the wires to the switch and make sure that the connections are firm. Reassemble the lamp by reversing the order in which it was dismantled.*

Replacing a light switch

To control the light from a single point you can use either a one-way or a two-way switch. In large rooms and on staircases it is often useful to be able to switch the light on and off at two places, for which you need a two-way switch.

A one-way switch has two terminals at the back and the two separate switch cable cores are connected to these. A two-way switch has three terminals, marked C, L1, and L2. For two-way control, one switch is installed at each switching position. The light is linked to one switch in the usual way using two-core and earth cable. The two switches are then connected by three-core and earth cable. The red core links the two C terminals, the blue core links the two L1 terminals, and the yellow core links the two L2 terminals. Two-way switches can be used for one-way control, using terminal C and one L terminal.

Wiring a switch for one-way control

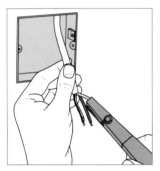 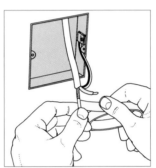 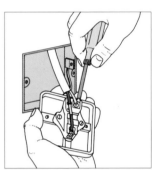

1 *Make sure that the cables are trimmed to the right length and use a pair of wire strippers to bare about ¼–½in (6–12mm) of wires at the centre of each core.*

2 *Connect the earth core to the terminal inside the mounting box and mark the black core of the cable with red PVC tape to remind you that it is live.*

3 *With a simple one-way switch, connect the red core to terminal L1 and the black core to terminal L2. Ensure that the wires are firm, then screw the switch to the wall.*

Replacing a ceiling light

Roses should always be fixed securely to the ceiling, either to the underside of a joist or to a batten fixed between the joists, above the ceiling surface. The cables enter the rose through knock-out panels in its base before being connected up to the terminals. The connections differ according to whether the ceiling wiring is done with junction boxes or by the loop-in method. If there is a junction box for the light fitting, there will only be one cable at the rose itself – the switch cable should be connected to the junction box in the loft. With a loop-in rose, the number of cables makes the job a little more complicated, so follow the instructions for connection carefully.

Fitting the rose

With a loop-in system (shown here), there should be three or four cables at the rose. The two circuit cables are the ones that connect two junction boxes or roses, the switch cable links the light to the switch, and there may be a branch cable, to which another rose is connected. After pulling the cables through the holes in the rose, strip a small piece of casing from each cable. The live, neutral and earth cores are grouped together in the rose terminals. The exception is the switch neutral, which is connected to the live flex core. The live flex core is connected to the switch return terminal of the rose, and the neutral flex core is connected to the neutral terminal of the rose. At the other end of the flex, the two cores are connected to the lampholder.

Fitting a ceiling rose

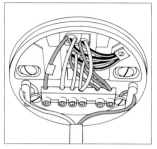

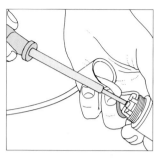

1 *First pull the ceiling cables carefully through the hole in the back of the rose.*

2 *Connect the live, neutral and earth cores to the appropriate terminals in the rose.*

3 *Connect the other ends of the live and neutral flex cores to the terminals in the lampholder.*

Replacing a socket

Every socket on a power circuit has three connections with the circuit cable. The live core is linked to the socket's live terminal (marked L), the neutral core to the neutral terminal (marked N), and the bare earth to the earth terminal (marked E or ⊥). On a ring main, there will be two separate three-core cables to be connected to the socket – two cores should be connected to each terminal.

On a spur there will only be one cable. On either a spur or a ring circuit, the connections must be in a fireproof enclosure. This is normally provided by the metal or plastic box on which the socket is mounted.

First check that the core cables are of the correct length and strip them with cable strippers if necessary. The earth core in power cable is uninsulated, and before connection you should cover the earth cores with green-and-yellow PVC tubing. It will then be insulated and clearly identifiable.

Wiring a socket in a ring circuit

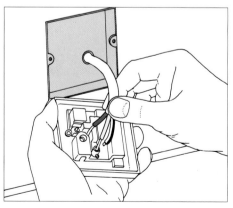

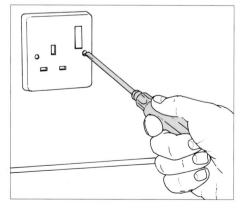

1 *Connect the cables to the terminals on the back of the socket, pairing up the two live cores, the two neutrals and the two earths.*

2 *When the cables are connected, push the main cable back into the wall and fit the socket on to the mounting box with the two fixing screws.*

Fluorescent lights

Fluorescent lights last much longer if they are left burning and not constantly switched on and off. Manufacturers rate the life of the tubes by the number of times they are switched on: a 40-watt fluorescent tube, for example, turned on for three hours each time, will last for about 12,000 hours. In practice, most fluorescent tubes have a working life of about 7500 hours, usually lasting for between three and five years.

These lamps are designed to be used at temperatures on or above 50°F (10°C) and the life of a fluorescent lamp is considerably reduced at low temperatures. If you intend to use this type of lighting outside or in a cold room, enclose the lamp in a glass fitting, to insulate it from the cold.

Fluorescent lights require special fittings. The pins of straight tubes fit into a socket at either end of the fixture, while the pins of a circular tube plug into a socket and are held in place by spring clips. The fittings for most tube types contain starters, although rapid-start tubes do not use them. All fittings for fluorescent lights contain a ballast for each tube. Normal ballasts (heavy coils of wire) consume a certain amount of power. Electronic ballasts are now available which use less power and are lighter in weight. They start the lamp almost immediately and eliminate flickering.

Replacement tubes, starters and ballasts must be exactly the same type and rating as the original. You will need an adaptor for a fluorescent tube with a direct current. When a new lamp is switched on, the light usually flickers and swirls along the tube. This should soon disappear, but if it does not, consult the troubleshooting box opposite.

Starter-type fluorescent tube
To fit a new starter, push it into the socket and give it a half-turn clockwise to secure it. To remove the starter, press it down and twist it anti-clockwise.

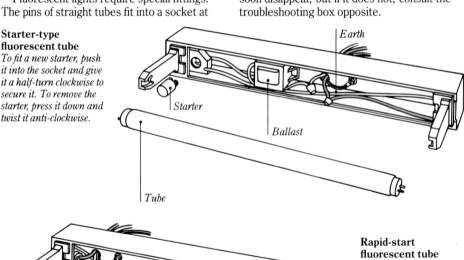

Earth

Starter

Ballast

Tube

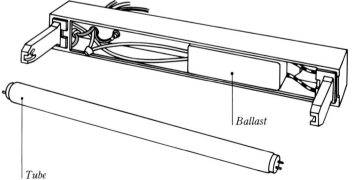

Rapid-start fluorescent tube
Replace a straight tube by aligning the pins with the socket slots on either end of the fixture, push it in place and secure it with a quarter-turn. Some lampholders have slotted rotating discs. When fitting a new tube, make sure that the slots in the discs align with the slots in the brackets.

Ballast

Tube

Fitting a fluorescent light

Fittings such as fluorescents, rise-and-fall units and close-ceiling units require a method of connection that is slightly different from that used for pendant fittings. The flex from the fitting is connected to the circuit wiring via a multi-way connector block. This must be housed in a non-combustible enclosure, provided by recessing a metal or plastic box (called a BESA or terminal conduit box) into the ceiling or wall.

Once the flex and circuit cables are connected, the backplate of the fitting is fixed to the BESA box. The box can be screwed into a recess chiselled into the underside of a joist, but it is easier to attach it to a batten fixed between two joists in the ceiling.

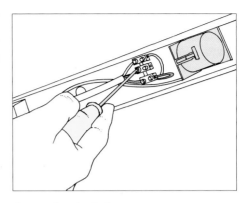

Connecting the fitting
The connections between the fitting's flex and the circuit cables are made with either three or four connectors, depending on whether the wiring uses a junction box or the loop-in method.

TROUBLESHOOTING FOR FLUORESCENT LIGHTS

Tube will not light
Make sure that the fuse or circuit breaker is not blown or tripped, and that there are no loose or broken connections. If it is intact, try replacing the starter. If this does not work, renew the tube. As a last resort, replace the ballast.

Light flickers and swirls inside the tube
This usually happens with a new tube and will disappear with use. If it persists or the tube is not new, the starter motor may be faulty and need replacing. If replacing the starter does not cure the problem, you will need to replace the ballast.

Light blinks on and off
The tube may not be properly seated in the socket; remove it and examine the pins. Straighten bent pins with long-nosed pliers and return the tube to the socket. Lightly sand the pins and socket contacts if the light still blinks, brushing out the residue with a toothbrush. Tighten any loose connections. If the problem persists, replace the

starter, and if then this too does not solve the problem, replace the ballast.

Fixture hums but otherwise works properly
Check that the connections are not loose. If they are firm, replace the ballast with a special low-noise type.

Electrodes glow at each end, but the tube will not start
If the glow at each end of the tube is white, the starter motor is faulty and will need to be replaced. If the glow is red, however, the lamp is nearly dead and should be replaced.

Ends of tube are discoloured
A brown colour at the ends of the tube is normal. If the colour is black and the tube is new, replace the starter. If an old tube starts to blacken about 2in (50mm) from the ends, the electrode material in the tube is evaporating and the light will soon fail, so replace the tube. If the tube is discoloured on one side only, remove it, turn it over and return it to the socket. If the

tube is new and one end darkens before the other, reverse the tube end to end in the socket.

Tube burns out too fast
The tube has probably been turned on and off too often. Replace the tube and leave the light on for longer periods. If the trouble persists, replace the starter, and then the ballast. Check all connections and make sure that they are secure.

Tube lights up at half brightness
This happens with old tubes which are in need of replacing. Renew the tube, and the light should work at full brightness.

Tube glows at one end only
The tube holder at the dark end of the tube may be faulty. Try fitting a new tube, but if that does not cure the problem, call a professional electrician, as the holder has probably short-circuited.

Make sure that the power is switched off before making any repairs.

Appliance fault-finding

Most electrical appliances give years of reliable, trouble-free service, but when they receive hard and regular use over the years, some breakdown is to be expected. Faults are always irritating, not least because we take smooth running for granted, yet many problems can be solved quickly and easily.

Basic faults, such as disconnected wires and blown fuses, can be corrected in a matter of minutes and it is always worth checking these as a matter of course before consulting a specialist. Many internal faults in basic household appliances can also be easily put right when you know how to do it.

Detecting basic faults

When an appliance stops working, the most usual cause is loss of receiving power. The plug and flex, which convey the current to the appliance, may have become disconnected, or the fuse may have blown. It is worth making a few basic checks before looking for more specific faults.

Checking the wiring
Open the plug and check that the colour-coded cores are securely connected to their correct terminals (brown or red core to live, blue or black core to neutral, and green-and-yellow or green – if a third core is present – to earth). Then check that the flex is firmly anchored in the cord grip to prevent the cores from

dislodging. It is always wise to throw away an old cracked, chipped or discoloured plug and replace it with a new, modern one.

Checking the fuse
The fuse should blow if there is a fault in the appliance, but it may also fail if it needs replacing. Try fitting a new fuse of the correct rating, reassemble the plug and plug it in. If the appliance works, the fuse needed replacing. If the fuse blows again, isolate the appliance for repairs. Another way of testing the fuse is to unscrew a metal torch, and hold one end of the fuse against the metal casing and the other against the bottom of the battery. A sound fuse will light the torch, a blown one will not. Use a 3 amp fuse for appliances that use up to 700 watts, a 5 amp fuse for lighting circuits up to 1kW and a 13 amp fuse for appliances such as TVs, kettles, irons, heaters and washing machines, which use up to 3kW.

Checking the flex
First examine the flex for signs of damage. If there are no obvious signs of a break, check the flex connections within the appliance. If you need to open the appliance casing to do this, unplug it first. If the flex is worn, do not use insulating tape to repair it. Instead, you should replace it, taking care to buy the right type and rating. If the flex is inconveniently short, take the opportunity to fit a longer length. Alternatively, use a flex connector to join two flexes, or use an extension lead. Choose bright-coloured leads for use outdoors. Coiled leads, like telephone flexes, can be bought in various bright colours and are very useful for outdoor appliances; they are easier to handle than straight flexes.

POINTS TO REMEMBER

- Switch off any electrical gadget before examining and mending it, otherwise you may inadvertently start the machine as you examine it, or get an electric shock.
- Switch off at the wall before unplugging. Failing to do so is potentially dangerous, particularly if the plug or appliance is faulty.
- Operate the appliance according to the instructions given in the booklet supplied with it, which are there for your guidance.
- If the fault is not immediately apparent, call in an engineer and do not tamper with the inner workings of the device unless you know what you are doing. You might damage more than just the appliance, and you will certainly invalidate the manufacturer's guarantee.
- Always check the basics first before looking for more serious faults. Tighten the terminal screws in the plug and check the fuse.

CORRECTING FAULTS IN SMALL APPLIANCES

COFFEE PERCOLATOR (GRAVITY)

Symptom: Coffeè does not keep warm.
Cause: Failed warming element.

Cure: Replace the warming element.
Remove the base screws and pull off the rubber feet and the bottom plate. Unscrew the nut holding the element guard and remove the old warming element. Then remove the screws from the top unit, pull off the casing and remove the reservoirs. Use long-nosed pliers to disconnect the lead wires from the terminal board and slide out the main element. Remove the retaining rod and separate the element from its pan. In some models, the entire heating arrangement can be replaced as a single unit. In others, the two elements are fitted individually.

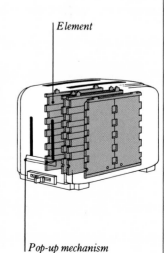

Main element

Top unit

Warming element

Symptom: Ready light does not work.
Cause: Failed light.

Cure: Replace the light.
Disconnect the leads from the terminals within the base. Push out the old light. Insert a new light and reconnect the leads.

TOASTER

Symptom: Toaster will not heat.
Cause: Failed element.

Cure: Replace the element.
You will have to work carefully and methodically, or you will upset the pop-up mechanism. Open the toaster and have a look at the mechanism. If you can see how it works, unscrew the old element and fit a new one. If the toast will not pop up, you will have to take the toaster to a specialist, since the mechanism is very intricate.

Element

Symptom: Toast does not brown.
Cause: Faulty thermostat.

Cure: Replace the thermostat.
Take the toaster to a specialist electrical repair shop or return it to the manufacturer.

Pop-up mechanism

CORRECTING FAULTS IN SMALL APPLIANCES

ELECTRIC IRON
Symptom: Iron will not heat/
control lamp is not lighting.
Cause: Damaged flex.

Cure: Replace the flex.
Fit a braided, non-kink flex of the
correct rating for the iron.

Flex connections

*Thermostat
contacts*

Symptom: Iron will not heat/
control lamp glows.
Cause: Failed element.

Cure: Replace the element.
Locate the cover-fixing screws
and lift the cover off to expose
the element. Disconnect the flex
connections from the element
and remove the element from
the soleplate. Find an exact
replacement for the element, fit
it into position, reconnect it to
the flex connections, replace the
cover and screw it back on.

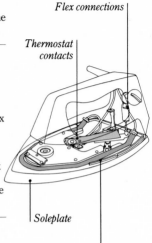

Soleplate

Symptom: Iron overheats
or underheats.
Cause: Failed thermostat.

Cure: Replace the thermostat.
Thermostats are tricky to
replace, so take the iron to an
electrical repair shop.

Elements

UPRIGHT VACUUM CLEANER
Symptom: Vacuum overheats/
loss of suction.
Cause: Failed drive belt.

Cure: Replace the drive belt.
Remove the cover plate from the
front, then turn the cleaner over
and remove the metal cover.
Prise out the roller, slip off the
old belt and fit a new one of the
same type and size around the
roller. Replace the roller and
metal shield, turn the cleaner
right way up and hook the belt
over the drive pulley, following
the diagram on the casing.

Drive pulley

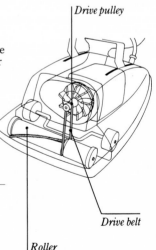

CYLINDER VACUUM CLEANER
Symptom: Loss of suction.
Cause: Punctured hose.

Cure: Replace the hose.
Bind the hose with insulating
tape, or replace it.

Drive belt

Roller

Symptom: Intermittent power.
Cause: Worn carbon brushes.

Cure: Replace the brushes.
Take the appliance to a specialist.

CORRECTING FAULTS IN SMALL APPLIANCES

SEWING MACHINE
Symptom: Motor hums but machine does not operate.
Cause: Bobbin or take-up assembly jammed.

Cure: Clear the bobbin. Remove the bobbin and the bobbin carrier and clean them to make sure that there are no lint or thread particles which will clog the machine. Make sure that the thread is wound tightly and evenly around the bobbin.

Cause: Faulty motor.

Cure: Replace the motor. Take the sewing machine to an electrical repair shop or return it to the manufacturer.

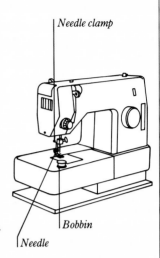

Needle clamp

Bobbin

Needle

Symptom: Needle breaks/ machine does not stitch properly.
Cause: Wrong or bent needle/ needle incorrectly positioned.

Cure: Reposition/replace needle. Check the position of the needle and reposition it if it is not inserted in the clamp correctly. If the needle is the wrong size or bent, replace it with a new one of the correct size.

KETTLE
Symptom: Slow heating.
Cause: Build-up of hard water scale.

Cure: De-scale the kettle. Mineral deposits or scale can be removed using proprietary products, although these are very strong. An alternative is to cover the element with vinegar and bring it to the boil. Allow it to cool before emptying the kettle and rinsing it thoroughly several times. Boil the kettle and pour the water away at least once before using the kettle again. To prevent scale from building up again, keep a metal de-scaler inside the kettle to collect the scale.

Element

Coupler housing

Symptom: No power.
Cause: Faulty element.

Cure: Replace the element. Hold the element with one hand while you unscrew the coupler housing. Slide off the washers and pull the element out through the top of the kettle. Fit the new element in position and reassemble the kettle.

CORRECTING FAULTS IN LARGE APPLIANCES

ELECTRIC COOKER
Symptom: Ring will not heat.
Cause: Faulty ring.

Cure: Replace the ring. Disconnect the cooker, then lift the hob and undo the box-like cover to gain access to the ring terminal. Remove the screw on the element fixing plate, free it from the hob and disconnect the faulty ring from its terminals. Fit the new ring by reversing the operation. Call the service engineer for faulty controls or a failed grill.

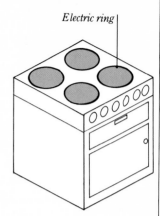

Electric ring

GAS COOKER
Symptom: Automatic lighter fails.
Cause: Blocked pilot jet.

Cure: Unblock the pilot jet. Use a long pin to clear debris in the jet.

WASHING MACHINE
Symptom: Leaks.
Cause: Perished inlet hose.

Cure: Replace the inlet hose. The inlet hose may perish if the stop taps are not turned off when the machine is not in use. Turn off the mains, remove the old hose and fit a new hose with new threaded couplers. Fit the couplers on to the supply pipe at one end of the hose and on to the machine inlet at the other.

Internal hose

Cause: Perished internal hose.

Cure: Replace the internal hose.
To replace an internal hose, use a screwdriver to undo the worm drive or rubber clips holding the old hose in place. Smear a little petroleum jelly over the spigots before slipping the new hose into position.

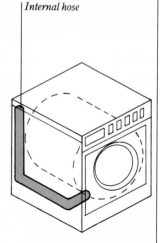

Cause: Perished door seal.

Cure: Replace the door seal. The door seal usually fits in a channel around the door. Remove the old one and press the new one into place. If the seal links the cylinder of the machine with the casing, leave the repair to a service engineer.

CORRECTING FAULTS IN LARGE APPLIANCES

TUMBLE DRYER

Symptom: Over-heating/slow drying.
Cause: Build-up of fluff in the filter.

Cure: Clear the filter. Fluff and fibres collect in the filter, so try to clean it out every time the machine is used or at least once a week. All other faults should be dealt with by the service engineer.

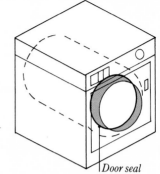

Symptom: No power.
Cause: Loose connection.

Cure: Check the plug and flex. Reconnect any loose cores.

Door seal

SPIN DRYER

Symptom: Drum will not revolve/pump will not work.
Cause: Faulty drive belt.

Cure: Fit a new drive belt. Turn the machine on its side, unscrew the bottom plate and examine the drive belt. If it has become dislodged from its groove, adjust it into its correct position. If the old belt has snapped or worn thin, replace it. Match the length and thickness of the old belt, stretch the new belt over the pulleys and fit them into the grooves.

Drum drive belt

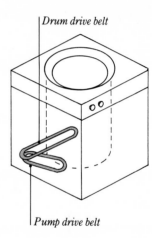

Symptom: Excessive vibration.
Cause: Worn bearings.

Cure: Replace the bearings. Consult the service engineer.

Pump drive belt

DISHWASHER

Symptom: Slow washing.
Cause: Clogged waste filter or inlet holes.

Cure: Clear any obstructions. Empty the perforated metal or plastic filter at the bottom of the cabinet. If the machine has a rotor arm that sprays water into the cabinet, lift it off and clean it under a tap to prevent the hard water scale from forming around the inlet holes. If inlet or outlet hoses have perished, replace as for a washing machine.

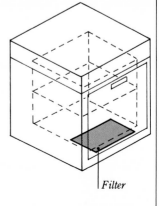

Symptom: Dishes will not dry.
Cause: Faulty blower or element.

Cure: Replace it with a new blower or element. Consult the service engineer.

Filter

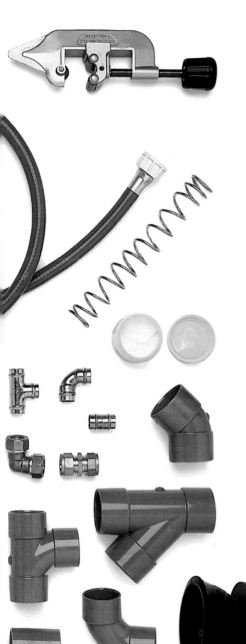

CHAPTER SEVEN

PLUMBING

The plumbing system consists of a network of pipes carrying hot and cold water around the home and taking waste material away. These pipes, together with the sinks, basins, baths and WCs they serve, usually need little maintenance. But when something does go wrong – whether it is a burst pipe or a blocked drain – a great deal of damage and inconvenience can result. With a basic knowledge of how household plumbing works, however, most of the necessary repairs are straightforward.

You can avoid some problems by taking care of the plumbing in your home. For example, lagging pipes will reduce the likelihood of freezes and bursts in cold weather (for more information on insulation, see pages 190–7). Remember that new water by-laws require appliance fittings, such as taps and ball-valves, to be fitted with servicing valves so that the water can be turned off in an emergency, preventing wastage.

Tools and materials

Two fairly large, adjustable spanners and a ½in (12mm) or ¾in (19mm) wrench, for removing and repairing taps, will all be useful for plumbing work. A crowsfoot spanner is ideal for use in confined spaces. If you are working with copper pipes, a pipe cutter is better than a hacksaw for cutting the ends square. Use bending springs or hire a bending machine for larger sizes.

Fine steel wool and a strip of emery cloth are useful for cleaning the ends of copper tubing. Plumbers' mastic should be used for bedding joints and PTFE tape for wrapping around threaded joints to ensure that the connections are completely watertight.

There are two basic types of pipe: supply and waste pipes. Supply pipes carry water to the taps and fittings in the home. Waste pipes carry water from waste outlets to the drains. In older homes both types were often made of lead, but copper is now the most popular material for supply pipes and plastic for waste pipes. Both materials are flexible and easy to cut, but copper is perhaps more versatile, as it can be bent to fit. Some modern cold water pipes are made of rigid plastic.

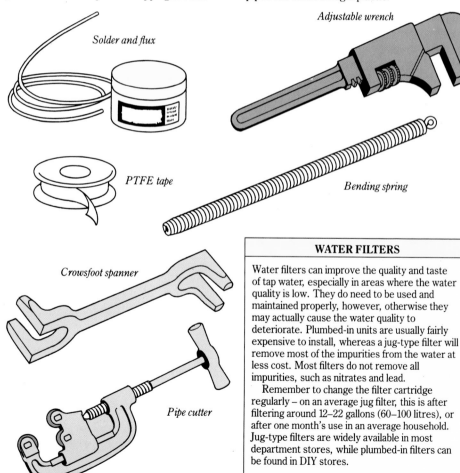

Adjustable wrench

Solder and flux

PTFE tape

Bending spring

Crowsfoot spanner

Pipe cutter

WATER FILTERS

Water filters can improve the quality and taste of tap water, especially in areas where the water quality is low. They do need to be used and maintained properly, however, otherwise they may actually cause the water quality to deteriorate. Plumbed-in units are usually fairly expensive to install, whereas a jug-type filter will remove most of the impurities from the water at less cost. Most filters do not remove all impurities, such as nitrates and lead.

Remember to change the filter cartridge regularly – on an average jug filter, this is after filtering around 12–22 gallons (60–100 litres), or after one month's use in an average household. Jug-type filters are widely available in most department stores, while plumbed-in filters can be found in DIY stores.

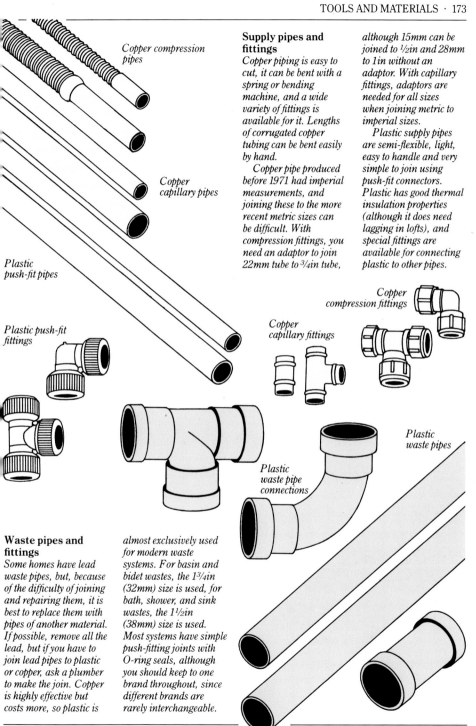

Copper compression pipes

Copper capillary pipes

Plastic push-fit pipes

Plastic push-fit fittings

Supply pipes and fittings

Copper piping is easy to cut, it can be bent with a spring or bending machine, and a wide variety of fittings is available for it. Lengths of corrugated copper tubing can be bent easily by hand.

Copper pipe produced before 1971 had imperial measurements, and joining these to the more recent metric sizes can be difficult. With compression fittings, you need an adaptor to join 22mm tube to ³/4in tube,

although 15mm can be joined to ¹/2in and 28mm to 1in without an adaptor. With capillary fittings, adaptors are needed for all sizes when joining metric to imperial sizes.

Plastic supply pipes are semi-flexible, light, easy to handle and very simple to join using push-fit connectors. Plastic has good thermal insulation properties (although it does need lagging in lofts), and special fittings are available for connecting plastic to other pipes.

Copper compression fittings

Copper capillary fittings

Plastic waste pipes

Plastic waste pipe connections

Waste pipes and fittings

Some homes have lead waste pipes, but, because of the difficulty of joining and repairing them, it is best to replace them with pipes of another material. If possible, remove all the lead, but if you have to join lead pipes to plastic or copper, ask a plumber to make the join. Copper is highly effective but costs more, so plastic is

almost exclusively used for modern waste systems. For basin and bidet wastes, the 1³/4in (32mm) size is used, for bath, shower, and sink wastes, the 1¹/2in (38mm) size is used. Most systems have simple push-fitting joints with O-ring seals, although you should keep to one brand throughout, since different brands are rarely interchangeable.

Plumbing systems

The household plumbing system is divided into three distinct parts: the cold-water system, the hot-water system and the drainage system. Although the actual layout will vary from home to home, most domestic plumbing systems work in the same way, and once you have a working knowledge of the basic principles involved, you will be able to carry out simple repairs and maintenance. Remember that large parts of the system are hidden from view – water storage tanks are usually in the loft, while the drainage system takes away waste below ground.

POINTS TO REMEMBER

- Prepare yourself for emergencies by getting to know where the stopcocks and control valves are so that you can turn off the water quickly.
- Tell other members of the household where the stopcocks and control valves are so that they can act quickly if you are not there.
- Use a spring or pipe-bending machine to bend metal pipes, otherwise they will kink at the bend.
- After cutting metal pipes, rub the edges with a fine file to remove metal waste that may make joining the pipe difficult.
- If possible, replace old lead pipes with modern copper or plastic ones.
- When replacing lengths of pipe, check the size carefully – you may need an adaptor to join metric pipe to pipe measured in inches.

The cold-water system

There are two basic types of cold-water system – direct fed and tank fed. With the direct system, the taps are fed from the water authority's main supply. With the tank system, the main supply is taken to a tank, called a storage cistern, in the loft and the cold taps are fed from the cistern. With the direct system it is still necessary to have a small storage cistern, holding a reserve of water to feed the hot-water system.

The direct system has two drawbacks. Because there is no storage tank, there is no back-up if the supply of cold water is interrupted. Also, the direct-fed cold taps work at a higher water pressure than the hot taps, making it impossible to install a conventional shower mixer valve. However, you can fit an instantaneous electric shower, which will run off the cold-water supply alone.

Most water authorities prefer a tank-fed system, with the kitchen cold tap connected directly to the mains supply, to provide a source of drinking water. The cistern, which has a capacity of at least 50 gallons (225 litres), feeds all the cold taps except the one in the kitchen, as well as the WC cisterns. It also has an outlet pipe to feed the hot-water system. The only drawback with tank-fed systems is that drinking water should be taken only from the kitchen tap. To prevent debris from falling into a storage system, water by-laws now require that new and replacement cold water storage systems should be provided with a

cover that is dust-proof and insect-proof, but must not be air-tight.

The hot-water system

The most common household hot-water system is the indirect type. This has two parts. The first part (the "primary circuit") consists of a boiler that heats water. This water passes through a pipe into a coil inside a tank and back again to the boiler. The second part carries the heated water from the tank to the hot taps throughout the home. With a boiler of the correct capacity, a hot-water radiator system can be run off the primary circuit. A small storage system in the loft, called a feed-and-expansion tank, makes good any small water loss by evaporation from the primary system. With a direct system, hot water from the boiler is stored in the tank.

The drainage system

Houses that are more than 30 years old usually have a soil pipe for the waste from the WCs and a separate waste pipe for the waste from the baths, basins, showers and sinks. These often connect at an underground inspection chamber, from which the combined waste is taken by drains to the sewer under the road or to a septic tank.

In newer homes, single-stack drainage systems, with one soil pipe, are generally used. With this modern type of drainage system, separate branch pipes connect all the WCs, sinks, baths and basins to the stack.

Plumbing repairs

Modern pipes and fittings are easy to take apart and re-assemble, although repairs to old-fashioned lead pipes are more difficult and are best carried out by a professional. If you have old lead pipes, it is probably best to get them replaced – copper and plastic are much easier to maintain.

Before embarking on repairing or replacing fixtures, make sure that you know what sort of plumbing system your house has and turn off the water at the stopcocks and valves. For smaller jobs, such as clearing a blocked waste pipe, WC or drain, you will not need to turn off the water supply to the house.

Clearing a blocked drain

Drain blockages are indicated by overflowing gulleys, water leaks from around inspection chambers, and WC pans that are either obviously blocked or fill higher than usual before the water level slowly drops back to normal. It is easy to clear a blocked gulley with your hand in the way shown below, but the best method to clear it is to use the type of vacuum cleaner suitable for wet or dry cleaning, so that bits of debris are not pushed further along the drainage system.

Unblocking a gulley

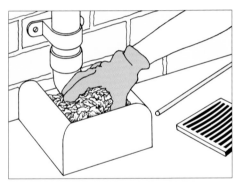

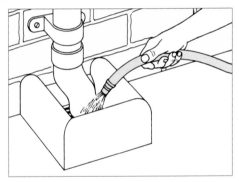

1 *Lift the cover grip to give access to the trap. Break up any sediment in the trap with a stick or trowel and remove it by hand.*

2 *Once all the debris has been cleared, flush the gulley clean. Use a small hosepipe and squirt water down the drain under pressure.*

EMERGENCY ACTION

If you have a water leak or a burst pipe, the first thing you should do is to turn off the water supply to stop the flooding and then isolate the fault for repair. Once this has been done, remember the following points:

• Turn off central heating boilers and water heaters.

• Turn off the whole cold-water supply at the stopcock where it enters the house.

• Once the cold-water supply has been turned off, drain the pipes by turning on all the taps until no more water runs out.

• The water in the hot-water tank, the radiators and the closed system between the boiler and the hot tank can only be drained by opening the appropriate draincocks – ask a plumber if you do not know where these are.

• If water is pouring from an overflow pipe, check the ball valve in the tank or cistern (pages 180–1).

• For more information on repairing leaks, see page 178.

• Make sure that you get to know where all the stopcocks are in your house so that, if an emergency does arise, you do not waste precious minutes in searching for them.

Clearing a blocked waste pipe

If working a rubber plunger over the outlet does not free the blockage, clear out the waste trap, as this is where the blockage is most likely to be. Place a basin or bucket under the trap ready to catch the contents. Traps vary in design. Old-style traps have a drain plug, which you take off to remove debris. More modern traps, especially those made of plastic, may not have a drain plug. There may be several sections which unscrew for cleaning, or the whole base may unscrew. Use a length of wire to clear the trap. If cleaning the trap fails to cure the blockage, clear the pipes on either side with a length of wire. Put out anything that is blocking the pipe, so that it does not block the pipe further along.

Clearing a U-bend trap

1 *Holding the trap steady with a piece of wood, unscrew the drain plug – if it has a square head, you should use a spanner, if there are two protrusions, these are turned with a steel bar.*

2 *If you cannot pull out the debris with a piece of hooked wire, use an adjustable wrench to remove the whole trap and clean it thoroughly, pulling out any debris in the pipes.*

Clearing a plastic trap

1 *Unscrew sections of the plastic trap, using a bucket to catch the debris that will fall out. It should be possible to unscrew the trap by hand.*

2 *Probe the pipes with a piece of wire if you find that there is still a blockage, pulling out anything which may be obstructing the pipe.*

Clearing a blocked sink

If your basin, sink or bath is blocked, you may be able to clear it with a plunger, rather than dismantling and clearing out the trap (page 176). When using a plunger, you will need to block the overflow hole to prevent air and water from escaping so that all the suction is concentrated on the blockage. Similarly, if the sink is a double one, you will need to plug the drainage and overflow holes in the second sink to create the vacuum.

Remove the plug and scoop out any excess water into a bucket with a cup or mug, leaving only about 1in (25mm) in the bottom. When the blockage has been dislodged, the remaining water will drain out.

Using a plunger

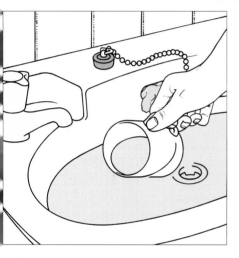

1 *Block the overflow hole with a rag to prevent air and water from escaping. Remove the plug and bail out the excess water using a cup.*

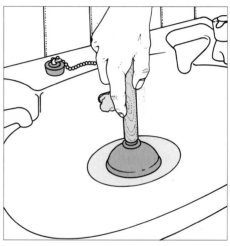

2 *Place the plunger firmly over the drainage hole and work the handle briskly up and down. The pool of water will drain out when the blockage is dislodged.*

Removing air locks from pipes

If you turn on a tap and the water comes in spouts or does not come out at all, it is quite likely that there is an air lock in the pipes. Wrap a mallet in a cloth and tap gently along the pipe to shift an air lock. Pay particular attention to bends in the pipes or areas where the pipe is not absolutely horizontal.

If you cannot remove the air lock with this method, try attaching one end of a hose to the problem tap (usually a hot-water tap) with a hose clip. Fit the other end of the hose to a mains cold-water tap, such as the kitchen tap.

Turn on first the faulty tap and then the mains tap; the pressure from the mains will push the air out of the system and back into the tank or cistern. If you have a mixer tap, remove the spout and press a cloth tightly up against the spout hole. Turn on the hot tap and then the cold tap to remove the bubble.

From time to time, especially in old houses, there may be a hammering and banging noise when you turn on the tap. This is probably because the pipes are not properly supported, especially where they come through a ceiling or floor. Vibration can be stopped by securing the pipes with pipe brackets to a fixed wooden batten. If the pipes are not loose, you may have an air lock in the system.

Plumbing-in a washing machine

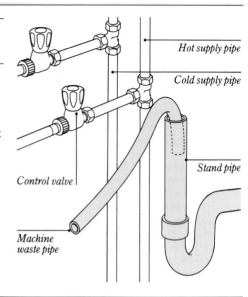

Hot supply pipe

Cold supply pipe

Most washing machines must be connected to hot and cold supply pipes. They need control valves, incorporating integral check (non-return) valves. If the control valve does not have an integral check valve, fit a double-check valve into the supply pipe by the control valve.

Take short lengths of ⅜in (15mm) pipe from the Tee-connectors in the supply pipes to the washing machine's control valves. The flexible supply pipes of the washing machine are connected to the outlets of these valves with hose union nuts. The waste can discharge directly through the wall above a gulley, it can be connected to the kitchen waste by a "swept-Tee" fitting, or it can be connected directly to a single-stack drainage system.

Control valve

Stand pipe

Machine waste pipe

Curing leaks

The most common cause of leaky pipes is frost damage. This can have the effect of pushing fittings apart or of causing a split in the pipes themselves. Metal pipes also leak because they become corroded.

Push-fit joints that have separated can be simply pushed together. For compression fittings that are parted by frost, slacken the cap nut, push the pipe back into place and retighten the cap nut. If the problem is in the pipe itself, cut out the affected section and insert a new length, using straight connectors at each end. Plastic pipe is ideal for this.

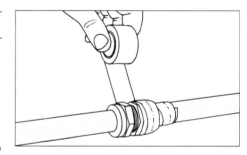

Mending pipes
To repair a pipe temporarily, drain it, dry it out and then bind it with waterproof mastic repair tape. For a permanent solution, cut out the affected pipe and insert a length of plastic pipe using straight connectors.

TIPS FOR THAWING PIPES

- Do not use a blowtorch – it is very easy to start a fire, especially in a loft. Use a fan heater to raise the temperature in the loft and thaw the pipe slowly in case of leaks.
- An electric hot-air paint stripper is ideal for thawing pipes, but be careful when using it near insulating materials.
- If you do not have a paint stripper, try a hairdryer, which

will work more slowly, but will still be effective.
- Thaw out first the areas that are most likely to be frozen, such as unlagged areas and bends in the pipes.
- If the frozen pipe has obviously burst, turn off the water supply to the pipe before thawing it, to avoid creating a flood and giving yourself an even worse problem.

- If the pipe has only recently frozen, thaw it as soon as possible. If you leave it, a burst will almost certainly occur, which will involve replacing the pipe and clearing the flood.
- Unfreeze the pipe slowly if there is a risk that the ice has already cracked the pipe, as the water will appear more slowly and it will be easier to cope with the resulting flood.

Replacing a tap

Before beginning work, you will need to empty all the water from the pipe. Turn off the stopcock controlling the water supply and turn on the tap to drain away the water in the pipe. To remove the old tap, unscrew the tap connector, which is attached to the tail of the tap, and, using an adjustable wrench, undo the back nut, which holds the tap to the fitting. Then lift the tap out of place.

Apply a little non-setting mastic to the underside of the new tap before putting on the plastic bedding washer that fits between the tap and the top of the sink or basin. Put the tap in place, fit a fibre washer on the tail from beneath and replace the back nut.

If you are fitting the tap to a thin surface such as a steel sink surround, put a "top-hat" washer over the tail to act as a spacer before fitting the fibre washer. Wrap the lower part of the tap tail with three or four turns of PTFE tape. Finally, fit the tap connector and a new fibre washer. It is good practice to fit a servicing valve in the supply pipe so that the water can be turned off in an emergency.

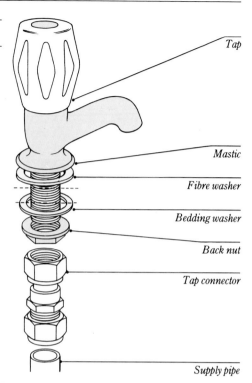

Tap

Mastic

Fibre washer

Bedding washer

Back nut

Tap connector

Supply pipe

Replacing a washer

A tap that drips when you turn it off needs a new washer. Basin and sink taps have ½in (12mm) washers, while bath taps require ¾in (19mm) washers. Start by turning off the water supply and opening the tap to drain the pipe.

The two main types of tap are the traditional capstan-head tap and the modern shrouded-head design. The method used to replace the washer varies slightly, depending on the type of tap, but once the shroud has been removed from the shrouded-head type, the headgear unscrews in the same way as that on the capstan-head tap.

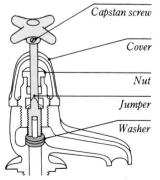

Capstan screw

Cover

Nut

Jumper

Washer

Capstan-head tap (left)
Remove the cover to reveal the hexagonal nut of the headgear. Unscrew the nut to reveal the jumper holding the washer. Fit a new washer or washer and jumper unit, and replace the cover.

Shrouded-head tap (right)
If the tap is a modern, shrouded-head type, either pull off the head shroud or remove the central fixing screw that holds it in place. The headgear then unscrews like that on a conventional tap.

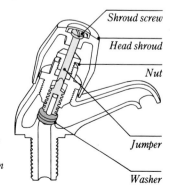

Shroud screw

Head shroud

Nut

Jumper

Washer

Repairing WCs

There are a few specific jobs which can easily be performed to maintain your WC. Here is a quick guide to recognizing the faults and deciding on the remedies. If the overflow is dripping, you probably need to replace the ball-valve washer. If the cistern will only flush with repeated pressing of the handle, replace the flap valve. If water is pouring from the overflow, the ball float is likely to be leaking and will need replacing. If your cistern is leaking, make a temporary repair by emptying the cistern, drying it out and inserting a wad of epoxy putty. Replace the cistern with a new one of the reduced flush type.

Clearing a blocked WC

This job is easier with special equipment and you may prefer to leave it to a specialist drain cleaner. If you do it yourself, start by finding the site of the blockage. Lift the drain inspection covers, beginning with the one closest to the pan. If the chamber is empty, this indicates that the blockage is between this chamber and the pan, probably at the pan itself. If the first chamber is full you will need to clear the drains using a set of special drain-clearing rods.

It is a good idea to get a helper to stand by the first inspection chamber while you clear a WC pan, to retrieve anything that might have been lodged in the pan, causing the blockage. If it is not retrieved immediately, it may block the drains farther down the pipe.

Unblocking a WC pan

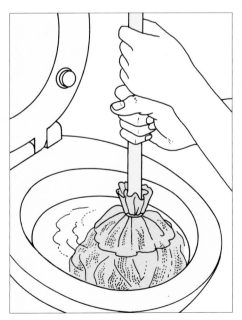

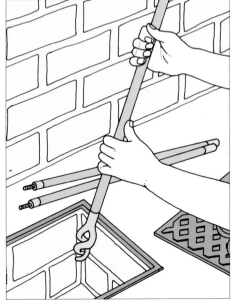

1 *First try pushing flexible drain-clearing wire down the WC pan, or try plunging the pan using an old mop with a plastic bag tied around the head.*

2 *If this does not work, open the nearest inspection chamber and use drain-clearing rods to clear the pipes. Alternatively, call in a specialist drain cleaner.*

Repairing a ball valve

If there are drips from the cistern overflow, examine the mechanism inside the cistern: the ball-valve washer or diaphragm probably needs replacing. The way you remove the washer or diaphragm depends on whether the valve is made of brass or whether it is a modern plastic valve. It is most likely that you will have to replace a brass valve, similar to that shown below right, which involves turning off the water supply and taking apart the valve and piston assemblies.

Replacing a valve washer

With a brass valve, turn off the water supply and remove the split pin holding the float arm to the valve assembly. Unscrew the cap end of the valve case and ease the piston assembly out of the valve. The washer is at the end of the piston. Undo the end of the piston or simply prise the washer out of place. Fit a new washer either by replacing the cap or by easing the new washer carefully under the lip of the cap so that it rests flat in the recess. Rub the piston with wire wool so that it slides easily in the valve case and then replace the float arm and the split pin.

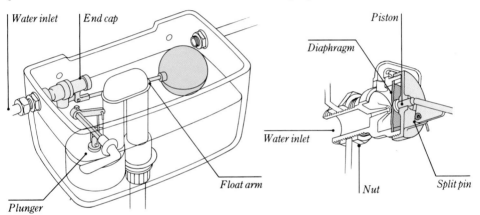

Water inlet *End cap* *Piston* *Diaphragm* *Water inlet* *Float arm* *Nut* *Split pin* *Plunger*

Replacing a flap valve

If the WC handle has to be depressed several times to make the cistern flush, the flap valve, which controls the amount of water that leaves the cistern, probably needs replacing. With a modern plastic ball valve, the water flow is controlled by a rubber diaphragm. After turning off the water supply, remove and replace the diaphragm by loosening the large knurled nut just behind the float-arm pivot.

Tie up the ball valve to stop the water flowing in and empty the cistern by flushing. Disconnect the flush pipe and slacken the large nut holding the siphon assembly. Remove the metal link connecting the handle, lift the plate and remove the siphon. A new plastic flap valve can be slipped in before refitting the assembly.

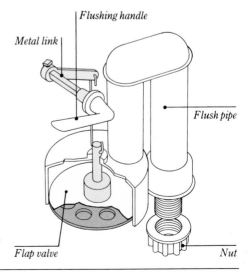

Flushing handle *Metal link* *Flush pipe* *Flap valve* *Nut*

· CHAPTER EIGHT ·

HEATING
AND INSULATION

Most homes require heating of some sort,
and today most people opt for central
heating. Once installed it is more efficient,
more versatile and usually cheaper to run
than an assortment of portable electrical
appliances. Other types of system include
electric storage heaters, gas fires and
wood-burning stoves.
Much of the warmth created by your
heating system disappears through the
walls, roof, windows and doors of your
home. Insulation offers a way of saving
this warmth, which in turn saves you
money on heating bills.

Heating

If you are planning a new central heating system, assess your requirements carefully. Before you consult a firm of heating engineers, work out which fuel you prefer, how many radiators you need and what form of control you require. Do not skimp at this stage. It is easier to fit plenty of radiators when the system is installed than to extend the system later. Remember that extending a system may not be as simple as adding a new radiator: you may also have to change to a bigger-capacity boiler. Most systems need little maintenance, and jobs such as bleeding a radiator and flushing out the system are quite straightforward.

When planning central heating, select a boiler that will give you sufficient capacity for your present and future needs. The other important factors when choosing a boiler are the type of fuel and where you are going to install the boiler. Some gas and oil boilers have a balanced flue, which both supplies air for combustion and removes exhaust gases. This type must be sited on an outside wall. Other types require a conventional flue, and in most cases a metal tube must be passed up the chimney to line the flue and divert exhaust gases. Most modern home boilers are compact; wall-mounted designs are available.

Types of fuel

Central heating systems can be powered by gas, oil, or solid fuel. Gas is generally the cheapest fuel and is very versatile. It can power a variety of boilers, including concealed back-boilers and compact wall-mounted models, some of which are available to fit in single kitchen cupboard units. Gas makes no

mess, does not have to be stored, and is easy to control, which makes it very economical.

Solid fuel is both widely available and competitively priced, but a lot of space is required for storage. The boilers require a flue and need regular attention – you usually need to top up the fuel supply at least once a day. The flues also need to be cleaned frequently. Control is less flexible than with gas or oil. Oil can vary in price and must be stored outside.

Types of control

The versatility of any central heating system is affected by the amount of control you are given over the heat. You should be able to control easily both the temperature and the time when the system is working.

Programmers and timers
These vary in sophistication, but most offer two separate on-off switchings every day and a manual override.

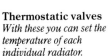

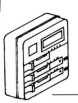

Room thermostats
Every system has a room thermostat to give overall temperature control.

Thermostatic valves
With these you can set the temperature of each individual radiator.

Tools and materials

The tools needed for repairs to your heating system are mainly wrenches and spanners, which you may already have in your tool kit. The only specialized piece of equipment that you may need is a small key used for bleeding radiators (page 187).

Adjustable spanners and wrenches are particularly useful for heating repairs which involve plumbing work, such as replacing a radiator or repairing leaking pipes. Most adjustable spanners are bulkier than the fixed-size open-ended or ring spanners, but they are also weaker and should be used carefully.

Adjustable ring spanners have a metal shaft with two pivoting heads, which tighten against the shaft as you turn the spanner. You do not have to remove the spanner between turns with this design.

Pipe wrenches are used for gripping pipes and rods; footprint wrenches have an adjustable pivot and grip the pipe when the handles are squeezed. Stilson wrenches are very strong, with spring-loaded jaws, but may damage the pipe. The self-grip or mole grip wrench has a locking device that allows it to grip flat or circular metal objects very firmly. The jaws are controlled by an adjusting screw, and extreme force is applied when the handles are closed.

Adjustable spanner

Multiple ring spanner

Adjustable box spanner

Self-grip wrench

Footprint pipe wrench

Front-rack wrench

Single-slot screwdriver

Stilson pipe wrench

Heating systems

A central heating system has a single heat source from which warmth is distributed to the places where it is needed around the home. The way in which the heat is circulated defines the type of system. Wet systems work by circulating hot water around a number of radiators; dry systems circulate warm air around the home through a network of ducts.

With wet systems, a central boiler heats water which flows to the radiators, where it gives off heat, and returns to the boiler. Most systems have two pipes, one to take hot water to the radiator inlets and one to collect water from the outlets. Older systems may have a single pipe to feed and collect water from each radiator in turn, with the drawback that only the first radiator receives water that is fully hot. The majority of systems also have a pump which sends the water around the circuit, but some older systems rely on the tendency of hot water to rise to create the flow. Small-bore pipes of ⅝in (15mm) diameter are usually used to link the boiler and the radiators.

Dry systems, on the other hand, use air to carry the heat around the home. The most common type uses a central boiler and a fan to blow heated air through ducts under the floors to each room. Most systems of this type need to be installed when the house is built, although there is one type, called a stub-duct system, which can be put in later. This discharges warm air to several points close to a central shaft. The other type of dry system is electric underfloor heating. This is also built in when the house is constructed. It consists of large heating elements laid in each solid floor slab which heat the air above.

Other heating systems

There is a wide choice of appliances that offer alternatives to central heating. These include an extensive range of portable electric heaters. They are efficient, easy to move and not expensive to buy, although electricity itself is a costly fuel to use for heating.

Radiant heaters are the cheapest. Convector heaters can take a long time to heat a whole room and are best used for providing

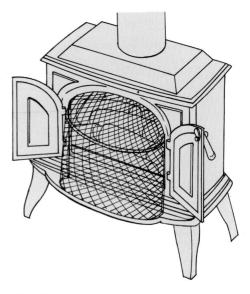

Wood-burning stove
Attractive and economical, this type of stove gives a good heat source if you have a plentiful wood supply. Old-fashioned and modern designs are available.

background heat. Like convectors, electric oil-filled radiators are also slow-acting. Fan heaters are probably the quickest-acting type, although they are not cheap to run and tend to make the air in a room very dry.

Electric storage heaters are a sophisticated form of convector heater linked to a timer. They are more economical than other forms of electric heating because they use cheap-rate electricity, but they suffer from the major disadvantage that their reserve of heat may be almost exhausted by the evening.

Modern gas fires provide a combination of radiant heating and convection. They must be connected to a suitable flue, to remove the by-products of combustion. Gas convector heaters can use a balanced flue, a short duct leading directly from the back of the heater through the outside wall. This means that gas convectors can be installed almost anywhere on an exterior wall.

Wood-burning stoves are worth considering if you have a regular access to supplies of cheap or free wood. Paraffin and bottled-gas heaters are useful as stand-by appliances.

Curing a leaking valve connection

If the leak is where the radiator is connected to a valve, try tightening the nuts linking the fitting to the pipe and the radiator. Use two spanners, one to tighten the nut, the other to brace the fitting as you work, so that you do not damage the pipework. If this does not cure the leak, isolate the radiator by closing the valves at either end, undo the connections and remake them. Put a large bowl under the valve to catch the water.

Connecting a radiator valve

1 *Close the valves at either end of the radiator, using a small spanner for the lockshield valve. Note how many turns are required to turn it off. Put a large, shallow container under the leaking valve to catch the contents of the radiator, and undo the coupling nut. Keep an eye on the water as it flows out, to ensure that it all goes into the container.*

2 *As water flows out, open the bleed valve slightly using a radiator key. When all the water has run out, clean the ends of the connector with wire wool and reassemble it. When opening the lockshield valve, use the same number of turns of the spanner as you used to close it. If you open it too little or too much, the radiators will heat unevenly.*

Bleeding a radiator

One of the most common problems with a wet central heating system is a radiator that is not as warm at the top as it is elsewhere. This is usually caused by a build-up of air in the radiator, due either to air dissolved in the water or to corrosion within the system which produces gas that collects in the radiators. The solution is to "bleed" the radiators by opening the bleed valve with a special radiator key, which will allow the air to escape. Make sure that you have a bucket and cloth ready to catch any escaping water, and close the valve again as soon as water starts to appear. The system will then top itself up from the feed-and-expansion tank.

Bleeding a radiator
Open the air-bleed valve at the top of the radiator using a special key. Close the valve as soon as water starts to escape. The radiator should now heat evenly.

Replacing an old radiator

Radiators sometimes leak along the bottom seam. If this is happening, rust or corrosion has probably taken hold inside the radiator and you should replace it. To remove the old radiator, start by closing both the valves and disconnecting the radiator at both ends (page 187), then lift the radiator off its brackets. You should remove its fittings, which may also be corroded. Replace the radiator with one of the same capacity. Do not attempt to fit a larger-capacity radiator, as your boiler may not be powerful enough to cope.

Use as many turns of the spanner to open the lockshield as it took to close it or the system may heat unevenly. As the radiator fills, air will escape from the bleed valve. Close this valve when water starts to escape from it.

Fitting a new radiator

1 *Fit two new couplers, a bleed valve and a blanking nut to the new radiator and lift it into place on the wall brackets.*

2 *Connect the radiator to the lockshield and hand valves and wind PTFE tape around each end to seal the connection.*

3 *Once all the connections are sealed, open the bleed valve and the two valves at the bottom so that the radiator fills with water.*

Repairing leaking pipes

If there is a leak in the pipework or where the pipe enters the radiator valve, drain the system. First turn off the boiler and the pump, and then stop water entering the system, either by tying up the ball valve in the feed-and-expansion tank or by turning off the appropriate stopcock. Attach a length of garden hose to the system draincock (usually placed near the boiler or on the lowest run of pipework) and take the hose to an outside gulley. Open the draincock with a spanner, then open the radiator bleed valves, starting from those on the upper floors, working down.

Replacing damaged piping
Cut out the damaged pipe and insert a new piece, joining it with compression or capillary joints. Refill the system by closing the draincock and bleed valves and restarting the water flow at the feed-and-expansion tank. When the system is full, bleed the radiators, as there will probably be air trapped inside.

Flushing out a central heating system

The feed-and-expansion tank will need to be drained and flushed through periodically, to remove any rust or sludge that could damage the pump or cause cold spots in radiators. The system is definitely in need of flushing if, to cure uneven heating, you find it necessary to bleed the radiators fairly frequently.

To flush out the tank, tie up the ball valve to close the water supply valve. Open the draincock and drain all the water out of the tank into a bucket or sink, using a length of hosepipe attached to the drain outlet. Close the draincock and untie the ball valve to refill the tank. Keep draining and refilling the system in this way until the water coming out of the draincock is reasonably clear. Finally, put anti-corrosion liquid into the water, to prolong the life of the radiators.

Flushing out a boiler

The amount of dirt that gets into your boiler will depend on the water supply, but as a general rule this is a job that will rarely need to be done. To drain the boiler, first turn off the burner, then shut off the water supply inlet to the boiler. Attach a hose to the drain outlet at the base of the boiler and put the other end into a sink, drain or several buckets, whichever is more convenient.

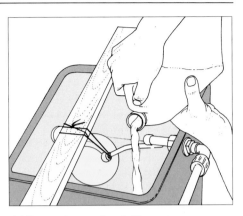

Adding anti-corrosion fluid
To introduce a corrosion inhibitor to the circulating water first tie up the ball valve in the feed tank. Drain off about 4½ pints (20 litres) of water through the draincock to empty the expansion tank and part of the pipework. Pour the recommended amount of corrosion inhibitor into the tank, restore the water supply to top up the system, and start the pump so that the water and the anti-corrosion fluid circulate.

Open the draincock and, when water begins to flow through the hose, open the bleed valves on the radiators. After the sediment has drained out, flush the boiler through with clean water from the water supply inlet. When the water draining out of the boiler is clean, close the draincock and refill the boiler. The burner can be turned back on once the boiler is full. Leave the bleed valves open until you hear water filling the pipes, then close them. You will need to bleed all the radiators once the system has been on for a few hours.

Replacing a pump

A central heating pump may become blocked as a result of corrosion within the system. If it fails, replace it with one of identical specifications. Disconnect the old pump from its power supply and drain down the system before unscrewing the couplings at each side and removing the old pump. Some pumps have isolating valves on either side which can be closed so that you do not have to drain the entire system. When you fit the new pump in place, fit new sealing washers. Reconnect the power supply and bleed air from the pump by turning its bleed screw.

POINTS TO REMEMBER

● Plan a new heating system carefully, taking the fuel costs and your own present and future requirements into account.
● Repair small leaks quickly; they will worsen if left unattended.
● Insulate loft pipes and lag hot-water tanks to avoid bursts and save fuel (pages 196–7).
● Flush out a wet central heating system once a year to remove any rust that may have accumulated, or it will affect the efficiency of the system and encourage corrosion.
● To improve the efficiency of radiators, fit a sheet of aluminium foil or radiator wall panels against the wall behind them, particularly on outside walls. This will prevent the heat from escaping through the wall and reflect it back into the room, thereby helping to cut your fuel bills.

Insulation

If your home has no insulation, you may be wasting three-quarters of the money you spend on heating. With proper insulation, it is possible to cut down this loss by almost half.

You can insulate almost every part of the structure of your home. Some areas are responsible for a greater heat loss than others, and so are more important to insulate. Certain areas are also easier and cheaper to insulate than others. For example, it is simple, and relatively inexpensive, to insulate a loft, which might be responsible for up to one-quarter of the entire heat loss. Windows lose less heat and double glazing is an expensive form of insulation. Of course, your own insulation requirements will vary according to the type of home you live in. In general, the more outside walls you have and the larger the area of the roof, the more insulation will be required.

Insulation can save you trouble as well as money. If you lag your pipes and water tanks, they will be unlikely to freeze and burst. If you also insulate your hot-water cylinder you will save money on heating water.

Reducing heating costs

An uninsulated house will lose heat not only through windows, doors and roofs, but also through walls and floors. Surprisingly, most heat is lost through uninsulated walls on a standard, two-storey, detached modern house, but the proportions lost through the different surfaces will vary with the type of building, whether it is a bungalow, house or flat.

Roofs
As much as 25 per cent of the heat can escape from an uninsulated roof. This can be cut to 8 per cent by the simple method of insulating the loft with glass-fibre blanket material or loose-fill insulation. Loft insulation can have the further advantage of protecting the water pipes in the roof. If they are covered by glass-fibre or loose-fill material, there is no need for them to be separately lagged.

Walls and floors
Potentially the greatest heat loss can occur through the walls. They can be responsible for losing as much as 35 per cent of the heat produced in the home. If you have cavity walls, the best method is to have the cavities filled with insulating foam by a specialist company. If this is not possible, you can dry-line the walls with sheets of insulated plasterboard.

Up to 15 per cent of the heat can escape from under the floor. One of the simplest ways to cut this down is to fill underskirting gaps by fitting strips of beading to the bottom of the skirting boards (page 117).

Windows and doors
Ordinary single-glazed windows can be responsible for losing 15 per cent of the heat. This can be reduced to 5 per cent by double glazing, but the cost of installation hardly justifies the saving on heat. But you can save some warmth cheaply by fitting draught excluders to windows that fit badly. Draughts under and around doors can cause a heat loss which you can reduce by making sure the doors fit well and have the necessary draught excluders fixed to the bottom of the door or around the door frame.

POINTS TO REMEMBER

• Whichever part of the home you are insulating, leave some ventilation – otherwise you run the risk of condensation.
• When insulating a loft, leave the area under the cold-water cistern uninsulated so that a little warmth comes through from the room below to prevent the cistern from freezing.
• Cover water tanks with a lid and insulate this with the same material as the rest of the tank.
• Wear stout gloves and a protective face mask when working with glass-fibre insulation material to avoid scratches and inhalation.
• Make sure that windows and doors are draughtproof, but maintain an adequate air supply for fuel-burning appliances, as they need a steady supply of oxygen.

PROPORTIONAL HEAT LOSS FROM A HOUSE

The diagram below shows the proportions of heat loss for which the parts of a typical house are responsible. The proportions vary for other types of building. A bungalow loses proportionally more heat through the roof and less through the walls, while in a ground-floor flat there is less heat loss through the ceiling than there is through the roof of a house.

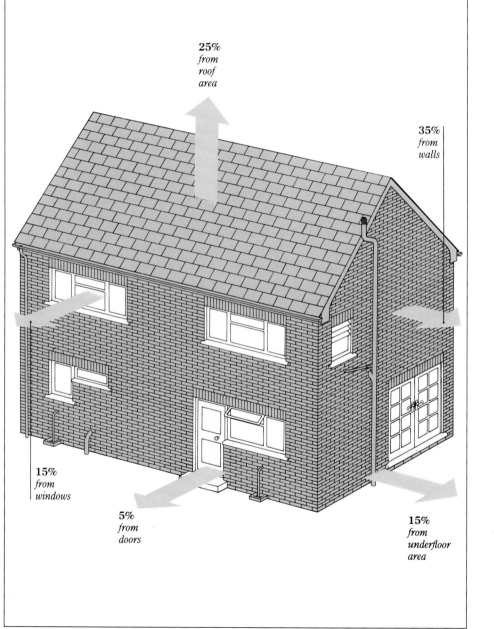

25%
*from
roof
area*

35%
*from
walls*

15%
*from
windows*

5%
*from
doors*

15%
*from
underfloor
area*

Types of insulation material

A wide range of materials is used for insulation. Some of the most common materials are glass fibre and expanded polystyrene, which have excellent heat-saving properties and are made up in various forms for insulating different parts of the home. Aluminium foil, which reflects radiant heat, is also a useful material. The types illustrated below are all simple to install, but there are some types of insulation, such as foam cavity-wall fillings, which require special equipment and should be installed by a professional. Although expensive, these are very effective and worth the investment.

Wall insulating materials

Builders use blown glass-fibre or other mineral-fibre material for cavity-wall insulation. This is often inserted in slab form during new building work. Beads of expanded polystyrene are also used. Some types of glass-fibre matting are backed with building paper, poly-thene or foil. This enables them to be stapled within the framework of a timber stud wall. Use expanded polystyrene wall veneer for insulating walls and reducing condensation.

Roof and loft insulation materials

The most popular method of insulating lofts to stop heat escaping through the ceiling is to lay glass-fibre matting. This consists of cotton-wool-like filaments and is supplied in rolls. It comes in several thicknesses, from 6in (15cm) and 4in (100mm) for new work to 3in (75mm) for adding extra material to areas that are already insulated. It is also ideal for lagging water tanks and cisterns. Similar mineral-wool matting is also available. Other alternatives in the loft are beads or slabs of expanded polystyrene and vermiculite, a material that expands to form spongy, lightweight granules. For lining the roof in a loft area, you can use either building paper or fibre boards.

Tank and pipe insulation materials

Glass-fibre matting is most commonly used for lagging tanks in lofts. For hot-water cylinders, jackets of insulating matting covered in plastic are the best solution. Buy one that is at least 3in (75mm) thick and that conforms to British Standards specifications. For pipes, use foam insulation, which surrounds the pipe and is taped into place. For corners and awkward areas, use self-adhesive pipe bandages, which are more flexible than foam insulation.

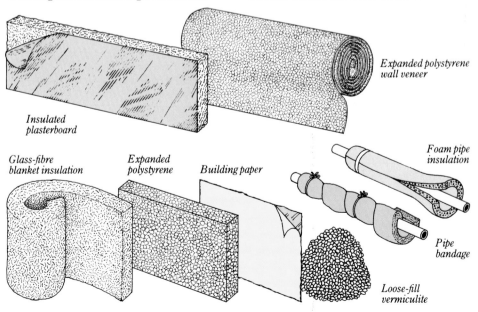

Expanded polystyrene wall veneer

Insulated plasterboard

Glass-fibre blanket insulation

Expanded polystyrene

Building paper

Foam pipe insulation

Pipe bandage

Loose-fill vermiculite

Types of draughtproofing

Heat loss from draughts can account for up to 16 per cent of the fuel bill. Double glazing can stop draughts from windows (page 146), but it is best to fit draught excluders.

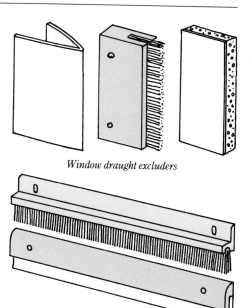

Window draught excluders

Door draught excluders

Doors
Draughts between doors and door frames can also be treated with draught excluder, provided that you use a durable type. Fit brush or tubular strips around the door frame. Position these so that the brush or soft tube touches the face of the door. For under-door draughts, treatments range from simple, self-adhesive plastic strips to two-part excluders with one part fixed to the threshold under the door and the other to the door itself.

Hinged windows
For hinged and pivoting windows, fit self-adhesive foam tape. Fix it to the rebate of the frame so that the window closes against it. On the hinge side, fit the foam to the side face of the frame – the same side on which the hinge flaps are mounted.

V-shaped strips of plastic, copper, or bronze are a good choice for hinged windows that receive a lot of use. These strips are compressed when the window is closed and form a seal. They are either self-adhesive or designed to be pinned to the fixed frame. For windows that are not opened in winter, press tubular strip into the cracks and remove it in the spring. It is reusable.

For frames with irregularly shaped gaps, use silicone rubber sealant, which comes in a

cartridge. This is squeezed into the gap around the frame, where it sets to the exact shape of the gap. The sealant will expand and contract with changing conditions. Its flexibility makes it ideal for metal-framed windows.

Sash windows
Nylon-pile strip is the best material to use for insulating draught-prone sash windows. It is supplied in a plastic or metal holder and you tack it around the frame so that the brush strip presses against the sliding sash. For sealing the meeting rails where vertical sash windows overlap, use sprung, V-shaped strips.

TIPS FOR INSULATING FLOORS AND CEILINGS

• The simplest method is to lay aluminium foil, or foil-backed building paper, beneath underlay or foam-backed carpet.
• Insulate a cold solid floor by laying polythene sheeting and polystyrene slabs, covered by a floor of tongue-and-groove edged chipboard.
• Insulate a wooden floor with fibre insulation board covered by hardboard, which will provide a

good finish for the floor covering (pages 118–19).
• If you do not want to raise the height of the wooden floor, insulate it by taking up the floorboards and inserting either glass-fibre matting or slabs of polystyrene cut to fit between the joists.
• Cover underskirting gaps with beading (page 117). This will prevent draughts, as well as

providing a finish to the edge of the floor.
• If there is no access to the floor above a ceiling, insulate the ceiling with material fixed between battens screwed to the ceiling, and cover the battens with panelling (page 109). A wood panelled ceiling will itself provide good insulation.
• Use thermal board for a heat-saving ceiling.

Lining a roof

In an old house with an unlined roof, draughts and blown-in rain can create problems. Lining the rafters with waterproof or foil-backed building paper can provide a solution. It will both keep out the rain and help cut heating bills. Foil-backed building paper is best. It provides much better standards of insulation than ordinary waterproof building paper.

Staple the lining to the rafters in horizontal strips, starting at the apex of the roof and working down to the eaves. If you are using foil-backed paper, the foil should face inwards. To stop the paper from tearing at the fixing points, cut small squares of cardboard, place these over the paper, and staple through them. Overlap adjacent strips of paper by about 2in (50mm). Before fixing the last strip, tuck pieces of building paper into the eaves between the rafters. This will ensure that any water that is blown under the tiles will run down the lining and into the eaves, where it will disperse. If you do not do this, water will build up and cause damage to the roof timbers. The whole roof space must not be sealed from the outside air, however. Make sure that there is a ventilation gap at the eaves. Poor ventilation will increase the risk of rot and subsequent structural damage, for which the remedies are both difficult and expensive.

Putting up the lining

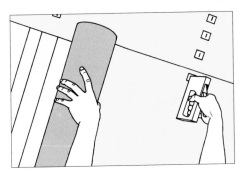

1 Staple through small squares of cardboard so that the paper is not torn by the staples.

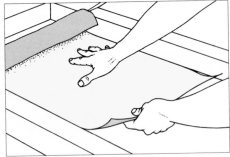

2 Tuck paper into the eaves to direct water away from the roof timbers.

Lining and insulating a roof

When you want the entire loft space insulated – for example, if you intend to convert the loft into a spare bedroom or occasional room – fit a more substantial insulating lining. This involves attaching strips of waterproofing material to the roof itself, then adding insulating material between the rafters and, finally, if a neat finish is required, putting up lining boards. Make sure that the roof is still adequately ventilated.

Before you start work, examine the roof timbers for signs of woodworm and dampness (pages 214–21) and take remedial action before fitting the insulation. If you are working in a loft with no floor, lay a few planks across the ceiling joists to form a temporary walkway so that you do not accidentally put your foot through the ceiling, and make sure that the loft is well-lit so that you do not miss your footing.

The best waterproofing material to use is roofing felt attached with battens tacked to the sides of the rafters, but building paper and plastic sheeting can also be used to prevent water from entering. The insulating material can be slabs of expanded polystyrene, cut to fit between the rafters and held in place by small nails driven into the sides of the rafters, or rolls of insulating matting tucked between the rafters and held in place with bamboo canes.

Fitting the insulation

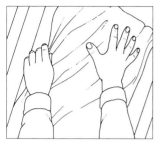 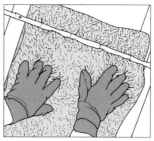 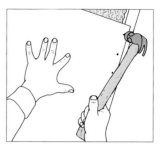

1 *Fix strips of waterproof material between the rafters running from the apex to the eaves. Leave an air space between the felt and the underside of the roofing battens.*

2 *Fit the insulating material under the lining. Polystyrene slabs are held by nails driven into the rafters; matting is tucked between the rafters and held with bamboos.*

3 *To give a neat finish, attach fibre insulating board, vapour-checked plasterboard or tempered hardboard to the rafters. Doing this will add to the insulating effect.*

Insulating a loft

Glass-fibre and mineral wool in roll form are the most popular materials for loft insulation because they are very easy to lay. Loose-fill materials are also available, but they are not suitable for use under unlined roofs, since the granules can be blown around by winds or the draughts created when you open the hatch.

Examine the roof timbers for signs of woodworm and damp and treat any problem areas, then vacuum the loft, taking care not to damage lath and plaster ceilings. When working in a loft, walk only on the tops of the joists, or lay a few planks along them. When laying blanket insulation, wear plastic or rubber gloves, and loose-fitting, long-sleeved clothing, to avoid contact with the skin. A dust mask is also an essential precaution.

Laying glass-fibre matting

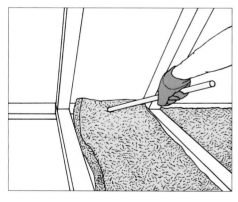 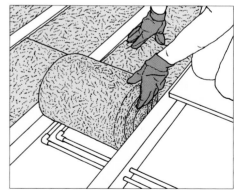

1 *Unroll the matting, butt-joining ends of rolls. If the roof is unlined, tuck the insulation into the eaves to cut out some of the draughts. If the roof is lined, keep the matting clear of the eaves to allow air to circulate and prevent condensation.*

2 *Take the matting over water pipes that run along the loft floor, so that you do not have to insulate them separately. Do not take the matting under water tanks: a little rising warmth from the room below will help to prevent them from freezing.*

Lagging tanks and cisterns

Water-storage and feed-and-expansion tanks in the loft can be insulated to prevent the water from freezing. Insulate the sides and tops, but leave the bases uninsulated, so that gentle warmth can rise from the rooms below. If you are insulating the loft, do not fit insulation under the tank for this reason. Cover the tank with a close-fitting lid, and fit the insulation to this, so that it does not fall into the water.

When fitting a lid, you will need to accommodate the expansion pipe that discharges over the tank. To do this, drill a hole through the lid and insulation beneath the point where the expansion pipe ends, and fit a large funnel in the hole. This will catch any water from the expansion pipe and direct it back into the tank without wetting the insulation material.

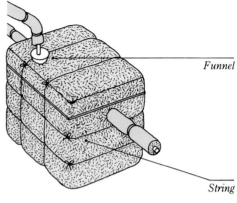

Funnel

String

Fitting glass fibre
Wrap the matting around the sides and hold it in place with loops of string. Make a wooden lid wrapped in polythene, and cover this in matting.

Lagging a hot-water cylinder
The heat losses from an uninsulated cylinder are very great, so ideally it should be lagged with a purpose-made jacket at least 3in (75mm) thick. If your cylinder has an old jacket, measure its thickness – the filling frequently disintegrates and drops down to the bottom of the jacket, leaving the hottest part of the tank almost uninsulated.

To fit a new jacket, drape the segments over the cylinder and loop them around the pipe at the top. Arrange them neatly around the pipes connected to the cylinder, and leave the top of the immersion heater uncovered. Loop the fastening tapes around the cylinder to keep the jacket in place.

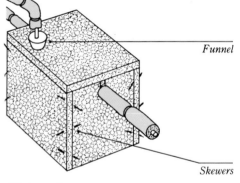

Funnel

Skewers

Fitting polystyrene
Slabs of polystyrene at least 1in (25mm) thick can also be used. Hold them in place with cocktail sticks or meat skewers pushed through the corners.

Lagging pipes

To help prevent them from freezing and bursting, insulate all exposed pipes in the loft space, including overflow and expansion pipes, even though these are normally empty. It is also worthwhile insulating long runs of hot-water pipes, especially if they are fitted under floors. This will keep the water from the hot-water tank hotter and will prevent the waste that occurs when hot water in the pipes cools down quickly, even when you have only drawn off a small amount at the tap.

The ideal material for lagging pipes is moulded foam, although you may also need to use blanket-type material at stopcocks, valves and tight or difficult corners. Some types of foam insulation have a press-to-close fastener which is very quick and easy to use. Otherwise, hold the insulation in place with adhesive tape.

Fitting the insulation

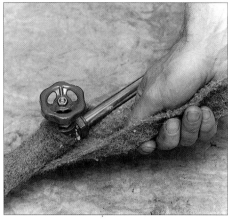

1 *Foam insulation can be bent around large angles, but at tight bends and elbows it will need to be cut to make a 45° mitre joint so that it fits properly. Similarly, cut the insulation at T-joints to make a neat 45° angle. If the type of foam insulation you are using does not have press-to-close fastening, hold the tubing in place with adhesive tape.*

2 *Pre-formed foam insulation can be difficult to fit properly at stopcocks and valves so that it does not leave a gap. In this case, use the traditional, blanket-type material, cut into strips and wound in an overlapping spiral around the pipe. The best way of securing this type of insulation material is by tying it at intervals with string.*

Insulating a basement

Insulation in the loft can prevent heat from escaping; in the basement it can prevent cold and damp from entering. Line the walls of the basement with a wall insulation material backed with building paper, plastic or foil for waterproofing. If your basement is the home for duct work for your central heating system or for long stretches of water pipe, it is worth insulating them individually as well as the space itself. Besides covering the water pipes, insulate the ducts as well by wrapping them in pre-formed foam or blanket insulation.

If the basement has a bare dirt floor, cover it with plastic sheeting. Roll it out, overlapping each strip by at least 6in (15cm). Use sand or bricks to keep it in place. If the basement is unused, insulate the ceiling in the same way as for lining and insulating a roof (pages 194–5). In heated basements, attach battens to the walls, then fix insulated plasterboard to the battens (pages 97–8).

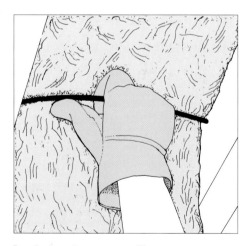

Insulating a basement ceiling
In an unused basement, use the same principle to fill the space between the ceiling joists as you did to insulate a roof (pages 194–5), holding insulating matting in place with bamboo canes. Never compress the material, as this will reduce its capacity to insulate. Wear rubber gloves to handle the matting.

· CHAPTER NINE ·

EXTERNAL REPAIRS, DAMP AND ROT

Roofs, gutters and external walls need to be kept in good repair to protect the home. Basic roofing maintenance and repairs, for example replacing tiles, are not difficult, but it is essential to pay attention to safety. Most people prefer to leave large projects involving external walls to a professional, but there are a few smaller jobs that are quite straightforward. The most useful of these are pointing (repairing the mortar joints in brickwork) and patching up areas of rendering and pebbledash.
Homes that are not well maintained are potential victims of damp. Signs of damp should be checked for regularly and treated immediately. Rot and woodworm need not be serious problems if they are diagnosed and treated in time.

Roofs and gutters

The roof is one of the most important parts of any building. If you keep it in good condition, it will protect your home from wind and rain, preventing damp from getting into the rooms below and rot from establishing itself in the timbers. Because of their exposed position, roofs often need repair. Tiles and slates get damaged and the covering of flat roofs starts to crack. The gutters, which are important in keeping rainwater away from the walls and stopping damp, should also be kept in good repair. Basic roofing repairs, such as replacing slates and tiles, are not difficult, as long as you pay attention to safety.

Tools and materials

The main tools used for repairing roofs are a hammer and nails for fixing slates and tiles in place, and a bricklayers' trowel for removing broken tiles. A slaters' rip is a more specialized tool, used specifically for removing old slates. An ordinary gardening trowel is useful for clearing blocked gutters, while the best way of cleaning swan necks and downpipes is with flexible drain-clearing rods. A screwdriver and screws are used for fixing gutter support brackets to the fascia board.

Ladders
To gain access to roofs and gutters, you will need a ladder or scaffolding tower and, possibly, a roof ladder. Choose a double or triple extending ladder. A triple extending ladder is easier to store and to erect single-handed. Aluminium alloy ladders are lighter than timber ladders. The treads should be wide enough for comfort and positioned so that they form flat surfaces when the ladder is at the correct angle. At the top and bottom of each section there should be rubber safety grips, so that the ladder cannot slip.

Scaffolding towers cost more than ladders, but they can be hired. They take longer to erect than a ladder and are more difficult to move, but they provide a working platform that is safe and secure. They are essential for extensive roof work and gutter replacement, and useful for other work on roofs, gutters, external walls and upper-floor windows.

Roof ladders are essential for work on all roofs except the flat, bitumen-felt type. They are usually made of light aluminium alloy, and have small wheels that enable the ladder to be pushed up the roof to the ridge. Roof ladders vary in length. Choose one that just fits the distance between the ridge and the eaves of your roof. They can be hired or, if you have a spare sectional ladder, you can convert it to a roof ladder using a bolt-on wheel-and-hook set.

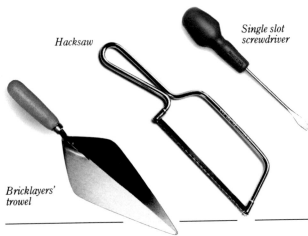

Hacksaw

Single slot screwdriver

Bricklayers' trowel

POINTS TO REMEMBER

- Always take care when working at a height – never try to cut corners to save time.
- Wear soft, rubber-soled shoes that give a good grip.
- For work on a roof, use a roof ladder – never walk directly on a slate or tile roof.
- For major jobs, such as slate or tile replacement and fixing new gutters, work from a scaffolding tower fitted with safety rails and toe boards.
- Support ladders and scaffolding with strong boards.

USING LADDERS

Ladders are potentially dangerous, so use them with care and follow these safety tips.
• Never lean out from the top of a ladder.
• Use a ladder stay to hold a ladder away from guttering and prevent it from slipping sideways – never lean a ladder directly on a gutter.

• Make sure that a ladder is resting at the correct angle and that the foot cannot move.
• Tie the top of the ladder with rope to a large eye bolt fixed in the wall or fascia board.
• When using a scaffolding tower, tie it with strong rope to an eye-bolt screwed into the brickwork.

Building a scaffolding tower
Put the tower on firm ground, or position the feet on thick, wide boards. When the tower is 3ft (1m) high, check with a spirit level that it is vertical. If it has screw feet, you can adjust the tower's stability easily. If not, pack one or more of the corners with strong, wide boards. If the tower is over 16ft (5m) tall, tie it to the building. Screw an eye-bolt into the brickwork just below the

eaves and secure the tower to this, using strong rope. Stabilizing outriggers provide good additional support for a tall tower. Fit safety rails and toe boards to the tower before you start to use it.

Using a roof ladder
Push the ladder's wheels up the roof towards the ridge. Then invert the ladder and check that the hook is secured firmly over the ridge of the roof.

Roof ladder

Scaffolding tower

Three-tier ladder

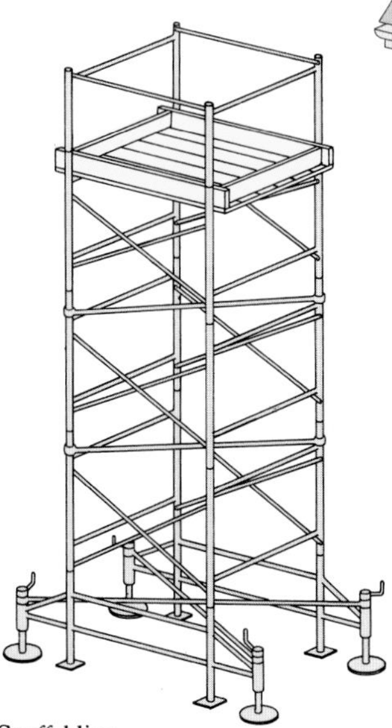

Using ladders
Place the ladder at the correct angle to the wall. For every 10ft (3m) of height up the wall, it should be 3ft (1m) away from the base. If the top of the ladder has a stay, allow for this when positioning it. Stand the foot of the ladder on firm, level ground. If the ground is soft, put it on a thick, wide board. Anchor the base of the ladder to a stake driven into the ground.

Types of roof covering

The main materials used for roofing are tiles and slates, which are often used on pitched roofs, and bitumen felt, which is used on flat roofs. Slates are often used for roofs on older houses. A slate roof in good condition will give excellent service. New slates are available for repairs, and secondhand slates in good condition form a cheaper alternative. Imitation asbestos-based slates are also suitable both for repairs, and for replacing a complete slate roof. Slates vary in size, so measure a slate from your roof before buying replacements.

Plain tiles are rectangular, have a curved surface and have two holes at the top for fixing nails. They usually also have two projections (known as nibs) at the top, which hook over the tiling battens to hold each tile in place. If the tiles have nibs, nails are only used for fixing in exposed places. Plain tiles are usually 10½×6½in (26.5×16.5cm), but there are many types and colours. At the eaves and ridges, special shorter tiles are used to maintain the correct overlap, and there are special wider tiles for use at the edges of the roof. Interlocking or single-lap tiles are sometimes made of clay, but concrete versions are common on new homes and in replacement roofs. Sizes and styles vary.

Flat roofs are often covered with bitumen felt. This material is also sometimes used on sloping roofs.

Slate roof construction
Each slate is fixed by two nails to a horizontal timber batten which is nailed to the rafters. To ensure that the covering is waterproof, alternate rows of slates are staggered and each row overlaps by half the one below it. At any place on the roof there are there-fore at least two thick-nesses of slates. Old slate roofs are rarely lined with underfelt.

Plain tile roof construction
Plain tiles are hung overlapping to give a double thickness. Their nibs hook over horizontal tiling battens which are nailed to the rafters. The tiles are attached to the battens with nails. Not every tile is nailed; every fourth row should be nailed, together with the tiles along the edges of the roof, at the eaves and at the apex.

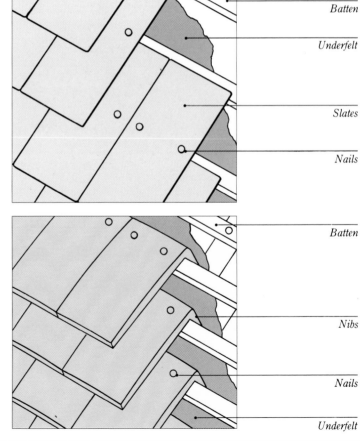

Batten

Underfelt

Slates

Nails

Batten

Nibs

Nails

Underfelt

Interlocking tile roof construction
These tiles are laid in a single layer and interlock at the edges. Like plain tiles, they have nibs that hook over the tiling battens and they are also attached to the battens with nails.

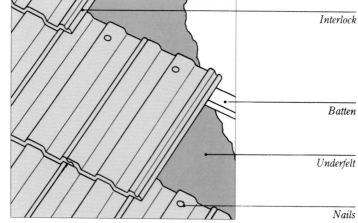

Interlock

Batten

Underfelt

Nails

Wood shingle roof construction
Overlapping sheets of roofing felt are fixed to the battens. The shingles are nailed in overlapping courses on top of this.

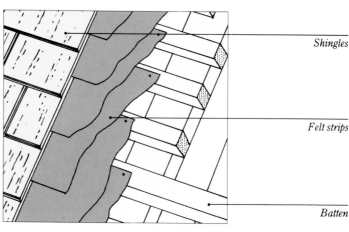

Shingles

Felt strips

Batten

Bitumen felt roof construction
On flat roofs the felt is usually fixed in three separate layers, bonded together with bitumen. The first layer is nailed to the roof boards and the subsequent layers are bonded to it. Flat bitumen-felt roofs are usually finished with light-coloured stone chippings that reflect the sun's heat.

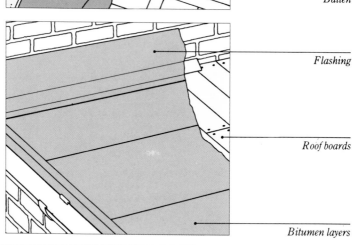

Flashing

Roof boards

Bitumen layers

Replacing a slate

Remove any broken pieces of slate with a slaters' rip. Slide it upwards under the broken slate, and move it to one side until you can feel the fixing nail. When you pull the rip down, the barb on the end will hook around the nail, pulling it out of place or cutting through it. Once both nails have been removed, pull out the remaining pieces of the damaged slate.

To secure the new slate in position, a strip of lead about 8in (20cm) long and 1in (25mm) wide is nailed to the roof timbers with 1½in (38mm) aluminium or galvanized nails, then bent back up over the lower edge of the slate. Double over the end of the lead strip so that it is not easily flattened, for example by melting snow sliding down the roof. The nail that fixes the lead strip in place should pass into the timber batten to which the lower row of slates is fixed.

Fixing the slate

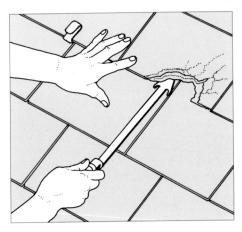

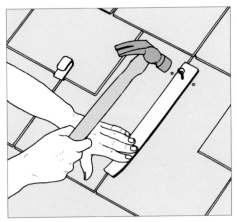

1 *Slide a slaters' rip up under the broken slate and hook the barb around one of the fixing nails. Pull the rip downwards to remove the nail. Repeat the process for the other nail, then pull out the remaining broken pieces of slate.*

2 *Cut a strip of lead to the right length and nail it to the timber batten between the two slates in the row below. Push the replacement slate into place and bend the protruding end of the lead strip back over the bottom of the slate to secure it in place.*

TIPS FOR REPAIRING BITUMEN-FELT ROOFS

● To recondition an old roof, first scrape off the stone chippings, then deal with any serious cracks or blisters, and, finally, recoat the roof.

● Recoat a roof by treating the entire area with a bitumen primer, adding a coat of roofing bitumen, pressing down an open-weave glass-fibre mesh, adding further coats of bitumen and, finally, applying chippings over the whole roof.

● Prepare an area for repair by scraping away the chippings and drying out the area, using a hot-air paint stripper.

● After preparing a cracked area, press down the crack firmly with a wooden wallpaper seam roller. Paint the area of the crack with flashing-strip primer and, when this has dried, press metal-backed self-adhesive flashing strip over the crack so that it is completely waterproof.

● If the roof is covered with chippings, paint the repair with liquid bitumen to seal it and sprinkle chippings over the surface of the roof while the bitumen is still wet.

● If there are blisters and bubbles, make two cuts at right angles across the centre of the blister, turn back the edges and treat it in the same way as a crack; the edges will overlap slightly when you press them down with the wooden roller, because the blister will have stretched the surface of the felt.

● Use patches of self-adhesive flashing strip to complete small bitumen-roof repairs.

Replacing a tile

To avoid leaks, you should inspect your roof regularly to check that there are no cracked or broken tiles. As well as looking at the roof from the outside, go into the loft while it is raining and check for leaks. Replace cracked, crumbling or broken tiles with new ones as soon as possible.

The method is similar whichever type of tile you have, except that interlocking tiles require extra fixing – either with 1¼in (32mm) aluminium alloy nails, driven through the fixing holes, or with clips. With both types of tile, make sure that you have removed all the broken pieces before fixing the new tile in position on the roof. When removing a broken tile, first lift the tiles in the row above, using two wedges cut from scraps of wood.

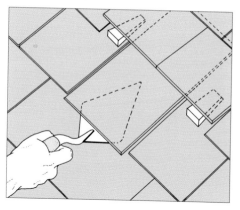

Fixing a plain tile
Slip the point of a bricklayers' trowel under the tile and lift it over the tiling batten. Push the new tile up until its nibs hook over the batten. Two wooden wedges lift the tiles in the row above.

Repairing flashing

Flashings seal the joints where a roof meets a brick wall. Traditional flashings are made of sheet lead or zinc. The top edge is usually tucked into the brickwork; if this pulls out, leaks can occur. Rake out the old mortar, tuck the flashing back into place, holding it firm with lead strips, dampen the joint and press fresh mortar into place. If there are tears, cracks or holes in the flashing, clean the areas with a wire brush, paint the surrounding areas with flashing-strip primer and, when this has dried, fit self-adhesive flashing strip to cover up the holes and create a waterproof seal.

Badly corroded flashing is best replaced with a self-adhesive strip. This involves preparing and priming the surface carefully first to ensure that the strip adheres firmly.

Fixing self-adhesive flashing strip
Press a strip of flashing to cover the roof by about 4in (100mm) with 2in (50mm) on the wall. Apply a second strip to cover 6in (15cm) of the wall and overlap the first. Flatten creases with a wallpaper seam roller.

Replacing a split shingle

Replace damaged shingles immediately, to prevent moisture from getting into the roof timbers. Remove the shingle, using a mallet and chisel to split it into narrow pieces. Work these free of nails, then slide a slaters' rip under the row above to remove the old nails. Fit a new shingle about ½in (12mm) smaller than the space to allow for expansion. Tap it into place, using a hammer and a wooden block to protect it. Secure the new shingle with galvanized roofing nails.

The guttering system

The gutters on a house are intended to catch all the rain falling on to the roof and to channel it towards a downpipe and into a drain. This system is needed to protect the walls and prevent water from running down them. Any blocked or damaged guttering could result in water pouring down the wall during heavy rain, which will encourage dampness and even mortar and brick decay.

The basic system consists of gutter channelling fixed so that it falls slightly towards an outlet. This is connected, by means of a swan-neck fitting, to a downpipe that either discharges directly into a rainwater gulley or stops just short of a gulley and discharges its water through a shoe, which directs the water away from the wall. Sometimes another pipe is fed into a downpipe by means of an open-ended, funnel-shaped inlet called a hopper.

Half-round guttering, available in both metal and plastic, is fixed to the fascia board at the eaves by means of brackets. Ogee-shaped guttering, made of cast iron or steel, is a more angular design with a flat back that allows the gutter to be screwed directly to the fascia board. Most modern guttering systems are made of plastic, because it does not rust and is easier to handle than cast iron. Sometimes, seamless aluminium gutters are used on new homes and in replacement work. Asbestos cement gutters were also once made, but are no longer available.

Gutter and downpipe sizes vary according to the area of roof they drain. It is important for gutters and downpipes to be large enough to deal with heavy rainfall. A generally adequate size for half-round guttering is 4in (100mm), with circular downpipes 2⅔in (68mm) in diameter. Square-section guttering systems usually have a greater water-carrying capacity than half-round systems. If you are uncertain about which size of guttering or downpipes to use, consult the manufacturer of the systems you are considering.

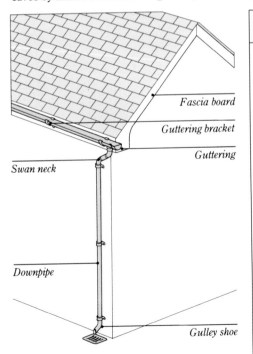

Fascia board

Guttering bracket

Guttering

Swan neck

Downpipe

Gulley shoe

TIPS FOR REPAIRING LEAKING GUTTER JOINTS

- Before starting to repair a leaking joint, clean out the gutter with a wire brush and allow it to dry thoroughly. This will provide the clean, dry working surface necessary if the repair is to be successful. If the join is next to a downpipe, make sure that you brush away from the opening, to prevent debris from falling down it.
- On a metal gutter, use non-setting mastic injected into the joint from the inside and outside, or remake the joint with strips of thick mastic or metal window putty.
- Self-adhesive flashing strip can also be used to seal joints in metal guttering. Stick the flashing on to the outside of the guttering.
- If you find a leaking joint in a plastic gutter, unclip the affected section and simply replace the sealing gasket.
- Cracked joints in plastic gutters can also be repaired with waterproof tape bound around the crack and 2in (50mm) beyond on either side.
- Check for blockages below a leak and clear them (page 207).
- Clean a leaking downpipe joint during dry weather with non-setting mastic or a waterproof mastic bandage.

Clearing a blocked gutter

If a gutter is overflowing or there is a severe water leak from a downpipe, there may be a blockage in the gutter, in a downpipe or in the rainwater gulley. Start by clearing out the gutter, using a garden trowel to scoop out the debris. To avoid pushing debris into the downpipe, work away from the pipe outlet towards the stop end. When you have cleared the gutter, pour a bucket of water along it from the stop end and check that it drains quickly. This test may highlight other faults, such as leaking joints. After clearing a metal gutter, let it dry and apply two coats of black bitumen paint to the inside.

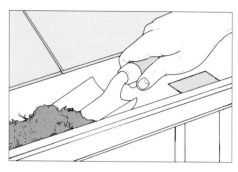

Scraping out the debris
When cleaning out a gutter, work away from the downpipe outlet. Use a garden trowel or, to make the job easier, cut a scrap of hardboard or plywood to the shape of the gutter to act as a scraper.

Clearing a blocked downpipe

Place a tray under the downpipe outlet to catch the debris and prevent it from being washed into the drain and blocking that. Clean the swan neck, either by removing it and flushing it through or by loosening the debris with drain-cleaning wire. Probe upwards through the rainwater shoe. Clear the straight sections of the pipe with a rag tied around a stone and secured to bamboo canes. If the pipe is often blocked, fit a wire cage over the top outlet to prevent debris from being washed down it.

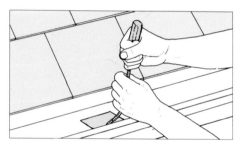

Clearing a swan neck
Try clearing the swan neck by pushing flexible drain-clearing rods down from the top. This may force debris down, so put a container under the shoe to prevent it from falling into the drain.

Repairing a sagging gutter

If the gutter has sagged so that it is lower than the top of the downpipe, water will not drain away properly and puddles will collect in the gutter. The most likely cause of this is that the fixing screws holding the gutter in position have corroded and worked loose and so are not supporting it properly. The solution is to put in new gutter-fixing screws. With an ogee gutter, you will need to drill new holes for the screws along the fascia board; with a half-round type, remove the old brackets and replace them with new ones.

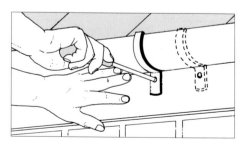

Refitting a half-round gutter
Cut through the old screws with a hacksaw blade and remove the old brackets. Put up new brackets with new fixing screws. Move the fixing positions along the fascia board slightly and drill new screw holes.

External walls

Brick, stone and concrete are the most common materials for external walls. They all vary greatly in appearance, although they can be disguised by the addition of rendering or pebbledash. Smaller jobs, such as pointing (repairing the mortar joints in brickwork) and patching up areas of rendering and pebbledash, are quite straightforward. It is also possible to paint external walls. Brick and stone walls are usually attractive enough to leave bare, without painting, but painting can considerably improve the appearance of a rendered or pebbledash wall. It is important to prepare the wall carefully (by brushing off stains and loose material, filling holes and applying primer) and to use a paint that is suitable for exterior masonry. When stains on walls are caused by damp, the damp must be treated.

Tools and materials

Tools needed for repairing external brickwork include a club hammer, which is ideal for heavy-duty work such as demolishing walls and driving a chisel, and a pointing trowel for repointing brickwork. A wooden float and plasterers' steel trowel are useful if you have to repair rendering.

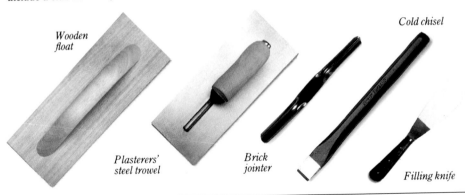

Wooden float

Plasterers' steel trowel

Brick jointer

Cold chisel

Filling knife

Repairing pebbledash

Cut away all the loose rendering with a bolster chisel and club hammer. Mix some rendering and apply it in two coats. While the second coat is still wet, throw on the stones, using a small trowel, until you have thoroughly coated the area to the same density as the rest of the wall. Press the stones to firm them into the rendering, using a small piece of board or wooden float.

If you intend to leave the wall as it is, you will have to choose stones to match. Otherwise paint the wall when the pebbledash is dry, to disguise the repair.

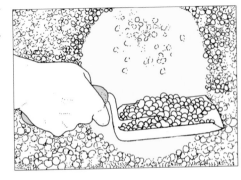

Putting on the stones
Using a small trowel, throw the stones so that they stick to the rendering.

External wall fault-finding

Brickwork can be stained in a number of different ways. Stains are quite often caused by damp, which you should eradicate, both to get rid of the stains and to prevent structural damage (pages 214–19).

Algae, moss and mould are caused by dampness, which you must cure to prevent them from recurring. Moss can be lifted with a scraper, while algae and mould are best removed by scrubbing with a stiff-bristled brush. When the wall is clean, apply a coat of fungicide solution. Wear rubber gloves while using this liquid. After 24 hours, wash and brush the wall with clean water.

To remove water stains, first cure the cause of the dampness and leave the wall to dry out. Seal the wall with a coat of alkali-resistant primer, to make sure that the stain is not visible through fresh paintwork.

With a dusty surface, treat the wall with a proprietary stabilizing solution. Brush on a generous coat and allow 24 hours before painting the wall. Remove ingrained dirt by scrubbing with a solution of sugar soap and

POINTS TO REMEMBER

- For a small area of pointing buy ready-mixed dry mortar.
- Before pointing or repairing rendering, scrape out all the loose material and dirt.
- Brush water into the joints before pointing – otherwise the moisture will be sucked out and the pointing will crumble.
- Keep the mortar mixture fairly dry – it should not run out of the joints.
- Make sure that you never wash walls that are covered with efflorescence.

water. Rinse off the solution and allow the wall to dry before painting. Small areas of loose dirt can be scrubbed off using clean water.

Efflorescence is a powdery deposit, sometimes spread over considerable areas, which is often found on new homes. It will disappear naturally as the wall dries out. The powder consists of salts from the brickwork or mortar which are drawn to the surface, together with moisture. You can buy a chemical treatment to cure this problem, but it is sufficient to clear away the powder with a dry brush as it appears. Do not try to wash the salts away, as this will only make the problem much worse.

Repairing rendering

Use a bolster chisel and a club hammer to cut away all the loose rendering. Mix some render, using one part Portland cement, one part hydrated lime in powder form and six parts clean plastering sand and water, to make a butter-like, lump-free consistency. Render mix sets quickly, so make no more than you can apply in about twenty minutes. Before applying the rendering, dampen the wall well.

Applying the rendering

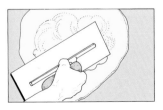

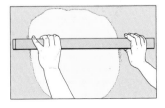

1 *Use a trowel to spread the first coat on to the wall and work upwards from the bottom of the patch, pressing the lower edge of the trowel hard against the wall and sweeping it up with firm strokes.*

2 *Take the first coat to within ¼in (6mm) of the surrounding render surface. Before the render sets, use the side of the wooden float to score lines on the rendering, to create a key for the next coat.*

3 *Apply the second coat on the following day, working from left to right and from top to bottom. Draw a piece of straight-edged wood across the repair to level the patch with the surrounding rendering.*

Pointing a wall

Old mortar that is cracked and loose will let in rainwater and cause dampness on interior walls. Chisel away all the old mortar and brush out all the dust from the cracks between the bricks, taking care not to damage them. If it is only a small area of your brickwork that needs repointing, buy a small bag of dry mortar mix, to which you only need to add water. If the area to be pointed is larger, it is worth buying your ingredients separately and mixing your own mortar of one part cement, one part lime and six parts soft sand. Add a little water, but keep the mix on the dry side – if it is too runny, it will be weak and may run down the wall, which will cause stains.

In hot weather, keep the joints soft for a few days by sprinkling water on them. If you do not do this, the heat will dry the joint out too quickly, so that it will start to crumble.

Applying mortar

1 *First chip away the old mortar, using a slim cold chisel and a club hammer. Avoid damaging the bricks. Brush all the flaking pieces of mortar and dust from the cracks.*

2 *Immediately before pointing, brush out the joints with water, to ensure that water is not sucked from the mortar by the dry bricks, causing it to crack or crumble again quickly.*

3 *Using a hawk and pointing trowel, press rounded slices of mortar into the vertical joints. Trim away the excess with the edge of the trowel, then press mortar into the horizontal joints.*

4 *Finally, trim off the excess mortar from the horizontal joints with the edge of the trowel, matching the finish with the pointing on the rest of the wall to disguise the repair.*

Repairing timber cladding

Wooden cladding on external walls often cracks or splinters and is subject to rot. If only a small section of cladding is damaged, it is quite easy to cut out part of a board and replace it. If a whole board is badly cracked or rotten, it is best to take it out and replace it with a new one. The easiest cladding to repair is the type made from simple, overlapping bevelled boards. Tongue-and-groove and shiplap boards can also be replaced in the same way, but you will need to cut the tongue or lap off the board to make it easier to fit.

It is important to finish off the repair carefully, to prevent water from entering behind the boards and restarting the rot. Use wood putty to fill the gaps at each end of the board, and then protect it with either a wood preservative or primer and paint to match the rest of the wall.

Repairing damaged cladding

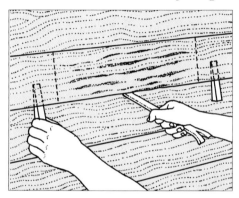

1 *Tap in wedges behind the damaged section, levering it out with a wrecking bar. You will need to slide a hacksaw blade up under the board to cut through the nails holding it to the wall.*

2 *Using a thin piece of wood to protect the board below, cut through the exposed part of the board with a tenon saw. Finish cutting the top part of the board with a pad saw.*

3 *Split the damaged board into pieces with a chisel to make it easier to remove. Take out the wedges. Hammer the replacement board in place, using an offcut of wood to protect it.*

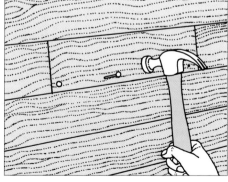

4 *Nail the new section of the boards above and below and fill the gaps at the side with wood putty. Finally, protect the board with either a wood preservative or primer and paint.*

Repairing a wooden sill

Wooden window and door sills tend to rot and need repairing or replacing. If the damage only affects part of a sill, use a tenon saw or jigsaw to cut out a wedge-shaped section around the damage, taking care not to cut into the rest of the frame. Remove the section with a chisel. Cut a replacement piece of wood and, when it fits exactly, glue it in place. Drill and countersink holes for screws 4in (100mm) apart. Screw the section firmly in place and plane it flush with the rest of the sill. Finally, prime the replacement piece and paint the whole sill to protect it.

If the rot or damage extends along the whole sill, you will need to replace it. Measure the old door or window sill before removing it and cut a new hardwood sill to fit. If the sill extends under the door jamb, you may need to remove the door stop to make the repair.

Replacing a wooden sill

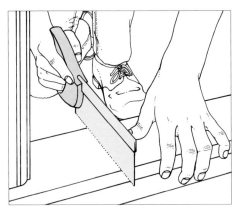

1 *Remove the existing sill by cutting out the middle with a tenon saw, and then sliding out the two end sections. Vacuum the area thoroughly.*

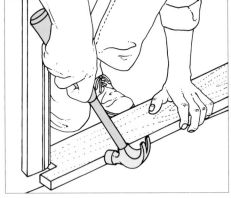

2 *Gently tap the new sill in place. Do not force it into position; if the fit is too tight, pull the sill out again and trim it until it fits.*

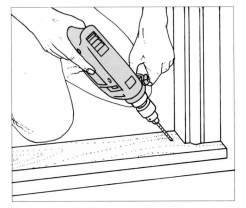

3 *Sills are usually made of hardwood so that they last for longer than softwood. To avoid splitting the wood, you will need to drill small holes for the nails.*

4 *Drive 2½in (65mm) nails in to fix the sill in place. Fill the nail holes and sand them flush, then prime and paint the sill to protect it from rot.*

Shutters

Shutters keep in more heat than curtains or blinds and, if they fit well, they can also help to insulate the house and keep out window draughts. In addition, well-made shutters can help to make the home more secure.

There are several different designs. Folding types for interior use range from elegant Georgian and Victorian shutters, which tuck into the window reveal when not in use, to plantation shutters, which are louvred and based on the type used on houses in the southern United States. The louvres can be adjusted to let in more or less sunshine as you wish. Sliding shutters are available for both interior and exterior use. Other types of exterior shutters are hinged, made of either tongue-and-groove boards or louvred. If you intend to fit sliding or hinged exterior shutters on upper floors, make sure that any casement windows open inwards.

Folding shutters
Georgian and Victorian window shutters folded back into recesses at the sides of the window by day. At night, the shutters were unfolded and secured with iron bars. These shutters are usually panelled and fold back concertina-fashion – an idea that you can copy for any windows that are set in deep recesses. Plantation-style shutters, which also fold, are intended to filter light rather than to contain heat, and the slats are adjustable to admit different amounts of light.

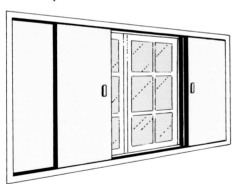

Sliding shutters
These come in two forms. One type slides within the window recess, guided by runners like those used for secondary double-glazing. With this arrangement, one shutter will slide behind the other and, when they are in place, only part of the window can be unshuttered at any one time. But it is easy to remove the shutters completely by lifting them out of their runners. The other type slides on runners fitted outside the window recess and can be pulled free of the window along the walls to either side.

Sliding shutters can also be fitted from floor to ceiling if they are attached to the type of track intended for use with sliding doors. The shutters can run either in a single groove or one behind the other.

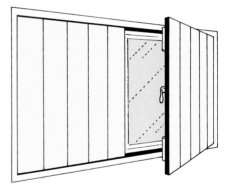

Exterior shutters
On the ground floor, external shutters can be closed and opened from the outside and secured with a hasp and padlock. On the upper floors, external shutters are difficult to use unless the windows open inwards. One compromise is to fit working shutters downstairs and decorative fixed shutters on the floors above.

Exterior shutters are available ready-made, but the choice is limited and, as it is important that the shutters match the style of the house, it is better to make your own. Tongue-and-groove board is a good material to use for making up into panels. In warmer climates, louvred shutters can be kept securely closed and the windows left open during the day, to shade the room while allowing air to circulate.

Damp-proofing

A ny home that is not well maintained is a potential victim of damp. The roof, walls, windows and doors are battered by the elements, the floors and walls may be attacked by rising damp from below the ground, and inside the house the plumbing pipework represents another potential source of dampness. The result can be anything from spoiled decorations to a very damp environment, which can cause poor health for the occupants of the home and major structural damage as timbers start to rot. Another source of dampness in the home is condensation, caused by moisture that gets trapped in a room. It is often produced in a building that is well insulated but poorly ventilated.

To protect your home from rising damp, a damp-proof course – a waterproof barrier in the brickwork – must be fitted in the walls. Although most people prefer to leave the job of installing a damp-proof course to a specialist company, there are a number of other ways in which you can protect your home from damp. Many of the potential sources of damp are in parts of the home that are not normally noticed, for example, the tops of chimney stacks and the guttering system. It is essential to keep these areas in good repair, and many of the jobs involved, such as keeping the gutters unblocked, are quite simple. The difficulty is being aware of the causes of damp, so that you can make repairs before much damage is done.

The causes of damp

A damp patch in a room can usually be linked quickly with a nearby structural fault. For example, a wet patch at the top of a wall in an upstairs room may be caused by a leaking gutter or downpipe, while a stain on a wall near a window could be caused by rain being blown through a gap between the frame and the wall. But sometimes a damp patch inside the home is some distance from its cause on the outside of the building. For example, water leaking through a crack in a roof tile can drip on to the roof timbers and run along for several yards before dropping on to the ceiling below.

Damp patches on a ceiling may be caused by leaks, overflows or bursts in the plumbing system. Keep pipes and tanks well insulated to help prevent them from freezing and bursting in the winter.

Slipped, cracked or missing tiles or slates are the likely problems on the roof. The best way to identify cracks is to climb into the loft on a rainy day and look and listen for any drips. Check for and replace any defective flashing. Failures in gutters and downpipes are caused by blockages which should be cleared. Rusted metal or faulty joints will result in leaks, and a sagging gutter will not drain properly.

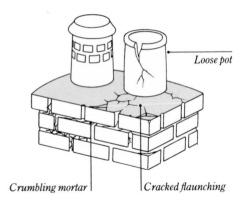

Loose pot

Crumbling mortar | *Cracked flaunching*

Chimney stacks
Damp patches on a chimney breast can often be traced to rainwater coming down the chimney. This is frequently a problem if the fireplace has been blocked up without allowing for ventilation – the flue must be ventilated to keep it dry. Repoint mortar joints between the bricks of the chimney stack that show signs of crumbling and replace any missing patches of rendering or pebbledash. Replace or refix loose or broken pots soundly into the flaunching that surrounds their bases. If the flue is no longer in use, insert a special capping pot that lets in air but keeps out rainwater. Any cracked flaunching should be repaired to keep out damp and to keep the chimney pots securely fixed. Replace any loose or defective flashing; this seals the joint between the base of the stack and the roof.

CAUSES OF DAMP

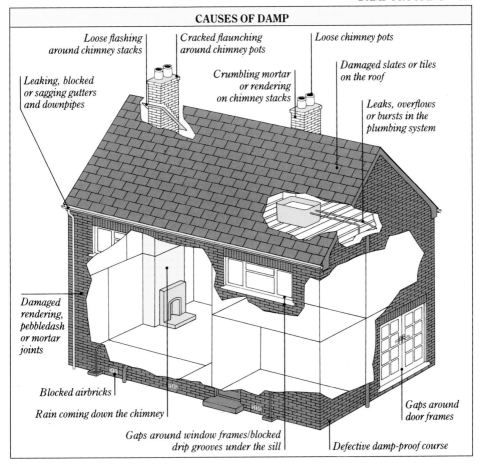

Loose flashing around chimney stacks

Cracked flaunching around chimney pots

Loose chimney pots

Leaking, blocked or sagging gutters and downpipes

Crumbling mortar or rendering on chimney stacks

Damaged slates or tiles on the roof

Leaks, overflows or bursts in the plumbing system

Damaged rendering, pebbledash or mortar joints

Blocked airbricks

Rain coming down the chimney

Gaps around window frames/blocked drip grooves under the sill

Gaps around door frames

Defective damp-proof course

On the walls, look for cracked, loose or missing patches of rendering or pebbledash. Defective mortar joints between bricks and cracked or flaking brickwork can also admit rainwater. Make sure that there is a clear gap, preferably at least 6in (15cm), between ground level and the damp-proof course. The damp-proof course must not be bridged by a pile of earth or a rockery.

Check for gaps between the frames of doors and windows and the wall where rainwater could seep through. These should be filled to keep out draughts as well as water. If rainwater blows underneath a door, fit a weatherbar. Clear out the drip groove in the underside of the sill; if it is blocked, rainwater can run across and soak through the wall.

Airbricks
Keep these clear and make sure that earth is not piled against them to restrict the airflow. They provide essential ventilation for timber floors.

Defences against damp

Most homes built in the last fifty years have damp barriers built into their masonry and so are less likely to suffer from damp than older buildings. Modern homes have cavity walls made up of two layers of bricks with a space between them, which prevents rainwater from coming through. The two layers are joined together at regular intervals by metal wall ties. At the base of each wall, about three or four courses of bricks above the ground, the damp-proof course is fitted. This prevents moisture from rising up the wall. If the damp-proof course is faulty, or if one has not been installed, moisture will gradually rise several feet up the wall, causing considerable damage. Faulty damp-proof courses cannot be repaired, but a new one can be installed. Houses with timber ground floors are usually less prone to damp problems in the floor. If damp does occur, it is usually the result of a faulty damp-proof course or because airbricks on the outside walls are blocked. Airbricks ensure that the floor timbers are ventilated and dry, so make sure that they are kept clear.

If the roof, gutters and damp-proof course are kept in good condition, your home should be free from damp. But damp-proof barriers can break down and poor building practices can also cause problems. During bricklaying, mortar can fall into the cavity, land on the metal ties and form a bridge for damp to get to the inner layer of the wall. Another problem can be an imperfect link between the damp-proof membrane in a concrete floor and the damp-proof course in the walls.

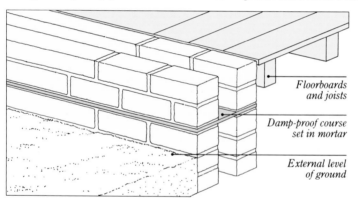

Damp-proof course with a timber floor
When there is a cavity wall and a timber floor, the damp-proof course is normally a thin strip of impervious material such as slate or bituminous felt. It is fixed in the mortar above ground level but below floor level.

Floorboards and joists

Damp-proof course set in mortar

External level of ground

Damp-proof course with a concrete floor
Solid concrete floors incorporate a sheet of waterproof material that stretches right across the building and links with the damp-proof course in the walls.

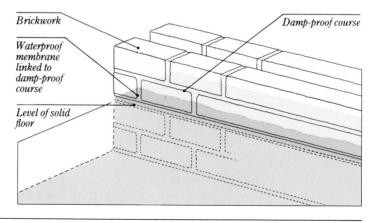

Brickwork

Waterproof membrane linked to damp-proof course

Level of solid floor

Damp-proof course

Damp-proof treatments

In most homes, especially modern houses, damp is prevented from rising more than a few inches up the wall by a built-in damp-proof course. A faulty damp-proof course cannot be repaired, but a new one can be installed. As well as the basic slate damp-proof strip, there are two other types: porous tubes and chemical injection. Slabs of bitumen are normally used instead of slates.

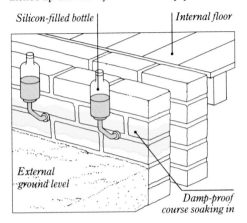

Silicon-filled bottle | *Internal floor*

External ground level

Damp-proof course soaking in

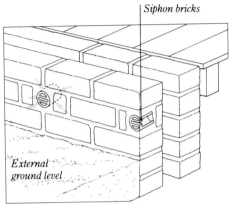

Siphon bricks

External ground level

Chemical injection
Drill a series of ½in (12mm) diameter, downward-sloping holes into the wall and introduce a silicone-based liquid. This is either put in under pressure from special injection equipment or left to soak in from special bottles fixed in the holes. You can hire equipment for pumping in the liquid.

Porous tubes
Earthenware tubes are fixed into the wall at an angle so that they slope downwards to the open air. Any moisture in the wall is absorbed by the tubes and cooled; this increases its density, causing it to flow outside and be replaced by fresh air drawn in, like a series of small airbricks.

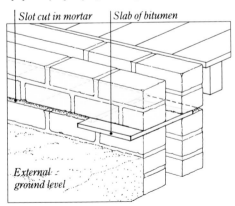

Slot cut in mortar | *Slab of bitumen*

External ground level

Bitumen slabs
A special chainsaw that can cut masonry is used to make slots in the brickwork. Slabs of bitumen are then inserted into the slot, making a damp-proof barrier which is similar to the traditional slate damp-proof course.

POINTS TO REMEMBER

- Make regular checks of outside walls at ground level to ensure that the damp-proof course is not bridged and ineffective.
- Keep gutters clear and in good repair to avoid leaks and penetrating damp.
- Examine regularly the condition of chimney stacks, pots and flaunching, and repair any faults or cracks straight away.
- To avoid condensation, ensure that ventilation is adequate, particularly if your home is well insulated and heated.
- Check the condition of your roof by examining it from inside the loft during heavy rain.
- Keep airbricks clear of all obstructions to ensure good sub-floor ventilation.
- If your house is very exposed to bad weather, or the bricks are porous, it may be worth protecting the walls with rendering, pebbledash or timber cladding.
- It is a good idea to check the outside of the roof regularly to make sure that there are no slipping or damaged slates or tiles.

Damp-proofing with chemicals

The basic method depends on the thickness of your wall. If it is 4½in (11cm) thick, drill holes 3in (75mm) deep in one side only. If the wall is 9in (23cm) thick, either drill from both sides or drill deep holes in two stages working from one side only. Drill a 3in (75mm) hole and insert some of the chemical solution, then deepen the hole to 7½in (19cm) and insert the rest.

If you are working on a solid wall from the inside, remove the floorboards nearest to the wall (pages 114–15) and remove any damp plaster to expose the brickwork. Drill the holes about 6in (15cm) below floor level and about the same distance above the ground outside. Once the solution has soaked in, the bricks become saturated and will sweat. Before replastering the inside wall, let it dry out completely: allow one month for each 1in (25mm) of wall thickness.

Putting in the chemical solution

 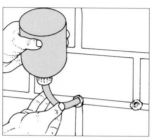 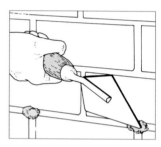

1 *Angle the holes when you drill so that they slope downward towards the centre of the wall.*

2 *Use the special bottles to apply the fluid, leaving it to soak into the gap in the wall.*

3 *When the cavity has been filled, remove the bottles and plug the holes with mortar.*

Types of condensation control

The key to curing condensation is to get the right balance between heat and ventilation in the home. But it is important to cut down the sources of condensation. Avoid paraffin heaters and unflued gas and oil heaters, reduce steam by covering saucepans and turning off the kettle as soon as it has boiled, and if possible avoid drying laundry inside the home.

Extractor fans
Portable fans simply recirculate the air in a room to keep it cool; an extractor fan will give you precise control over ventilation. Some simply suck air from the room; reversible types can be switched to remove air or blow air into the room from outside. Some types have shutters that automatically close when the fan is switched off, to prevent draughts. Make sure that you choose a fan that will be the right

size for the room. A huge fan in a small room creates a "wind-tunnel" effect, while a fan that is too small is almost useless. Before you buy a fan, calculate the cubic capacity of the room (length×width×height). Buy a fan that will give the right number of air changes per hour in a room of that cubic capacity. Kitchens need about 15 air changes per hour; bathrooms need about six changes per hour. Fit the fan as high as possible and preferably opposite a door so that air is drawn right across the room. If there is a solid-fuel-burning appliance in the room, allow sufficient air replacement for the fire, so that air and fumes are not drawn back down the flue and into the room.

Thermal insulators
Lining cold walls and ceilings with sheets of expanded polystyrene before wallpapering will eliminate condensation. Thermal insulation plasterboard, cork tiles, or tongue-and-groove edged boards will have the same effect. Special

anti-condensation emulsion paint is also available. This absorbs moisture when the humidity is high and releases it later when the air is drier.

Cooker hoods

These deal with cooking smells and steam very efficiently. There are two types. One extracts the steam directly to the outside air, the other filters the air and recirculates it into the room. Some models offer a choice between recirculation and extraction.

Dehumidifiers

When condensation is a serious problem, use a dehumidifier. This is a machine that works in a way that is rather similar to a refrigerator. It draws warm, damp air over a cold coil so that the water condenses, and then passes the air over a warm coil so that it is warmed again as it passes back into the room.

Ventilators

An open fire needs adjustable ventilators – ideally situated on either side of the hearth and fitted in the floor. With a solid floor, the ventilator should be fixed over the door leading to the hall.

A timber floor also requires ventilation. Airbricks are set in the walls for this purpose and they should be kept clear at all times. Blocked fireplaces should also be ventilated with an airbrick or a grille.

To power source *Motor* *Grille* *Controls*

Extractor fan

Extractor fans enable you to have precise control over the ventilation in a room and are useful in cutting down condensation.

Windows

Double-glazing with sealed units will solve the problem, although other types of double glazing may produce misting between the panes. This can be alleviated by placing a moisture-absorbing substance (such as silica gel) in the gap. The crystals need replacing regularly. Draughtproofing the inner window may provide a permanent solution to condensation. If this does not work, try ventilating the air gap between the panes by drilling downward-sloping holes in the outer frame and filling them with glass fibre. The best solution may be to fit a fan or vent.

Testing for condensation

Condensation is caused when moisture builds up and gets trapped inside a room. The most common sources of moisture in the home are cooking, washing and the breath of people in the room, but the presence of these factors alone does not cause condensation. It is when a home is so well insulated that moisture cannot escape that condensation occurs.

It is sometimes difficult to distinguish between condensation and structural damp. A steamed-up window is a sign of condensation, but a wet patch on a wall may be caused either by damp or condensation. If the wet patch

appears after rain, the problem is likely to be penetrating damp. If it develops on a cold, dry day when the windows are steaming, condensation is probably the cause.

If you are not certain of the cause of a damp patch, you can do a test with a piece of aluminium foil. Dry out the damp patch with a heater and stick a piece of foil to the wall with adhesive tape. Ensure that the edges are well sealed. If moisture reappears on the visible surface of the foil, it has obviously originated from within the atmosphere in the room, and the cause is condensation. If the moisture comes back on the face of the foil next to the wall, then it is caused by dampness coming through the wall.

Rot and woodworm

Rot and woodworm are the enemies of timber. If left unchecked, both can destroy woodwork completely. Where structural timbers are concerned, the damage can be far-reaching and very expensive to put right. So if there is any evidence of rot or woodworm in your home, eradicate it immediately.

It is possible to deal with small, isolated attacks of rot and worm yourself, provided that you are sure to treat or replace all the affected timber. But if the infestation has taken hold and spread, seek professional advice and assistance. A specialist company should offer a long-term guarantee on its timber treatment.

Types of timber infestation

Rot and woodworm may not be immediately apparent because they tend to start in places that cannot be seen – in concealed timbers beneath floorboards, in cellars and in lofts. But once you examine the timber closely, the signs of infestation are obvious.

Woodworm
Woodworm is the general name for a number of wood-eating beetles, of which the furniture beetle is the most common (page 15). The beetle lays its eggs in cracks in the wood. The larvae hatch out and tunnel through the wood for several years. Evidence of an attack is provided by the holes from which the beetle larvae emerge, together with small piles of dust around exit holes.

Dry rot
Attacks of dry rot usually originate in areas that are damp and poorly ventilated – floor joists, cellars and under sinks are common places. These places tend to be hidden, so the first sign may be a musty smell or the cotton-wool-like material appearing from below floorboards, skirtings or panelling. Once you have exposed the area, the dry rot will be obvious. The timber that has been attacked will be dark brown and cracks will have developed, breaking up the surface into squares. If touched, the wood will crumble easily.

The danger with dry rot is that it will transfer from wet to dry timbers. It does so because it is able to produce water-carrying roots that can be up to ¼in (6mm) in diameter. These roots can travel anywhere, even

Dry rot
First, matted fungal strands appear, which develop a silver-grey skin possibly tinged with streaks of lilac or yellow. A texture like cotton wool forms, followed by a pale grey, corrugated fruiting body resembling a pancake and surrounded by rust-red spore dust.

Wet rot
This form of rot has yellow-brown streaks or patches, accompanied by string-like strands that grow in a fern shape on timber or damp plaster. The wood becomes brownish-black and cracks along the grain, though criss-cross cracking is sometimes caused instead.

through brickwork, until they find dry timber which they can dampen to provide ideal conditions for growth.

Wet rot
The areas where dry rot can develop may also be prone to wet rot. In timbers such as window frames and doorsteps bubbling paintwork is sometimes the first clue to wet rot. Though equally serious, wet rot is easier to treat than dry rot, because it is always found in damp timber. But if you have wet rot, a dry rot attack may well be developing nearby.

Treating rot and worm

The initial cause of rot is dampness somewhere in the house structure. Wooden window and door frames are susceptible to rot, especially at the joints between the uprights and the sills. Leaking downpipes can cause penetrating damp, creating conditions ideal for both wet and dry rot. Rot may take hold in leaking roofs, also underneath floors where ventilation is poor. Rooms such as kitchens and bathrooms, where condensation is a problem, are particularly susceptible to rot. Woodworm attacks roof timbers, floorboards and joists as well as furniture.

The first thing to do is to cure the cause of the dampness (pages 214–19); there is no point in treating rot until the cause is removed. Once this is done, act quickly to treat the rot.

Treating woodworm

Woodworm attacks are most likely in rough-sawn, unplaned timber in lofts, understair cupboards and cellars. You should also check floorboards by taking up every fourth or fifth board (pages 114–15) and inspecting the underside. The most obvious sign of woodworm is small holes in the surface.

It is often difficult to tell whether the attack has died out or whether the problem is current. A current attack can be identified by light-coloured dust around the holes, but since structural timbers are often dirty, this can be difficult to see. If you are in any doubt, treat the timber by cleaning it and brushing, or by spraying it with woodworm fluid. If you find woodworm in the loft, treat all the loft timbers. You need not treat the other timbers in your home, such as floorboards, unless they too show signs of woodworm. If the damage is extensive, call in a specialist company.

Treating dry rot

Dry rot can have a devastating effect on a building, and treatment should be carried out with the utmost care and efficiency. If structural timbers have been affected, it is usually safer to leave the job to a specialist company than to attempt it yourself. Timber should be cut away at least 3ft (1m)

USING A WOOD-REPAIR SYSTEM

If only a limited area of wood has been damaged by wet rot, eradicate the rot and repair the timber, using a commercially available wood-repair system. This should contain a wood hardener, a filler and preservative tablets to prevent further decay.

A small area takes only about one to three hours to treat. Begin by digging away the worst of the rotten wood and then brush the quick-drying wood hardener over the entire area. You can then rebuild the shape of the wood with filler, before drilling holes into the surrounding wood and inserting the preservative tablets.

beyond the edge of the dry rot. If water-carrying roots have passed through the walls, plaster and mortar joints must be hacked out. If dry rot is discovered below the floorboards and in the joists, about 4in (100mm) of soil may have to be removed. As soon as the affected area is cleared the debris should be taken away and burned. If this is not done, red spore dust could recontaminate the property. Surface spores and strands can be destroyed simply by using a blowtorch.

The treatment involves spraying a fungicide over the affected areas and 7ft (2m) beyond. Two coats of fungicide are required, the second applied after the first has dried. New timber should also be coated and sawn ends dipped in timber preservative before fixing.

Roots in the walls are killed by drilling downward-angled holes, ½in (12mm) in diameter, on both sides of the brickwork. They should be 6in (15cm) deep and drilled at 2ft (60cm) intervals. The holes should be filled with fluid, which will eventually soak into the brickwork and destroy the roots.

Treating wet rot

Where there is a large amount of damage, it is best to leave treatment to a specialist company. First, any rotten timber should be cut out and the surrounding wood treated with two liberal coats of dry-rot fluid or wood preservative. New timber should also be treated with preservative. Small areas of damage can be repaired with wood filler. Where only a small amount of wood has been affected, make good the damage with a wood-repair system.

Chapter Ten

Home Safety
and
Security

Safety in the home is largely a matter of common sense. If you keep your electrical and gas installations in good repair, take steps to prevent fire and make sure that children are not able to reach any of the potentially dangerous items in the home, you will avoid most accidents. Find out how to turn off your electricity and gas supplies and read the instructions on emergency action for gas and fire emergencies.

There are two main ways in which you can protect your home from intruders. The first is simply to follow a number of simple procedures – such as locking the door when you leave the home, cancelling deliveries if you go away, closing windows when the house is empty, and leaving on lights and a radio when you go out in the evening. The second way is to fit extra equipment, such as window locks, better door locks and even alarm systems and security grilles. If you do both of these things, you will greatly reduce the risk of your home being burgled.

Safety in the home

Certain areas of the home are more prone than others to accidents. Most people know that the kitchen presents many potential dangers, but there are other parts of the home where accidents can easily happen if you allow them to do so. But by simply thinking in terms of safety and using items in the proper way, you can avoid most accidents. The important areas are electrical and gas equipment, which should be serviced regularly, and open fires.

DANGER AREAS IN THE HOME

Electrical appliances
Always switch these off after use, and unplug them where possible.

Electric blankets
These can be damaged if they get creased. Have them serviced regularly by the manufacturer.

Electrical wiring
Ask a qualified electrician or the electricity supply authority to check the wiring regularly.

Multiple adaptors
Avoid using these where possible. If you have to use adaptors, make sure that the socket outlets are not overloaded.

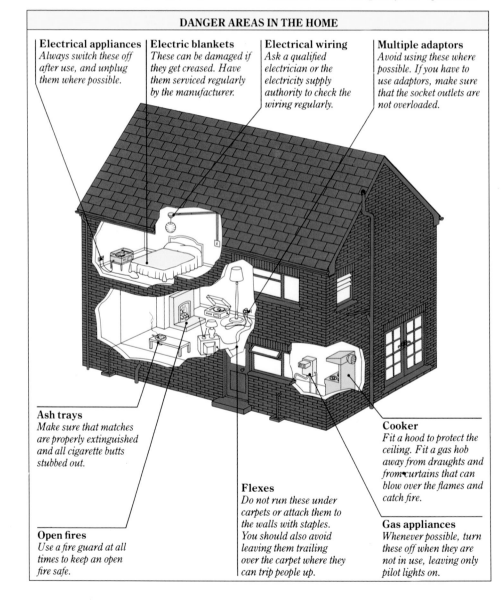

Ash trays
Make sure that matches are properly extinguished and all cigarette butts stubbed out.

Open fires
Use a fire guard at all times to keep an open fire safe.

Flexes
Do not run these under carpets or attach them to the walls with staples. You should also avoid leaving them trailing over the carpet where they can trip people up.

Cooker
Fit a hood to protect the ceiling. Fit a gas hob away from draughts and from curtains that can blow over the flames and catch fire.

Gas appliances
Whenever possible, turn these off when they are not in use, leaving only pilot lights on.

Types of fire-fighting equipment

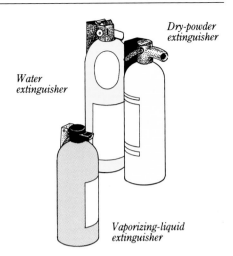

Dry-powder extinguisher

Water extinguisher

Vaporizing-liquid extinguisher

Small domestic fire extinguishers are useful, but they have a limited capacity, so they should be used promptly. For this reason it is worth installing a smoke alarm to warn you quickly of any fire. These alarms are battery-operated and can be mounted unobtrusively on a ceiling.

One of the most useful pieces of equipment is a fire blanket. Keep one in the kitchen, where it is ideal for putting out a fire of burning fat. Turn off the heat, cover the pan with the cloth, and allow the pan to cool before taking it outside. Never use water on a pan of burning fat or oil.

Fire extinguishers

Water extinguishers are coloured red. They are suitable for combustible materials such as wood and paper, but not for fires involving electricity, fat or oil. Water comes out of a jet, which should be directed at the base of the fire and kept moving across the burning material. Damp down the embers to prevent reignition.

Coloured blue, dry-powder extinguishers can be used on all fires, particularly those involving oil, fat and electricity. Choose one with at least 2lb (1kg) of powder. Direct the jet

of powder at the nearest edge of the fire and drive the flames away from you with a quick, sweeping action. The material can be removed with a vacuum cleaner, although you should discard contaminated liquids and clean electrical equipment thoroughly before you attempt to use it.

Vaporizing-liquid extinguishers are coloured green and can be used on any small fires, particularly electrical fires. The extinguisher should weigh at least 1½lb (680g). It is used in the same way as a dry-powder extinguisher.

EMERGENCY ACTION

If you suspect a gas leak:
• Extinguish all flames immediately, including pipes and cigarettes.
• Open all doors and windows to disperse the gas.
• Turn off all gas taps.
• Check whether an unlit appliance has been left on.
• Check whether a pilot light has blown out. If this is the cause of the problem, wait until the smell of gas has completely gone before relighting it.
• Do not operate electrical switches, as they can spark and ignite the gas in the air.
• If you suspect a leak, test for it using a fairly strong solution of concentrated washing-up liquid;

this will bubble where the gas is leaking. Call the Gas Board to come and repair the leak.
• Have any repairs to gas appliances carried out straight away by a gas fitter.
• If an obvious source of the leak cannot be found, turn off the entire supply at the gas meter and call the gas emergency service to deal with it straight away. Do not ignore it, thinking that you are mistaken; you may be right in your suspicion.

In case of fire:
• Get everybody out.
• Close all the doors behind you.
• Call the fire brigade.
• If anyone is still in the building,

tell the officer in the first fire engine: on no account should you go in yourself.

If you are trapped in a room:
• Check the temperature of the door handle – if it is hot, the fire is probably burning immediately on the other side, so do not open the door.
• Use blankets or mats to prevent smoke from entering under the door.
• Even in a smoke-filled room, 2–3in (50–75mm) immediately above the floor will be clear of smoke, where you can breathe.
• Go to the window and shout for help. Do not jump: wait for the rescue services.

Safety in the kitchen

More accidents occur in the kitchen than in any other room in the home. This is mainly because kitchens are busy places that are full of potential hazards to children, such as hot fat, sharp knives and jagged tins. So it is important to take precautions in the kitchen, especially if you have young children. Design the kitchen so that pans of hot fat or kettles of boiling water do not normally have to be carried across the room. If possible, keep young children out of the kitchen, using a safety gate on the door, especially when you are preparing or cooking food. Teach children safety habits from the very beginning.

Keep knives well out of the reach of children, whether on a wall rack or in a drawer. Bottles and cans should also be kept out of reach, well to the back of units and working surfaces. It is a good idea to fit a guard rail to a kitchen hob, to prevent children from reaching up and grabbing pan handles and upsetting the boiling contents over themselves. An alternative is to turn the handles away from the front and sides of the hob, but if you do so, be careful not to scald yourself or burn the handles when you are using more than one ring on the hob. Use an automatic kettle that switches off when the water boils. Keep bottles of disinfectant, bleach and other cleaning fluids on an upper shelf, well out of the reach of children, and preferably also out of their sight.

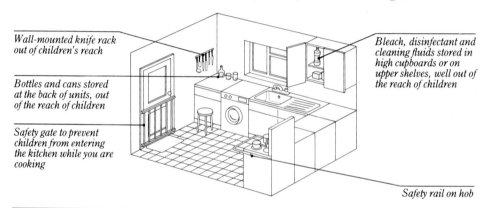

Wall-mounted knife rack out of children's reach

Bottles and cans stored at the back of units, out of the reach of children

Safety gate to prevent children from entering the kitchen while you are cooking

Bleach, disinfectant and cleaning fluids stored in high cupboards or on upper shelves, well out of the reach of children

Safety rail on hob

POINTS TO REMEMBER

- Get to know the positions of your main gas and water supply taps and the main emergency switch, so that you can turn them off in an emergency.
- Keep heater air grilles clear.
- Never drape clothes over a heater or leave them where they could fall on to the appliance.
- Always keep radiant fires at least 3ft (1m) away from curtains and furniture.
- Make sure that flues and chimneys used for gas and other fuel-burning appliances are kept clear of soot and debris.
- Keep paraffin heaters where they cannot be knocked over.

- Turn paraffin heaters off before refilling them.

Electricity
- Check your electrical equipment regularly, or get a qualified electrician to check it.
- Make sure that plugs have the correct fuses: you will need 3 amp for up to 700 watts and 18 amp for 700 watts–3kW.
- Ensure that all electrical equipment is correctly earthed.
- Use flex correctly; do not trail it across floors, run it under carpets or staple it to walls, floors or skirting.
- Only buy new electrical

equipment that bears the BEAB mark of safety.
- Have electric blankets serviced every two years by the manufacturer, regardless of how often they are used, and keep them uncreased and dry.

Gas
- Take prompt action if you detect any smell of gas.
- Have gas appliances serviced on a regular basis.
- Always have gas appliances professionally repaired.
- Change old-style, open-flue water heaters for modern, balanced-flue types.

Preventing burglary

Although it is impossible to make your home absolutely secure from the most determined thief, you can protect yourself and your possessions by following a few simple procedures. Mark valuable items with an ultraviolet pen, make a note of serial numbers, and take photographs of valuable items. Do not keep valuable papers such as house deeds in your home, and make sure that you are properly insured.

Security devices
There are several items that you can fit to your doors and windows to improve the security of your home. Mortise deadlocks should be fitted to the doors – the simple night latch found on most doors is not adequate, as it can be forced very easily. On windows, locks should also be fitted. In addition, it may be worthwhile installing a burglar alarm or, in a high-risk area such as a basement window facing on to a street, a security grille or bars.

Care with keys
Do not leave any identification on your keys and avoid carrying keys in a purse or handbag that may contain some form of identification. Even if a lost key is returned, a copy may have been made. If you lose a key that is marked with your address, the only solution is to change the locks or lock mechanisms. Do not be lured from your home by a call, purporting to be from the police, telling you to collect your lost keys. As you go out the caller may let himself in.

Dealing with callers
Beware of confidence tricksters. Old people, in particular, should be on their guard against callers who say they are from organizations such as the local authority or the welfare department. Many such ploys are used to gain entry to homes, and even if nothing is removed on the first visit, thieves can call again to take specific items. You should leave a strong door chain in place while you establish callers' identities, if possible telephoning their office to check on them. Ask them to come back later while you check their credentials.

Another common trick is for one caller to keep you talking at the front of the house while someone else enters through the back door.

SECURITY TIPS

- Glazed doors: There is a further security risk with any glazed door. It is worthwhile changing to a door made completely of wood, but if you want to keep the glass, replace it with strengthened glass (page 147) or fit a grille or bars.
- Doors: A solid hardwood door fitted with a mortise deadlock is best in terms of security. Lock all doors at night and whenever you leave your home unoccupied. Do not leave door keys where they can easily be found. Avoid such places as on a string attached to the back of the letterbox and under a paving stone, brick, flowerpot or doormat. When moving into a new home, it is worth removing the locks and fitting new ones.

- Doorstep evidence: Items such as milk bottles, newspapers and letters near the front door give a clear sign that a house is unoccupied. Notes left for tradesmen are also clues, so cancel all deliveries verbally whenever you go away.
- Lights: You can ask a neighbour to help by coming in each day to switch on and off lights and perhaps a radio or television set, to make the house look as if it is occupied. Alternatively, use a time switch to turn lights on and off. Light-sensitive or timer switches, which turn on one light when it gets dark and turn it off again after a set time, are widely available, inexpensive, and a worthwhile investment.

- Windows: Fit window locks and keep all your windows locked at night and whenever there is no one at home. Lock even small windows – burglars will push a small child through an open window who can then open other windows or doors.
- French windows: Because of their large area of glass and the way they fasten together in the middle, French windows are difficult to secure. Hinge bolts on both sides and mortise rack bolts in the middle will make them much more burglar-proof. An alternative is to fix security grilles or bars to either the inside or the outside of the French window. These will be secure against all but the most determined burglar.

Types of window lock

Windows provide a common route of entry and any that are accessible from the ground, via a tree, or by climbing on to a roof, should be well protected. Burglars do not normally climb in through broken glass. If they break glass it is usually in order to open a window or door through which they can then gain entry. To stop this, fit window locks. Alternatively, you can use immobilizers, which are attached to the existing catch and stop it being moved.

You should always remove the keys from window locks, but it is advisable to leave them nearby. Put them where they cannot be reached or seen by a would-be intruder, but where they can be quickly found from the inside in an emergency such as a fire.

Immobilizers for casement windows are available for fitting both to the cockspur handle and to the casement stay. Locks for casement windows include screws and locking bolts.

Metal casements can also be secured with a sliding wedge lock, which fits in the channel of the opening frame, and by stay screws, where the locking screw passes through one of the holes in the stay and holds a bar under the stay retainer. Sliding wedge locks are hidden and cannot be tampered with, so are ideal for metal windows, while stay screws are particularly useful for vulnerable metal fanlights.

A range of devices is available for locking the two halves of a sash window together or to prevent either half from being moved. The types include acorn stops, sliding window locks, dual screws and sash locks. Make sure that you buy locks that fit the width and thickness of the window frames and remember that some types allow you to leave the window locked slightly open for ventilation.

French windows present other security risks that can be overcome with bolts. Mortise rack bolts should be fitted to the top and bottom of the part that opens first; hinge bolts should be fitted on both parts.

Types of door lock

Outside doors provide a common route of entry for intruders and should be well protected with locks and bolts. On the front door two locks are needed – an automatic deadlocking latch to hold the door closed while you are at home and a mortise deadlock to keep it secure when you are out. The most important feature of a deadlock is that, when the key has been turned, the bolt is immobilized so that it cannot be forced back out of the door jamb.

You can get either a single- or a double-throw mortise deadlock. With the double-throw type, you can turn the key a second time to throw the bolt further into the staple, making it more secure. The deadlocking latch and the mortise deadlock will provide extra security if they are placed some distance apart on the door. The best positions are one-third of the way from the top and one-third of the way from the bottom of the door. Do not rely on a simple night latch to protect an outside door, as it is very easy to force from the outside.

Back-door protection

Burglars are more likely to attack a rear door than the front door, so this too should be well protected. Fit a mortise deadlock with a handle. For extra security, the back door should also be fitted with bolts. The simplest to fit are tower and barrel bolts. These are useless if they are fixed with weak screws into thin wood. In addition, they can be opened easily if they are installed near glass that can be broken. Mortise rack bolts are more secure. Fit one near the top and another near the bottom of the door frame.

Outward opening doors pose another security problem. The hinges are exposed, so that it is easy to knock out the hinge pins and force the door open. You can solve this problem by fitting two hinge bolts on the hinge side of the door, one a third of the way from the top, the other a third from the bottom. With this type of fastening, a fixed bolt engages in a hole cut in the door frame, so that the door cannot be lifted off its hinges. It also prevents the hinges from being forced. If you have a cat-flap, check that keys and bolts are out of reach if you put your arm through it.

Mortise locks

A mortise deadlock is the most secure type of lock for outside doors. It fits into a slot cut in the door. When locked, the bolt shoots across into another slot in the door post and the mechanism locks the bolt in position so that it cannot be forced out. Narrow versions are available for glazed doors, and two-bolt types for back and side doors. If you are working on a door that is hanging in its frame, wedge it open or ask a helper to hold it steady while you cut the slot in the door.

Fitting a mortise lock

1 *Mark the fitting position carefully, using the lock as a guide. With the door held firmly in position, drill a series of holes with a hand brace using a ½in (12mm) drill bit.*

2 *When you have drilled all the holes to the required depth, use a chisel to cut away the remaining wood and insert the body of the lock into the recess to check that it is a good fit.*

3 *Mark the size of the lock's face plate on the edge of the door and cut a rebate with the chisel. Next, cut a hole for the key. You may need a pad saw to make the hole the right shape for the key.*

4 *Finally, mark the position of the striker plate on the door post, cut a slot in the same way that you did for the lock and fit the plate as securely as possible, using long screws.*

Types of alarm system

Further protection for your home can be provided by a burglar alarm system. You should fit an alarm in addition to window and door locks. An alarm system operates from a central control panel and works from the electrical supply or from a battery. Usually, you set the system to operate as you leave home. There is a delay of about a minute to allow you to set the alarm and leave, and there is a similar delay to let you switch it off when you return. Many systems also incorporate a second switch, located in a hidden position inside the house, from which the alarm can also be operated.

With the most elaborate alarm systems, the wiring connects to a series of magnetic contacts attached to doors and openable windows. One half of the contact is fixed to the frame and the other half to the window. If the window is opened, the two parts separate, the electrical contact is broken and the alarm bell on the outside of the building is activated. As a second line of defence, magnetic contacts can also be fitted to internal doors. In addition, alarm-activating pressure pads can be installed under the carpet at points where a burglar is likely to walk. There are many magnetic alarm systems available, some of which you can fit yourself. They are not difficult to put in, but care must be taken to conceal all the wiring, pressure pads and magnetic contacts.

Another type of alarm system, which you can fit instead of or as well as a magnetic type, uses infra-red rays to throw an unseen barrier over a wide area. Similar alarms are available that use ultra-sonic waves and microwaves. The bell sounds when the barrier is broken. Some of these alarms can be triggered by draughts and normal air movements, although the best models are far more dependable.

A common problem with alarms is that they often sound by accident – because they have been set incorrectly, because they have been activated by children or animals or because the wind has blown open windows or doors. An alarm will only be effective if you and your neighbours always take it seriously.

Other security equipment

There are several items that you can fit in addition to window and door locks to improve the security of your home. Door viewers and door chains can protect you when answering the door to unknown callers. The various security grilles and bars that are available offer protection from all but the most determined thief and are particularly useful in areas where the risk of criminal activity is high. Viewers and chains are easy to fit, but bars are best fitted by a professional.

Door viewers and chains
A simple barrel tube containing a one-way lens giving a panoramic view allows you to identify callers before opening the door. Buy a viewer that is the right length for the thickness of the door. Fitting is simple: a hole is drilled through the door and the two halves of the viewer are slipped through and screwed together. A door chain may deter some burglars, but since it is only as strong as its securing screws, it is not difficult to force most chains by kicking the door. Door chains do have some value, however, and if you are going to fit one, use long screws rather than the small ones that are often supplied, and fit it in such a way that nobody outside can reach through the gap and take the chain off. Some chains are lockable and some models also incorporate an alarm that reacts if the chain is forced.

Grilles and bars
Mild steel bars can be fixed externally or internally. If they are used externally, the ends of the bars should be embedded 2–3in (50–75mm) deep in the brickwork. Inside, bars should be attached to a flat metal frame which can be bolted to the brickwork around the window. The bars themselves need to be strong enough to withstand forcing. A locksmith will be able to advise you on your own particular requirements, but you will usually need bars at least ⅜in (15mm) in diameter, spaced at intervals of 5in (12.5cm).

Working areas and equipment

A workshop or working area – whether a shed in the garden, a corner of the garage or simply part of a room in the home – is the ideal place to store the tools needed for home maintenance and improvement. The basic essentials for a work area are good light night and day, plenty of storage space, a work bench and a vice or clamps to hold the work steady. The area should also be free of damp. A number of socket outlets just above bench height will be needed for power tools, and heating will be needed in the winter. A fire extinguisher positioned near the door is a worthwhile safety precaution in the workshop.

A fixed worktop bench with cupboards or shelf space below is ideal for one end of the workshop. Bench-mounted tools, such as a drill stand or a small grinder, can then be permanently mounted. It is useful to fix a vice to one end of the bench. If you do not have the space for a permanent workbench, a folding bench is very useful and easily stored.

Timber and other materials need to be held still when they are being sawn, drilled or otherwise prepared. A bench-mounted vice is ideal for this and the best type for general purpose is the woodworkers' vice. Some types are permanently mounted to the bench, others can be clamped on and removed when necessary. The jaws are usually 7 or 8in (17.5 or 20cm) wide, with an opening capacity of about 8in (20cm).

Folding bench
This portable bench incorporates full-width jaws that act as a vice. The bench can also be used as a simple table, trestle or saw horse. When folded, it measures 31½×28½×7½in (80×72.5×19cm).

WORKSHOP STORAGE

● Hand tools: Store in accessible wooden racks, or use plastic or wire tool-hanging clips fixed on to sheets of perforated hardboard.
● Saws, hammers and pincers: Hang them on racks made by driving nails or dowels into battens fixed above the bench.
● Chisels, files and screwdrivers: Store them in a simple rack made from a strip of plywood about 3in (75mm) wide with holes drilled in to support the tool handles.
● Power tools: Cover benchmounted tools with cloths. Store portable tools in lockable cupboards or on shelves. Keep the cables wrapped around the tools when they are not in use.
● Cutters, blades and tool attachments: Drill and auger bits are best stored upright in wood blocks drilled with holes or small clear plastic boxes.
● Hardware: Store nails, screws, nuts and bolts in jars or labelled tins. Fix the lids of screw-top glass jars under shelves for the contents to be visible. Cutlery trays can also be used.

GLOSSARY

Air lock Pocket of air in the plumbing system preventing water from circulating properly.

Amp (ampere) Unit measuring the amount of current flowing in an electric circuit.

Ball valve Device that maintains a pre-set level of water in a tank or cistern.

Beading A narrow, decorative edging strip, usually of wood.

Bevel A slanting edge, such as the shape of a chisel blade.

Blind stitching An upholsterers' stitch used to pull stuffing to the side of the seat in order to form a firm edge.

Butt joint Where two edges touch without overlapping.

Buttons Forms covered with fabric are used to pull down deep upholstery. If you do not want to cover them yourself, a local upholsterer or supplier may be able to cover them.

Calico This thin, unbleached fabric is used to cover the second stuffing when upholstering chairs.

Cambric A cheap, black fabric stretched across the undersides of chair seats in order to give them a neat finish.

Came Lead framing used for holding stained glass.

Cantilever A rigid structure fixed at one end and overhanging its support at the other.

Capillary joint The type of joint used with copper tubing. The fitting is slightly larger than the pipe, leaving a small space that is sealed with solder.

Chalkline A piece of string coated with chalk, which is snapped on to a surface to leave a precise guide line.

Chamfer A sharp corner or edge, smoothed to a 45° angle.

Cistern An open-topped or lid-covered water-storage tank. Large cisterns are used for storing water, small cisterns store water for flushing WCs.

Compression joint The type of joint used with copper, and sometimes plastic, tubing. When the nuts are tightened they compress rings (known as "olives") to form a tight joint.

Conductor A substance, such as the metal core in a flex or cable, that will carry an electric current.

Cornice A decorative moulding covering the join between the ceiling and the wall.

Countersink To widen the outer edge of a drilled hole into a cone shape, until a screw-head can be sunk below the surface.

Coving A concave moulding covering the join between ceiling and the wall.

Cut floor brads Nails used to secure floorboards. They have L-shaped heads that are difficult to strike correctly, but they are unlikely to split the wood.

Dowel A headless wooden peg that is used to join two pieces of wood together.

Draincock A valve or tap that is used for draining water from the plumbing system.

Earth The pathway along which an electric current can flow safely to the ground if a fault develops.

Escutcheon A metal plate (usually brass or bronze) surrounding a keyhole. It often incorporates a pivoting cover. Some escutcheons for external doors come with a ledge for pulling the door closed.

Espagnolette bolt Used on French windows, two long sliding bolts slot into recesses at the head and sill of the frame. The bolts, which extend the full length of the door, are operated by a single central handle.

Flaunching A sloping piece of cement, e.g. around the base of a chimney pot.

Flush When two adjacent surfaces are perfectly level.

Flux Fluxes are used to clean and seal metal edges before they are soldered.

French polish A shellac-based coating for wood that can be burnished to a high-gloss finish.

Fuse Protective device that cuts off the current if the current is overloaded or a fault develops in the system.

Galvanized Metal coated with zinc to inhibit rusting.

Gauge (screw) A number indicating the diameter thickness of a screw, e.g. No. 8.

Gimp pins These small, coloured pins are used to fix gimp or braid to the seat rail.

Glaze A glass-like surface coating applied to ceramics to render them waterproof.

Glue size Thinned adhesive used to seal walls and ceilings prior to wallpapering.

Grouting A thin mortar, available ready-mixed or as a powder, that is used to seal the joints between tiles.

Gulley Earthenware trap into which waste and rainwater pipes discharge, which in turn empties into the drains.

Gypsum Calcium sulphate used to make plaster.

Hessian This coarse, brown fabric is woven from jute and is used in upholstery. Hessian is available in different weights; use a heavyweight 16oz (450g) type for seat platforms.

Inspection chamber Underground chamber topped by a manhole cover, that allows access to the drains.

Jumper The part of a tap that carries the washer.

Key To roughen a surface to improve adhesion before painting, tiling, plastering or rendering.

Lagging Insulating material used to cover tanks and pipes and to prevent heat from escaping.

Laid cord Thick jute or hemp cord is used to lace coil springs together.

Live The core of a cable or flex carrying current to where it is needed, or any terminal to which the live core is connected.

Marquetry Decorative veneers laid together to form abstract or pictorial motifs. Veneers made from exotic woods and shaded or stained veneers are often used.

Mastic A waterproof compound for sealing joints.

Mitre To trim the ends of two lengths of wood or plaster to a 45° angle, so that together they form a perfect right angle. A mitre box is used to make an accurate cut.

Mortar A mixture of cement, lime putty and sand used to bind bricks together in a masonry wall.

Mortise A recess cut in the edge of a door to house the protruding tongue of a lock.

Moulding A length of wood, shaped to form a decorative strip.

Neutral The core of an electrical cable or flex carrying current back to its source, or any terminal to which the neutral core is connected.

PTFE Thin plastic sealing tape that ensures watertight connections on screw fittings.

Piping cord This soft cotton cord is wrapped in top covering fabric and used to finish a seamed edge. It is available in three thicknesses – ¼in (6mm), ³⁄₁₆in (5mm) and ⅛in (3mm).

Plumb bob A small, cone-shaped weight attached to a line which, when held against a wall, gives a true vertical.

Pointing The mortar joints between bricks on a wall.

Primer A paint used to seal and key a surface before the undercoat is applied.

Push-fit joint Plumbing connections that simply push together.

Screed A layer of cement-based material used to level a floor.

Screed bead A straight or angled strip of wire mesh used to reinforce corners before plastering or to cover holes in plaster walls.

Scriber A tool used to trace off the edges and contours of an area on to decorating materials.

Scrim Strong, woven material, such as hessian, used to cover joins between pieces of plasterboard. In upholstery, scrim is a lightweight open-weave hessian used for covering the first stuffing.

Soil pipe Vertical pipe that takes sewage to the drains.

Solder An alloy used to make an effective, waterproof, electrically conductive metallic joint between two metals.

Stopcock Valve or tap on a water supply pipe that is used to cut off the water supply.

Stud partition A wall made out of a timber framework covered with plasterboard.

Template A pattern cut to specific dimensions and used as an outline for cutting the same shape from another material.

Thread The spiral ridges around a screw.

Through tiles Upholsterers' stitches which pull the stuffing down in the centre of a seat.

Toggle A small metal screw with a hinge or wings that open when pushed through a hole in a partition wall and so secure the screw in place.

Tongue-and-groove Wooden board or blocks with a groove down one edge and a protruding tongue down the other. The tongue slots into the groove of an adjacent piece for a secure fixing.

Top-stitching The act of sewing upholstery to make a firm, sharp edge to the top of the seat.

Trap Loop in a waste fitting that catches debris before it can enter waste pipes and drains.

Underlay A protective layer of strong material laid on a floor under a carpet.

Veneer An outer layer of decorative timber applied to a core of stronger but less attractive or cheaper wood.

Vent pipe Continuation of a soil pipe above roof level to ventilate the soil pipe.

Volt Unit measuring the electrical "pressure" driving the current round a circuit.

Wallplug An expandable plastic or fibre encasement for a screw, a wallplug is inserted into a hole drilled in a solid wall to provide a gripping surface for the screw. It can be cut to length.

Waste pipe Pipe that takes waste water to the drains.

Watt Unit measuring the amount of power consumed by an electrical appliance.

INDEX

Figures in italic refer to illustrations.

ACKNOWLEDGMENTS

Editor: Sydney Francis
Editorial Assistant: Joanna Swinnerton
Designer: Hilary Krag
Design assistant: Mark Davies
Illustrators: David Ashby, Rick Blakely, Kuo Kang Chen, David Day, Robin
Harris, Kevin Maddison, Fraser Newman, Les Smith
Studio: Del & Co.

Dorling Kindersley
Managing editor: Jemima Dunne
Managing art editor: Derek Coombes
Editorial assistant: Tom Fraser
Designer: Rachel Griffin
Production: Helen Creeke

Contributors: Elaine Brumstead, David Day, Albert Jackson

Photography
(t=top, b=bottom, l=left, r=right, c=centre)
Jon Bouchier: 12–13, 15, 20, 21, 31, 32, 33t and c, 34, 35, 43, 62, 63, 66, 73, 88,
89, 90, 91, 93, 96, 97, 98, 99, 101, 103, 105, 107, 112, 113, 114, 115, 117, 118,
119, 123, 124, 128, 130–1, 132–3, 134, 135, 138–9, 147, 148, 149, 153, 176, 185,
187, 188, 197, 200, 208, 210, 220, 229, 231.
Bridgeman Art Library: 59.
Crown Paint: 6–7.
Martin Dohrn: 12–13, 22, 33b, 37, 38, 41, 56, 57, 74.
Nick Harris: 61, 67, 69.
Tessa Musgrave: 70, 71.

For their generous assistance in supplying articles for the photographs on pages
10–11, 54–5, 86–7, 110–11, 126–7, 154–5, 170–1, 182–3, 198–9 and 222–3, the
authors and publishers would like to thank the following:

Amtico: vinyl tiles.
Black & Decker: drill bits, torches, curly cable and square smoke alarm.
Chadha & Sons: block plane, claw hammer, bevel-edge chisel, bending spring,
hosepipe for washing machine and adjustable spanner.
English Abrasives Ltd: sandpapers, sanding block, gloves and goggles.
First Alert Home Fire Safety Products: kitchen fire blanket.
Douglas Kane Ltd, OBO: masonry nails, door seals and tapes.
Knobs and Knockers: brass drawer furniture, door plates, knockers, keyhole
covers and catches.
The Loft Shop: wooden roofing shingles.
Mothercare: fireguard, kettle guard and round smoke alarm.
Omega Lighting Ltd: light bulbs.
Polycell Products Ltd: window locks.
M. E. Short Ltd: orac ceiling roses and mouldings.
Smith & Sons Ltd: tools.
Swan Electrical Products: jug kettle.
Wincanders (Great Britain) Ltd: wooden parquet flooring.
World's End Tiles: trellis tile.